THE SANTA FE TRAIL

A Historical Bibliography

THE SANTA FE TRAIL
A Historical Bibliography
By Jack D. Rittenhouse

THE UNIVERSITY OF NEW MEXICO PRESS Albuquerque

FOR CHARLOTTE

Designed by Bruce Gentry

First edition

ACKNOWLEDGMENTS

Few literary works require the help of so many people as does a bibliography, and without the aid of others compilation is impossible. For the original inspiration of this work I am indebted to the late Henry Raup Wagner, whom I knew briefly during membership in the Zamorano Club, and to Dr. Lawrence Clark Powell, who encouraged my entry into bibliographic work. I owe a special debt to Professor Ray Allen Billington of the Huntington Library and Art Gallery, Professor Rodman W. Paul of the California Institute of Technology, and Dr. Archibald Hanna, Curator of the Western Americana Collection at Yale University Library, for their review of the manuscript in its early stage.

Gratitude is due for guidance received from the works of Professor Max Moorhead of the University of Oklahoma, Michael D. Heaston of Wichita State University, and Professor Otis E Young of Arizona State University. Donald Powell of the University of Arizona helped me find many government documents. Outstanding in their help as librarians were Mrs. Portia Allbert and Mrs. Shirley Borglund of the Kansas State Historical Society library at Topeka, together with Nyle Miller, the Secretary of that Society. At the University of New Mexico Zimmerman library I received special assistance from Martin Ruoss and Norris Maxwell, and similar aid was given by Miss Maxine Benson at the State Historical Society of Colorado, Dr. Myra Ellen Jenkins at the New Mexico State Records Center and Archives, and Gilbert Campbell at the United States Air Force Academy. Professor Morris Taylor at Trinidad State Junior College in Colorado also located some essential books.

While the final labor of writing may be lonely, the search is often done among good companions, among whom were William E. Brown, then with the National Park Service, and a number of Americana booksellers including Peter Decker, Robert Kadlec, Glen Dawson, J. E. Reynolds, T. N. Luther, Ed Bartholomew, William Morrison, J. C. Dykes, Aaron Cohen, Dorothy McNamee, Bessie Wright, Michael Ginsberg, Richard Mohr, and especially Fred Rosenstock.

Jack D. Rittenhouse
Albuquerque

CONTENTS

ILLUSTRATIONS

Following page 56

THE SANTA FE TRAIL

A Historical Bibliography

TRAIL OF
COMMERCE AND CONQUEST

Nearly every history of the Santa Fe Trail begins with the same incident. Down the dirt streets of Franklin, a backwoods Missouri village, four men rode in from the west on January 29, 1822. Any arrival being news, their coming brought people into the streets, but for men returning from a five months' trading expedition the packs lashed to their horses seemed pitifully small. Then one of the traders lifted high a small rawhide sack and slashed it open with a knife. A shower of Spanish silver coins fell glittering to the ground. Thus were the possibilities of the Santa Fe trade and the trail announced to a community that was short of coin and full of restless men looking for adventure and profit.

The leader of the party was William Becknell. He and his companions had left Missouri on September 1, 1821, reached Santa Fe on November 16, and sold their trade goods to eager buyers. Their success started a regular trade across the route, and the wagons never stopped rolling until the railroad reached Santa Fe in 1880.

The annals of the Santa Fe Trail are long and diverse. The cast of characters included men as different as Coronado and J.E.B. Stuart, physician Adolph Wislizenus and gun-runner Albert Speyer, California land baron John Sutter and New York newspaperman William Rideing. The action involved massacres by men both red and white; raids by men of the Texas Republic and the later Confederate States; small parties that vanished without trace and trains of a hundred wagons stalled in terrible blizzards; poor men trying to get through with one

3

yoke of sick oxen, and great business firms such as Russell, Majors & Waddell. Riders along the Trail included governors, generals, archbishops, consumptives seeking health, and brides who blanched at teamsters' oaths. The tale contains enough adventure to fill a library, but adventure was only the color on the surface; below lay a deeper importance.

The Santa Fe Trail was a good deal more than a local route for trade; it provided access to a huge portion of the West and helped to shape the development of a quarter of a continent. As the first road to be surveyed west of Missouri, it set the initial pattern for roadbuilding across the West. As an avenue of commercial success and of information about the land and people of northern Mexico, it contributed to the expansionist doctrine of Manifest Destiny that led to war with Mexico. Expanding trade on the Trail brought the development of wagon freighting enterprises and stagecoach mail lines on a corporate scale never before conceived, using wagons of new and massive design. The problems of protecting Trail traffic from mobile Indian tribes initiated new national policies toward the Indians, brought into being new types of military units such as the U.S. Dragoons, and fostered the concept of satellite frontier forts served from great central supply depots. The Santa Fe Trail was in many ways a microcosm of westward expansion, and a study of its history is a study of much of the early frontier West.

This was all in the past, but that past is still close to those now alive. At points in northeastern New Mexico you can look out across a vista that appears today as it did to Coronado in 1541, to Pedro Vial in 1792, to Kit Carson in 1826, and to the wagonmasters of Alexander Majors in 1858. Frame your view properly and you will see not a house, a fence, or a sign of man's passing. Shift your view slightly and you can plainly see the remains of the old Trail, with so many variant ruts that the wide trace looks like a narrow field plowed a few summers ago.

Historians know that dates are only convenient bench marks on a map of time. In one sense it is correct to say that the Santa Fe Trail began with the 1821-22 expedition of Becknell and his men, but Becknell was not the first on the route; he was only the first to start regular commerce over an already beaten path. Who was the Leif

4

Ericson of the Santa Fe Trail? Was it Coronado, who in 1541 crossed northeastern New Mexico into a corner of Kansas before he abandoned his dream and turned back? Or was it someone among scores of others between Coronado and Becknell who tried to cross this unknown mid-continent? As far back as 1695, before St. Louis or New Orleans existed, the Spanish governor in Santa Fe heard vague news of Frenchmen venturing near from the northeast. In 1714 a Frenchman named Etienne Veniard Sieur de Bourgmont traveled far enough up the Missouri to hear Indian tales of possible commerce with New Mexico.

In 1719 a Spanish expedition set out from Santa Fe to explore toward Missouri, and the following year the governor of New Mexico sent a military expedition northeast toward the Platte River, where French voyageurs were reported forming an alliance with the Indians. When the expedition was defeated, the Spaniards established a protective outpost at El Quartelejo pueblo on the plains. Each side was aware of the other, across the wide barrier of empty land.

The first trading expedition known to have reached Santa Fe arrived there empty-handed. Two Frenchmen, Pierre and Paul Mallet, with seven companions, lost their pack animals during a river crossing but went on to the provincial capital in 1739. The Mallet brothers were welcomed by the New Mexicans who, fifteen hundred rugged miles from their colonial capital in Mexico City, felt isolated and neglected, but Spanish officials, fearing the effects of trade with outsiders, ruled against it. Nevertheless, contraband was welcome and Spanish border guards could be bribed. In 1744 Jacques Velo (or Belleau or Bellot) got as far as Pecos Pueblo before he was arrested. Other French-men reached Taos in 1748 to trade guns for mules, and next year brought three more Frenchmen: Louis Febre, Pierre Satren, and Jo-seph Michel Ravallo. One was from New Orleans, one from Quebec, and the third from a French post in Arkansas. Febre was a tailor and the others were carpenters. As Santa Fe had no artisans in either craft, all three settled down in the ancient city.

From this time on the visitors came in a stream. Felipe de Sandoval, a wanderer from Spain by way of Jamaica and New Orleans, arrived in 1750. Four more French traders came that same year, and their goods were seized and sold. In 1752 Jean Chapuis and Louis Feulli reached the mission at Pecos, and they too were imprisoned and their goods taken. In 1773 a Virginian, John Rowzee Peyton, was shipwrecked off the mouth of the Rio Grande and taken to Santa Fe as a prisoner. He escaped the following year and made his way overland to St. Louis, possibly by a route near that of the later Santa Fe Trail. In 1790 one of the French traders and scouts who were active along the upper Missouri River met Frenchmen who had been in New Mexico and eagerly questioned them about the possibility of trade with the province.

The first real trailblazer in the Southwest was Pedro Vial, a Frenchman in the employ of Spain. In 1786 he traveled from San Antonio northwest to Santa Fe, and about a year later he opened a similar trail from Santa Fe southeast to Natchitoches in Louisiana. In 1792 he was instructed to seek a route from Santa Fe to St. Louis and successfully completed this assignment. Vial deserves more credit than he has received.

These lonely venturings and random reconnoiterings may seem absurd to an impatient modern American who thinks he would simply have struck west or southwest without ado. He forgets the barriers then—not the puny border guard around the Spanish province, but the land itself. We have come to know that the land, the waters, and the sky determine much that man may do. Topography offers channels, fords, and gateways for those clever enough to find and use them but it also places great obstacles in their way. It was the nature of the land that isolated the market of New Mexico from the merchants of the east. Any understanding of the Santa Fe Trail and its trade must begin with an awareness of the land these men crossed.

From Santa Fe it is roughly seven hundred miles to San Antonio, nearly eight hundred miles to Kansas City, and about nine hundred miles to central Louisiana. On any of these journeys more than half the distance is across vast plains where in early days Indians were frequent and water was scarce. The first natural routes were the rivers, of which the three greatest in the region are the Missouri, the Arkansas, and the Red. The Missouri flows down through the Dakotas and Nebraska into Kansas, where, at modern Kansas City, it turns east to join the Mississippi near St. Louis. The Arkansas, middle of the three, leaves its snow-fed headwaters in Colorado and flows east along the lower edge of Kansas, making a great bend before it plunges southeast through Oklahoma and on to join the Mississippi in east central Arkansas. The Red, rising in northwest Texas and flowing southeast, played a negligible role in the Santa Fe trade.

It was convenient on the frontier to send cargoes coming down the Ohio, the Wabash, the Illinois, or the upper Mississippi to St. Louis, west along the Missouri to the site of Kansas City, then west-southwest across the Kansas prairies to meet the Arkansas at its great bend (see map in picture section). From there traders could take either of two routes: they could go up the Arkansas on the "Mountain Branch" into Colorado and drop down into New Mexico through Raton Pass. Or they could follow the Arkansas a short distance and take the dry "Cimarron Cutoff" across the plains of northeastern New Mexico. As caravans moved westward, they found that the land became a great open plain cut by small streams. On the Cimarron route there was little firewood, little water. A man could make it that way if he knew the waterholes; the land was not true desert, but it was inhospitable and unknown.

Other parts of the West were unknown, and by the Louisiana Purchase in 1803 the United States acquired a great parcel of mystery to be explored. Lewis and Clark set out in 1804 to go up the Missouri and across to the Pacific. On their return in 1806, as they passed the Kansas region, they were told that it might be possible to go overland to trade with Mexico. They duly noted this fact in their records. Meanwhile, also in 1804, a Kaskaskia trader named William Morrison sent Jean Baptiste La Lande overland to New Mexico with a supply of trade goods. La Lande reached Santa Fe, sold his goods, liked the place, and stayed there. In 1805 another trader named James Purcell, sometimes recorded as Pursley, also got to Santa Fe and stayed.

Lewis and Clark had barely returned from the Far Northwest when a second expedition, led by Zebulon Pike, was sent to explore the Arkansas River to its source and return by way of the Red. Pike traveled along the Arkansas in 1806, making careful notes and maps as he went. Beyond the great bend of the river he traversed country that later was part of the Santa Fe Trail, and some authorities call him rather than

7

Becknell the father of the Trail. When Pike reached the Rocky Mountains he turned south along them toward New Mexico. There he was taken into custody by the New Mexicans, who escorted him to Santa Fe (where he saw La Lande and Purcell) and on down to Chihuahua. He was released and made his way back to the United States in 1807, and in 1810 his book-length account of his journey was published in Philadelphia. This was the first report in English that described a possible route to Santa Fe, and there are indications that it soon was read by some Missourians.

While Pike was returning across Texas in 1807, Robert Fulton in the eastern part of the country was proving with his *Clermont* that river steamboats were practical. Fulton's invention would carry the goods down the Ohio and along the Missouri to the eastern end of the great Trail. It was also a great era of road building, with the construction of the Old National Road from Maryland to the Mississippi; the road continued as the Boon's Lick Trail across Missouri to the frontier settlements.

Encouraged by the success of Lewis and Clark, fur companies from St. Louis and the Boon's Lick country were soon extending their operations up the Missouri. From 1810 to 1840 the Mountain Men sent a flow of riches in furs back along the trails and rivers. In 1807 Jacques Clamorgan, a trader from St. Louis, made a successful trip overland to Santa Fe and went on down to Chihuahua. He was perhaps the first truly successful Santa Fe trader.

In 1812-15 the U.S. was in another war and expeditions to the West had to wait. But trappers along the Missouri, such as Manuel Lisa, paid little heed to the war and still felt the lure of Santa Fe. Lisa wrote to the Spaniards, offering to trade, and in 1812 he sent Charles Sanguinet toward Santa Fe with a load of merchandise. Everything was lost to attacking Indians.

At about the same time a group of Missouri frontiersmen, perhaps encouraged by news of unrest in Mexico led by the priest Hidalgo, decided to make a try overland to New Mexico. Robert McKnight, James Baird, Samuel Chambers, and at least seven others reached Santa Fe. But Hidalgo had failed and the Spanish authorities remained implacable; they jailed the Americans and confiscated their goods. Not

8

until 1821 was the last of the men, McKnight, released. Two other traders along the Arkansas, Auguste P. Chouteau and Jules de Mun, were seized and their goods confiscated in 1817, but Jedediah Smith, one of the truly great pathfinders of the West, escaped this fate in 1818 when he guided a pack train over what would be the route of the Santa Fe Trail to the point where it met the Arkansas. His caravan was to meet a Spanish merchant at that point, near present Fort Dodge, but the trader failed to show up and Smith led the party back home.

Debates of these affairs in Congress produced a report that was probably the first congressional document to deal solely with the Santa Fe trade. And in 1819 the United States and Spain signed the Adams-Onís treaty, which, among other matters, defined the Arkansas River as the boundary between the two countries in the Southwest.

When the War of 1812 was concluded, the United States resumed its official exploration of the West. Lewis and Clark had gone northwest, Pike southwest; a third expedition, headed by Stephen H. Long, was sent in 1819 straight into the Rocky Mountains. It returned in 1820 along the Arkansas and produced another official report of that route.

Then came the landmark year of 1821. The records reveal several claimants for the honor of being "first" that year into Santa Fe. Samuel Adams Ruddock reached Santa Fe from Council Bluffs on June 8, on a trip to the Columbia River country. Jacob Fowler and Hugh Glenn, two Mountain Men, were trapping the beaver streams north of Santa Fe that year. William Becknell reached Santa Fe on November 16. And another trader, Thomas James, arrived there two weeks later.

Becknell, usually called Captain Becknell, and his companions took several pack animals loaded with Indian trade goods when they left the Missouri River. His intention apparently was to trade with the Indians, not to go to Santa Fe. But at the Mexican border he learned from Spanish dragoons that Mexico had asserted its independence from Spain and that U.S. traders would be welcome; so naturally he went on to Santa Fe. History was made with every peso that changed hands that day. It must have been a dry winter, because the Missourians made it back home in forty-eight days.

As soon as spring came in 1822, Becknell headed again for New

9

Mexico, this time with at least three wagons, the first wheels to roll over the Trail. Jacob Fowler, coming down the Arkansas, noted in his wonderful journal that he saw the tracks of these wagons—an astonishing phenomenon at that time and place. Becknell and his party carried $3,000 worth of trade goods and made a profit of two thousand per cent on their investment.

From these two expeditions led by Becknell comes the continuing disagreement over the year in which the Trail was opened. At its eastern end, in Franklin, Missouri, a tablet states the year was 1821, but at its western end, in Santa Fe, a bronze plaque says the Trail began in 1822. And the same difference of opinion appears in written accounts. No one disputes the facts; all agree that the Trail as a route of regular commerce was opened by William Becknell, that he wandered into Santa Fe with a pack train of Indian trade goods in 1821, and that he returned in 1822 with a few wagons. But they disagree on the interpretation of these facts.

Those who prefer 1821 may quote Max Moorhead, who refers to "the launching of this first successful trade in 1821," or they may point to Margaret Long's book about the Trail, which says flatly that "the Santa Fe Trail began at Franklin on the Missouri River in 1821." Others depend on Dean Earl Wood's unequivocal statement: "1821. That was the year of the origin of the Santa Fe Trail." But the group that is staunch for 1822 argues that Becknell's second trip was the first to carry goods intended for civilian—not Indian—trade, that it was the first to use wagons, and that it was the first to travel west over the Cimarron Cutoff route that became the main branch of the Trail. And the monuments erected along the Trail by the Daughters of the American Revolution, following decisions made in separate states, generally carried the 1821 date on markers in Missouri but used 1822 on markers in Kansas, Colorado, and New Mexico.

Two other experts, Josiah Gregg and William E. Brown, offer their readers a choice. In his first chapter, Gregg says, "During the year [1821] Captain Becknell . . . went out to Santa Fe by the far western prairie route," then adds when mentioning Becknell's second trip in 1822 that "it is from this period—the year 1822—that the virtual commencement of the Santa Fe Trail can be dated." Brown recognizes that Becknell reached Santa Fe in 1821 but continues, "Becknell's second expedition [in 1822] . . . was in fact the true beginning of the Santa Fe Trade."

It is the antiquarians who debate whether one should accept the "first" trip in 1821 or the "virtual commencement" and "true beginning" in 1822. Becknell himself may have provided a reasonable solution: he reached Santa Fe first on November 16, 1821, and arrived back in Missouri with packs of Spanish coin on January 29, 1822. So we may say that the Santa Fe Trail was opened in 1821-22, justifying a sesquicentennial in 1971-72.

Two other expeditions had gone to Santa Fe in 1822. One was headed by Colonel Benjamin Cooper, the other by James Baird and Samuel Chambers, who had been imprisoned on their trading venture about ten years earlier but were ready to try again. Caught in a snowstorm along the Arkansas near the Cimarron Crossing, Baird and Chambers stayed through the winter. Their pack animals died, and the traders dug holes in the earth, cached their goods, then went on to Taos for fresh mules and returned for the merchandise. The holes remained a gaping landmark known for years as The Caches.

In 1823 only one caravan, led by Stephen Cooper, left Missouri for Santa Fe, but in 1824 Trail commerce really began with a well-organized caravan of eighty men, using twenty-five wagons and a small field piece. The party was guided by Alexander Le Grand, an elusive figure who turns up at random places in the history of the Southwest. Also along were Augustus Storrs, who became U.S. consul at Santa Fe the next year, and M. M. Marmaduke, a future governor of Missouri. The caravan carried $35,000 in trade goods, and the trip was successful in every way.

Missouri had been admitted as a state in 1821, but she was in financial difficulties; her banks had failed and her people were on the brink of a barter economy for lack of hard money and any reliable paper currency. One of her first senators was Thomas Hart Benton, a man of energy and eloquence, then in his early forties. Benton saw that Missouri's hope lay in her strategic position as gateway to the West. William Ashley's fur trading company was operating up the Missouri in 1822; Jedediah Smith and Thomas Fitzpatrick had just discovered

South Pass, opening up what would become the Oregon Trail; and Peter Skene Ogden had recently explored Great Salt Lake. These developments, together with the possibilities of the Santa Fe trade, pointed the way to the future for Missouri.

Benton became the champion of the West in Congress and remained so throughout his thirty years in the Senate. He now began pushing for development of the Santa Fe Trail, first asking Storrs and Marmaduke to send him information, which he had published as congressional documents. In March 1825 he carried a bill through Congress calling for a survey of the Trail, and before the year ended the survey party was at work in the field. The Santa Fe Trail was now a matter of national interest and no longer of importance to only a few frontier villages.

Diplomatic obstacles arose when the survey commissioners, headed by George Champlin Sibley, approached the Mexican border at the Arkansas. American frontiersmen considered the Trail a route of beneficial commerce and healthy enterprise, and the citizens of Santa Fe wanted badly the goods they hoped would come to them along the Trail. But the young government of Mexico viewed the Trail with serious misgivings. To them it was a potential military highway, a threat aimed straight at their northern border. Knowing that with merchandise would come also influence and the possibility of trouble, and that if trouble arose troops might use the Trail to protect U.S. interests, they felt the doubts and fears that had worried the Spanish viceroys in the days of the Mallet brothers and McKnight. But despite these misgivings, they eventually agreed to the survey.

The Sibley survey trip was more or less a fiasco. It surveyed the route first to Taos instead of to Santa Fe. Strictly speaking, Taos was a port of entry to Mexico, but it was difficult for wagons to reach that village, and once there they could not be taken on to Santa Fe. So the survey party laid out a branch road to Santa Fe. It was all unnecessary, really, because the wagonmen already knew the route and took the shortest way. The details of Sibley's survey were not published for guidance of caravans at the time. A few mounds were erected to mark the route, but they soon disappeared. Nevertheless the survey produced two things of significance: more national publicity for the Trail, and the signing of a treaty with the Osage Indians at Council Grove in 1825, providing for a semblance of peace along part of the route. That treaty was one of the first steps toward an Indian policy in the West.

Caravans continued along the Trail each year. At this stage anyone could take part in the trade. A man had only to buy enough goods to load a wagon, and if he lacked that much cash himself he could borrow it or persuade friends to join him in backing the venture. The assorted wagons gathered at Council Grove in late spring and journeyed on together as one great annual caravan. With the caravan in 1826 a runaway apprentice named Christopher "Kit" Carson made his first journey to New Mexico.

In 1827 serious trouble began with the Indians. They had appeared frequently to demand gifts ever since the first wagons lumbered over the Trail, but in 1827 the Pawnee Indians attacked a group of returning traders and made off with a hundred head of mules and other livestock. The next year there were two caravans, both big and both successful. The leaders were returning with a thousand head of mules and horses and were near the present Oklahoma-New Mexico boundary when Indians crept up on the sleeping men, seized their guns, and shot two: Daniel Monroe and the son of Samuel McNees. Young McNees died instantly; Monroe soon afterward. While the traders were burying their dead, a handful of curious Indians appeared on the opposite bank of the creek. Not knowing or caring whether these were the murderers, the enraged caravanners shot all but one, who escaped to tell his tribe. Thus began a bitter feud that was not ended for two generations. The traders journeyed on after gaining their immediate revenge, but they lost all of their livestock before reaching home.

Losing mules was the same as losing silver. In the first years of the Santa Fe trade, most of the hard money of New Mexico was carried to Missouri. That state, now recovered from its financial instability, had become known as the "hard money" state and Spanish coins circulated as readily as any other. Senator Benton became the champion of coin instead of paper money and was for years known as "Old Bullion." But mules were as good as money in Missouri. Before 1824 the records make no mention of mules in a state that later became nationally famous for them. The first ones came in over the Santa Fe Trail. Not until 1838 was jack-breeding stock brought in from the island of Malta. Until 1829 mules were used instead of oxen to draw the Trail wagons. And in all years the Indians preferred mules over coin as booty.

The deaths of Monroe and McNees, together with the loss of a thousand head of stock, threw a chill into Missouri traders. They demanded protection, and they got it—for a year. In 1829 Major Bennet Riley and an infantry escort accompanied the caravan as far as the Arkansas, *i.e.*, to the Mexican border. From there on a Mexican escort guarded the train to its destination.

By 1830 the Trail was well established between Independence, Missouri, and Santa Fe. The distance, reported variously in different accounts, was 775-780 miles. Because old accounts often tell of travelers starting from such places as Boon's Lick, Boonville, Arrow Rock, Franklin (Old or New), Blue Mills Landing, Fort Osage, Independence, Independence Landing, Westport, Cooper's Fort, Westport Landing, or Kansas (later Kansas City), a brief explanation is in order.

The Boon's Lick Trail leading west from St. Louis ended in a region known as the Boon's Lick Country, around the town of Franklin on the northeast bank of the Missouri River. In 1828 a flood washed away most of the town and New Franklin was built two miles back from the river. From Franklin travelers usually crossed by ferry to Arrow Rock, or sometimes to Boonville a few miles below Arrow Rock. Thus Franklin (Old or New), Arrow Rock, Boonville, or the Boon's Lick Country were essentially the same point. Cooper's Fort was a few miles northwest of Franklin.

When steamboat navigation began on the Missouri, most cargoes were sent by boat along the river and the freight and passengers could go by water to Blue Mills Landing or Independence Landing, then south about three miles to the town of Independence, which became the eastern terminus of the Trail around 1827. By 1833 caravans could save another ten miles by having their cargoes set ashore at Westport Landing, ten miles beyond Independence Landing, then carted a few miles south to the town of Westport. Strictly speaking, Independence and Westport were not on the river but were served by their respective landings. In later years Westport Landing became the town of Kansas.

14

later Kansas City, and the metropolis eventually absorbed Westport itself.

Actually, wagons came from many points on this turkey-track network, went on a hundred and fifty miles from Independence, and gathered to form the caravan or train at Council Grove. Along this initial stretch the wagons were joined at times by others coming down the side road from Fort Leavenworth, or they saw other companions depart where the Oregon Trail branched off from the Santa Fe Trail, about forty miles out of Independence. Before reaching Council Grove, travelers passed Round Grove and 110-Mile Creek (named for its distance along the Trail). Along this section the only obstacles were a few creeks and occasional quagmires. At Council Grove the main caravan was organized and all equipment was given a final check. There had been no towns since Westport; the land lay empty ahead.

The Santa Fe Trail was an easy trail compared to the difficulties along routes such as those across the Sierra Nevada into California. The caravans would encounter sand hills, long dry stretches, steep creek banks, rocky fords, and narrow passes. By combining two or even three teams, wagonmen could struggle past the worst spots; with care in planning each day's march a camp could be made near water, along most sections.

Beyond Council Grove the grass was shorter; the wagons entered buffalo country as they passed Diamond Spring and Lost Spring, crossed Cottonwood Creek, and forded the Little Arkansas. Around every place name along the route there grew a dozen legends in the life of the Trail. About 270 miles from Independence the wagons came to the Arkansas River at the top of its great bend, and the Trail continued along the north bank of the river, past Pawnee Rock, Pawnee Fork, Coon Creek and The Caches, finally reaching the Middle Crossings near the present town of Cimarron, Kansas. It was approximately the halfway point.

At this point the caravans had a choice of routes: the Mountain Branch or the Cimarron Cutoff. The Mountain Branch was used during the Mexican War and the Civil War because it was safer from attack; later when the railroad was being built, wagons went from the end of track over the Mountain Branch, along the north bank of the Arkansas to Bent's Fort, then forded the river and continued on to Trinidad, over Raton Pass, down to the village of Cimarron and on to Ocate Crossing and Fort Union. During most of the commercial years of the Trail wagonmen preferred the shorter Cimarron Cutoff. With trains averaging only twelve to fifteen miles a day, any shortcut was important, so most wagons forded the Arkansas at the Middle Crossings.

Once across the river on the Cimarron Cutoff the trains encountered sand hills, and then came a sixty-mile waterless stretch, the worst on the Trail, known as the Jornada. At its end they reached the Cimarron River, which they followed across the present Oklahoma Panhandle, passing the Lower, Middle, and Upper Springs and entering New Mexico just before they came to McNees' Crossing. From there they wound past Rabbit Ear Camp, Round Mound, and Point of Rocks. The route became more rocky as they came to the Canadian River and turned southwest to Wagon Mound. Then there was a good stretch of plains again until they reached modern Watrous, where the Cimarron Cutoff and the Mountain Branch rejoined. Along this section in New Mexico, from McNees' Crossing to Watrous, the old ruts are best preserved, for the Trail was not just one pair of ruts but several. Wagons traveled two to four abreast, so they could form a corral quickly in case of attack. Consequently the Trail often resembles a trace drawn by the fingers of a giant hand dragged across the plain.

Traffic was heavier as the combined routes continued on from Watrous, past Las Vegas, Bernal Springs, San Miguel (where they forded the Pecos), past ruined Pecos Pueblo, and wound along Glorieta Pass through the mountains and over the last rocky climb to the slopes into Santa Fe.

By 1831 tourists were beginning to appear on the Trail. In that year Albert Pike, a writer from Arkansas, went over the route and wrote lyrical descriptions of it. And in the same year a great Mountain Man met his death on the Trail: Jedediah Smith, ready to settle down and turn merchant, wandered away from a night's camp and was killed by Indians.

At about this time a major change occurred in the Santa Fe trade: it ceased to be an adventure for amateurs and became an occupation

16

for businessmen. New Mexico was becoming glutted with ordinary trade goods, so that a man could no longer venture west with a few mirrors, needles, pans, and knives and sell them at tremendous profits. Prices began to drop while Mexican taxes rose; small traders were lucky to break even. Profits were possible only for operators of several wagons, using hired help, and studying the market carefully so that only desirable merchandise was hauled. Instead of selling a wagonload of goods in the plaza, the trader made advance arrangements to supply specific stores at the end of the route. Mexican taxes were levied per wagon, and this suggested the use of larger vehicles.

The buying of merchandise also changed. Instead of securing goods haphazardly from frontier shops in Missouri, traders now bought from large wholesale outfitters at Independence or Westport. Some even ordered from New York or other eastern centers or, a few years later, from Europe and had goods sent direct to a Missouri point. Of still greater importance was the increase in trade with Chihuahua. Long before the Santa Fe Trail opened, there had been a Spanish trade route down the Rio Grande and on south to Chihuahua. Operators in the Santa Fe trade now found they could take this route down to a new market in which there was demand for their goods and silver coins with which to pay for them. By 1840 half of all the Santa Fe Trail freight was continuing on down to Chihuahua.

These changes were well along by 1831 when Josiah Gregg made his first Trail trip, for his health. He wrote undoubtedly the best contemporary account of the Trail and its trade, though he made only four round trips over the Trail before he left the trade in 1840. No student of the Trail can neglect Gregg's *Commerce of the Prairies*, published in 1844, but his description and statistics covered only the first twenty-two of the Trail's fifty-nine years; the adventure lay in the Gregg years, but the massive volume of trade and traffic came later.

The fur trade was reaching its peak around 1833. More and more men had been heading into the southern Rockies to bring out bundles of pelts. To accommodate the Mountain Men and trappers with supplies and to offer an outlet for their furs, Charles and William Bent, together with Ceran St. Vrain, built Bent's Fort on the upper Arkansas. This massive-walled adobe structure became a landmark on the Mountain Branch of the Trail and soon was a rendezvous for a group new to the frontier, the U.S. Dragoons.

The Dragoons were organized by order of President Jackson in 1833, because there was then no cavalry branch of the armed services and it had become evident that foot soldiers could not be effective in frontier warfare. The Dragoons were an elite corps of 1,832 men, at first commanded by Henry Dodge and later under such officers as Stephen Watts Kearny and Philip St. George Cooke. The men were mounted and could fight on horseback or on foot with sabre, carbine, and bayonet. The tactics they worked out in their first thirteen years and the manuals written for their use laid the groundwork for cavalry operations in the Mexican War, the Civil War, and the Indian wars.

In 1834 a detachment of Dragoons under Captain Clifton Wharton escorted a caravan along the Santa Fe Trail, the first such escort since Bennet Riley's service in 1829, and there were no more Dragoon escorts until 1843. But in 1835 the Dragoons made a long tour to present a show of force to the Indians of the West. The troopers rode north to the Platte River, followed it west to the Rocky Mountains, turned south down the eastern flank of those ranges to the Arkansas, then rode back along the Arkansas past Bent's Fort and over the Santa Fe Trail to their base at Fort Leavenworth.

A year later, in 1836, the Republic of Texas declared its independence from Mexico and defeated General Santa Anna at the Battle of San Jacinto. This portentous action had no immediate effect on the Santa Fe trade, although it tended to chill Mexican officials toward all Anglos, as U.S. citizens were called regardless of their color.

The Santa Fe trade continued to grow, despite Indian attacks such as those of the Pawnee in 1837 on a Bent, St. Vrain & Company train. In 1838 cost-conscious traders petitioned Congress for a free port of entry in Missouri. They asked that customs duties paid on imported goods landed in Atlantic ports and destined for the Mexican trade should be repaid by debenture or "drawback" when those bales and cases left Missouri in their original sealed condition. Seven years later this relief was granted.

Joseph Murphy, a St. Louis wagonmaker, was building bigger wagons for Trail use by 1840. The initial simple country wagons had long since

18

given way to the "Pittsburgh" wagon, a variation of the old Conestoga, but Murphy's new vehicles were juggernauts. Their wheels were seven feet high, with rims eight inches wide, the wagon tongue was fifty feet long, and the bed was so deep that a man standing inside barely exposed the top of his head. The payload was from two to three tons.

The mounting traffic of these great wagons soon became a matter of economic interest to the Texas Republic. Texas had claimed the Rio Grande as a boundary, placing the eastern half of New Mexico, including Santa Fe, within the young republic. This claim was not recognized by Mexico, and in 1841 Texas sent out the Texan-Santa Fe Expedition to secure the political, military, and commercial control of Santa Fe. More than three hundred men, calling themselves the Santa Fe Pioneers, left central Texas with twenty-one ox drawn wagons laden with merchandise and a supply of political handbills. In the group were George Wilkins Kendall, Thomas Falconer, and Franklin Coombs, all of whom later wrote narratives of the trip.

The expedition, often misinformed by its guides, moved slowly over an erratic course. By the time its advance party reached New Mexico, near present Tucumcari, the men were suffering from thirst and hunger. The Mexican governor, Manuel Armijo, aware of their approach and naturally incensed about it, sent out detachments who induced the Texans to surrender. They were then marched south to Mexico and prison, from which most of the men were released the next year.

Despite the immediate futility of the Texan-Santa Fe Expedition, it had profound effects on trade along the Santa Fe Trail in the years that followed. One consequence was the Snively Expedition. In January 1843 a Texan named Jacob Snively petitioned the Republic of Texas for permission to form a new expedition that would intercept and seize the goods of Mexican traders along the portion of the Santa Fe Trail—nearly three hundred miles along the Cimarron Cutoff—that lay within the territory claimed by Texas. The Republic authorized Snively's expedition with certain qualifications: the force was not to exceed three hundred men; the venture was not to be considered an official Texan enterprise; all actions were to be undertaken as in honorable warfare; and all goods seized were to be divided equally between the Texas government and the Snively men.

At the same time a similar pro-Texan force, headed by Charles A. Warfield, was formed in northern New Mexico. The Warfield Expedition included several Mountain Men, among them Rufus Sage. Snively's men moved north and Warfield's group marched east, heading for a rendezvous on the Santa Fe Trail just below the Arkansas. They were aware that the land north of the river was U.S. territory. At the end of May 1843 Warfield's men disbanded after a desultory and fruitless campaign and some of them, including Warfield, joined Snively. A few weeks later the Snively forces met a Mexican detachment in a short but decisive battle in which seventeen Mexican soldiers were killed. But the spoils of victory were meager, and the Snively command broke into separate detachments.

Philip St. George Cooke, then a captain in the Dragoons, was commanding a caravan escort at this time along the Trail above the Arkansas. His troops were on the alert because a Mexican trader, Antonio José Chávez, had been killed near the site of today's Emporia, in Kansas. Chávez' death had been blamed on Warfield's men, but it may have been the work of freebooters. Cooke moved rapidly south of the Arkansas to Snively's camp and ordered the Texans disarmed. The expedition then returned home and was disbanded. Enraged by the death of its soldiers and the killing of Chávez, the Mexican government placed a ban on all foreign traders coming overland into Mexico, but in response to an immediate outcry from Mexican citizens deprived of incoming goods the ban was soon lifted.

While Snively, Warfield, and Cooke were engaged in their encounters, John C. Frémont, on his Second Expedition to explore the Far West, traversed the Santa Fe Trail for the first time, following it along the Arkansas as far as Bent's Fort before heading on west. Two years later, on his Third Expedition, he used the Trail again and paused at Bent's Fort long enough to send young Lieutenant James Abert on a reconnaissance trip down through Raton Pass and on a wide loop eastward through the Canadian River country. Frémont went on to California and there became involved in the Bear Flag revolt against Mexican rule, and in 1846 young Abert was back through Raton Pass with a column of United States troops. Mexico's earlier fears that the Santa Fe Trail might be an avenue of conquest had become reality.

20

Expansionist fever had been rising in the United States for some years. The great migration westward over the Oregon Trail had begun in 1842-43 and was soon in full spate, and to the rallying cry of "54° 40′ or Fight" for the Far Northwest were added less noisy but equally intense ambitions for the annexation of lush California. Then in 1845 Texas was admitted to the Union, transferring to the nation her claim to the Rio Grande boundary which Mexico disputed. If President Polk could not achieve peaceful acquisition of the desired territories, war seemed bound to come.

Tension was high and debate fierce as the year 1846 began, but in New Mexico affairs were progressing normally. The spring trade over the Trail topped the million dollar mark. Then on May 13 Congress declared war with Mexico.

The major thrust and the first battles of the war occurred in South Texas, but United States forces also moved along the Santa Fe Trail into New Mexico. Stephen Watts Kearny organized the Army of the West at Fort Leavenworth and led it to the Arkansas and thence along the Mountain Branch of the Trail because, although this route was a hundred miles longer than the Cimarron Cutoff, it had more water and also Bent's Fort to be used as a staging area. Francis Parkman, returning from the Northwest, met the advancing troops along the Arkansas, and just ahead of them journeyed another visitor who later wrote about the West, Adolph Wislizenus, who was taking a pleasure trip along the Santa Fe Trail. He was with a caravan that included a trader, Albert Speyer, whose wagons carried a cargo of fine Mississippi rifles ordered by Mexico. They managed to get to Chihuahua ahead of the troops, but other traders following Speyer were scooped up by Kearny's advancing men.

The troops left Bent's Fort in early August and marched over Raton Pass, down to Las Vegas, and on to Santa Fe. They expected to meet Mexican resistance in every canyon, every village, and at every ford, but encountered none anywhere. Governor Armijo had ordered a retreat from his prepared position. On August 19 Kearny, now a brigadier-general, proclaimed in Santa Fe the United States' occupation of New Mexico.

Reinforcements came along the Trail to strengthen the Army of the

West. Included was the Mormon Battalion, an unusual unit that had been recruited from the great Mormon throng then encamped in Iowa on their way west. The United States government had promised to lend any possible financial aid in this Mormon migration, and the Mexican War offered an opportunity to redeem this pledge. Arrangements were made for a battalion of five hundred Mormons to accompany the Army of the West on its march to California; the wages of the men would aid their families, and the men themselves would reach the Pacific Coast.

When the Mormon Battalion, under Philip St. George Cooke, arrived at Santa Fe, a small group of men, feeling they were physically incapable of continuing the march, turned back over Raton Pass and set up a winter camp at what is now Pueblo, Colorado. Kearny led part of the Army of the West on across Arizona to fight in California, and Cooke and the Mormon Battalion followed him. Another large part of the Army of the West, under Colonel Alexander Doniphan, marched down the Rio Grande to capture Chihuahua. Sterling Price, later a Confederate commander in Missouri, stayed behind as the military commander in Santa Fe.

Throughout this campaign, traffic on the Trail was heavy as Missouri teamsters trundled great loads of supplies across the plains. Many men who otherwise might never have entered the Santa Fe trade came to know the Trail during the war and in the years that followed became major operators along its route. The end of the war, with the signing of the Treaty of Guadalupe Hidalgo in 1848, initiated the busiest thirty-two years of the Trail's life. Increasing quantities of supplies were needed for the garrisons at Santa Fe and other military posts in the Southwest. In 1848 James Brown secured the first government contract to haul supplies from Fort Leavenworth to New Mexico, and contract freighting became a major enterprise across the plains. Brown formed a partnership with John Russell, and in 1850 a hundred-wagon Brown & Russell train, trying desperately to get late supplies into Santa Fe before the full winter set in, was caught in deep snow in New Mexico. Brown went to Santa Fe and got more teamsters and animals but died soon afterward from the exposure.

Others were using the Trail in these years, some with unusual experiences. In 1848 young François X. Aubry, an enterprising freighter, made an unbelievable ride to win a wager. In September, using a relay of mounts, he rode from Santa Fe to Independence on horseback, covering more than 750 miles in five days and sixteen hours. And between late April and mid-September 1849 some 2,500 persons took the Santa Fe route to the California gold fields in order to avoid any risk of cholera. Mountain Man Jim Kirker guided one of the California caravans as far as Santa Fe.

With the passing of the fur trade and increasing preference for the Cimarron route, activity at Bent's Fort declined; so William Bent burned the grand old landmark and built a new post farther down the Arkansas. His brother Charles, who had moved to New Mexico, became the governor, and was killed at Taos during a wartime uprising in 1847.

Indian attacks still plagued traders and travelers on the Trail. At Point of Rocks in New Mexico, a physician named J. M. White and his family were killed, and at Wagon Mound in 1850 a ten-man party of mail carriers were killed and their mail scattered. For more than a hundred years treasure hunters have potholed the area in search of valuables that the mail was said, probably fictitiously, to contain.

When the Mexican War began, there was no U.S. fort except Leavenworth to serve the Santa Fe Trail, but with the increase in traffic and settlement that followed the war a series of forts were built. Altogether nineteen western forts were involved in the history of the Trail.

The oldest was the *Spanish presidio* at Santa Fe, established in 1610-11. In 1846 it was occupied by Kearny's troops, who promptly built a better defense a few hundred yards away and named it *Fort Marcy*. The second oldest fort was *Fort Cavagnolle*, built by the French in 1744 or 1745 at or near present Kansas City as part of a French plan to develop trade with Santa Fe. It was abandoned before 1760. *Fort Osage* was built on the northeast side of the Missouri River not far from Franklin in 1808. George C. Sibley in his survey of the Santa Fe Trail used Fort Osage as milepost zero. In 1827 Fort Osage was replaced by *Fort Leavenworth* as the major post at the eastern end of the Trail. Leavenworth was not located precisely on the Trail but was joined to it by a short military road.

During the Mexican War a post was needed midway between Fort Leavenworth and Fort Marcy, so *Fort Mann* was built in 1847-48, about eight miles west of present Dodge City. It was abandoned in 1850 when *Fort Atkinson* was built nearby. Fort Atkinson, predecessor of Fort Dodge and not to be confused with other forts named Atkinson in Nebraska and North Dakota, was first called Camp Mackay and then Fort Sumner; it became Fort Atkinson in 1851 and was abandoned in 1853.

In 1851 *Fort Union* was established astride the Santa Fe Trail east of Las Vegas, New Mexico. Before it was abandoned in 1891, its location was twice changed slightly. Fort Union became the principal supply and staging center for all military operations in the Southwest and was the hub of a great network of forts in Texas, New Mexico, and parts of Colorado, Kansas, and Arizona. Fort Leavenworth and Fort Union were linked by the Santa Fe Trail as their lifeline through all the Indian wars. Near Fort Union was a non-military trading post named *Fort Barclay*, built around 1849 by Alexander Barclay. He had been an employee of Bent and built his smaller fort on the model of old Bent's Fort.

In 1853 *Fort Riley* was built in Kansas. While not on the Santa Fe Trail itself, this fort—together with Leavenworth—provided troops who served along the Trail. In 1859 *Fort Larned* was built on the Trail in Kansas. First called Camp Alert, then renamed Larned in 1860, it was closed in 1878. Within sight of Bent's New Fort on the Arkansas the Army in 1860 erected a post at first called Fort Fauntleroy, then Fort Wise, and finally Fort Lyon. It is usually referred to as *Fort Lyon I*.

When the Civil War opened, the existing chain of forts serving the Santa Fe Trail included Leavenworth, Riley, Larned, Lyon I, Union, and Marcy. Before that war ended at Appomattox, the campaigns to control the Indians in the West had already started. Between 1864 and 1867 several smaller posts were built along the Trail to aid in these campaigns.

In 1864 *Fort Harker*, at first called Fort Ellsworth, was built near present Ellsworth, Kansas. It lasted until 1878. Also in 1864 *Fort Zarah* was built on the Trail near present Great Bend, Kansas. It was closed in 1869. In 1865 *Fort Dodge, Fort Aubry*, and *Camp Nichols* were built.

Fort Dodge, near present Dodge City, was a major post that lasted until 1882. Fort Aubry was a sod-house post built near present Kendall, Kansas; it lasted barely a year. Camp Nichols was built by Kit Carson along the Cimarron Cutoff where it nicks the edge of the present Oklahoma Panhandle, west of Boise City. It lasted only through a single summer. Both Aubry and Nichols were intended to be only temporary posts for short campaigns. In 1866 *Fort Stevens* was planned near Spanish Peaks in Colorado, not far from the northern end of Raton Pass, but the plans were cancelled before the fort was built. The last fort along the Trail was *Fort Lyon II,* built in 1867 near the first Fort Lyon. It was not closed until 1889.

Such a network of military posts needed a flood of supplies, and this opened the way for more rich contracts in government freighting. At the same time the government was beginning its surveys for railroads through the West. In 1853 two survey parties made the first leg of their trips over the Santa Fe Trail. John Gunnison's expedition sought one possible route through the Rockies, and the other expedition was that of E. F. Beale and Gwinn Harris Heap.

In that same year Alexander Majors began his wagon freighting operations along the Trail, and five years later he joined with two other wagonmen to form the famous firm of Russell, Majors & Waddell. Their name has been linked most prominently with the Pony Express, which never used the Santa Fe Trail, although Majors may have conceived his idea after seeing the postal couriers who carried dispatches over the Trail. By 1854 mail contracts were being awarded for two trips a month. Hockaday & Hall won the contract that year, away from David Waldo, who had held the contract since 1850 for mail carried once a month. Passenger stage lines began with the mail contracts. The Mexicans, whose role in freighting along the Trail has never been told adequately, were also active as freighters or outfitters during the entire life of the route. Names such as Manuel Escudero, Francisco Elguea, Francisco Perea, Antonio José Chávez, and Miguel Antonio Otero were among the most prominent on the Trail, and there were hundreds of Mexican teamsters with outfits small and large.

When the gold rush to Colorado started in 1858, the first groups headed west over the familiar Santa Fe route, and by the following year five hundred wagons a day were using the Trail to get to the new El Dorado. Later more direct routes through central Kansas to the Colorado camps lessened this traffic on the Santa Fe Trail. But freight volume continued to grow. In 1858 some $3,500,000 in goods was carried over the Trail, and by 1859 the volume had passed $10,000,000.

Then came the Civil War. Although the conflict between proslavery and antislavery forces had torn Kansas apart, it had little effect along the Trail, and at first the Civil War produced little activity there. "Buffalo Bill" Cody, scouting along the route for the 9th Kansas Cavalry, found only Indians. But before long the Confederates invaded New Mexico from Texas. Their first thrust carried them up the Rio Grande to capture the town of Mesilla and Fort Fillmore, and early in 1862 Brigadier General Henry H. Sibley took command of the Texans and fought his way north to take Santa Fe. His next goal was the seizure of Fort Union, with its great warehouses full of military supplies. When Colorado sent its 1st Regiment of Volunteers south through Raton Pass and along the Santa Fe Trail to Fort Union, the opposing small armies met late in March in Glorieta Pass on the Trail a few miles east of Santa Fe. The battle was a draw; each side retired confident that it had won. But the Union forces had sent a detachment around to the south to destroy the Confederate supplies, and the Texans found themselves unable to renew the fight the next day; they could only retreat homeward. The Civil War in the West was ended. Confederate guerrillas under William C. Quantrill occasionally attacked Union supply trains in eastern Kansas, with Dick Yeager leading the major forays, and similar groups under James Reynolds and Joel McKee were active along the Arkansas. In October 1864 the Battle of Westport, often called the "Gettysburg of the West," was fought in Missouri, but it was not a struggle solely for control of the Trail. General Sterling Price commanded the Confederate troops in this engagement, the largest west of the Mississippi. His defeat ended the fighting in the trans-Mississippi area.

During the war there was no loss in commerce. In 1862 $40,000,000 in goods and supplies went over the Trail in three thousand great wagons, compared to $450,000 in 230 wagons during 1843, the best year reported by Josiah Gregg. And the 1862 record was toppled when more than five thousand wagons moved over the Trail in 1866. In that year a former Mountain Man named Richens Lacy "Dick" Wootton hacked a better path across Raton Pass and turned it into a profitable toll road.

The tremendous increase derived in part from a wave of population moving westward, from growth in both demand and wealth in New Mexico, and from the broadening campaign against the Indians, which resulted in more forts and more troops to be supplied. Some of these new soldiers in 1864 were the "Galvanized Yankees," Confederate soldiers who had been captured and then released on condition that they fight for the Union side in the West. Supplies were needed also for the Navajo and other tribes interned in the Bosque Redondo camp below Fort Union.

But the end of the Santa Fe Trail was in sight. In 1866 the Kansas-Pacific Railroad reached Topeka, and the Atchison, Topeka & Santa Fe Railway was soon to start. The town of Abilene, Kansas, sprang into existence in 1867 as one of the first cowtowns, and the great herds began moving north from Texas to the railroads. The Kansas-Pacific reached Kit Carson, Colorado, in 1870, and three years later the Atchison, Topeka & Santa Fe was extended to Granada, Colorado, not far from the northern entrance to Raton Pass. The Cimarron Cutoff section of the Trail was already almost completely abandoned by wagon traffic; wagons and stagecoaches only shuttled back and forth between the end of the tracks and Santa Fe. After a six-year lull the last excitement occurred along the Trail as rival rail lines fought to be first through Raton Pass. The Atchison, Topeka & Santa Fe won and spilled down onto the plains and into Las Vegas. On February 9, 1880, the first train steamed into Santa Fe. The Santa Fe Trail was ended as a freight route. But some who saw the last freight wagons lived to see also the first motor cars as tourists took over the old Trail as a scenic route, and when the Daughters of the American Revolution began to erect markers along the Trail after 1906, they were guided by men who could point to spots they personally remembered.

It is clear that any bibliography of the Santa Fe Trail must include not only accounts of the Trail itself from 1821 to 1880, but the earlier years of the Spanish period as well. It must also include material on such related aspects as the explorations of Pike and others who touched the Trail, and the activities of the U.S. Dragoons and the Army of the West. It is not difficult to qualify those items that deal solely with the Trail, but on the related material a problem arises. It has been said that if one stands long enough on Times Square in New York City he will, sooner or later, meet everyone he ever knew. In the same fashion, nearly every person connected with the history of the West probably went over at least a part of the Santa Fe Trail at some time. But because, for instance, J.E.B. Stuart as a young officer saw brief service along the Trail, should every work dealing with Stuart be included? And should all the shelvesful of John Charles Frémont items be listed? To include everything would be to compile a bibliography of the entire West and much of the South. My basic standard, therefore, has been to list every known firsthand account by anyone who went over the Trail (and more than three hundred such items are listed) and every study of the Trail. On other Trail-connected personalities such as Carson, Frémont, Jedediah Smith, Joseph E. Johnston, John Sutter, and George C. Sibley, this bibliography contains only (and all of) the works that provide primary information on the connection of the men to the Santa Fe Trail.

Only published material has been listed, including some items published in microfilm or microfiche form. The best collections of manuscript materials are in the Missouri Historical Society library in St. Louis, the State Historical Society of Missouri at Columbia, the Kansas State Historical Society at Topeka, the State Historical Society of Colorado at Denver, the New Mexico State Records Center and Archives at Santa Fe, and the Mexican Archives. No scholar needs direction to the great collections at Yale, Bancroft, Huntington, Harvard, Newberry, Library of Congress, and the National Archives.

Some kinds of material have been omitted. General histories of states, counties, and towns are left out if they are only recent restatements of commonplace information, and so are popular magazine articles of a general nature. Fiction and poetry are omitted except for eleven entries intended to alert the researchers against works whose titles may falsely suggest serious history. The scope of this bibliography has been kept as large as possible so that it will benefit not only the advanced scholar but the smaller public libraries that serve the general public. As a guide to collectors and bookmen the first edition has been described wherever possible, and the latest reprint or paperback edition is also mentioned.

For those who here make their first acquaintance with the full literature of the Santa Fe Trail, I might suggest a few items of special worth. Making lists of "best" books on any subject is a pleasant coffee-table activity of doubtful merit, but most students of the Santa Fe Trail probably will agree that the thirty best writers about the Trail include James Abert, Louise Barry, Averam Bender, Ralph Bieber, William Brown, Bernard DeVoto, R. L. Duffus, Lewis Garrard, Josiah Gregg, Kate Gregg, LeRoy Hafen, Archer Hulbert, Henry Inman, David Lavender, Margaret Long, Noel Loomis, Susan Magoffin, Alexander Majors, Max Moorhead, Leo Oliva, Albert Pike, Kenyon Riddle, Marian Russell, F. F. Stephens, Stanley Vestal, Henry Walker, James Webb, Dean Wood, Walker Wyman, and Otis Young. A few of these —some early and some lacking the professional approach—have weaknesses, it is true, but in general these provide the foundation of Santa Fe Trail literature. They tell the story of a great pathway during the youth of the West.

A HISTORICAL BIBLIOGRAPHY

ABBREVIATIONS

advts. advertisements
b. born
biblio. bibliography
c copyright
ca. *circa*
cm. centimeters height
Cong. Congress
diagr. diagrams
Doc. Document
ed. edition, editor
Exec. Executive
facsim(s). facsimile(s)
ff. pages following
fldg. folding
frontis. frontispiece
H.R. House of Representatives

ltd. limited
lvs. leaves
n.d. no date shown
n.p. no place shown
p., pp. page(s)
Pt. Part
pict. pictorial
port. portrait
q.v. which see
rev. revised
Sen. Senate
sess. session
SFT Santa Fe Trail
t.e.g. top edge gilt
v.d. various dates
v.p. various places

Libraries mentioned, without indicating that they hold the only known copies:
KSH Kansas State Historical Society
N Newberry Library
UNM University of New Mexico

Bibliographies cited:
Graff: *Catalogue of the Everett D. Graff Collection of Western Americana,* Colton Storm, ed. (Chicago: University of Chicago Press, 1968).
Howes: *U.S.IANA,* Wright Howes, compiler (New York: R. R. Bowker Co., revised edition, 1962).
Wagner-Camp: *The Plains and the Rockies,* Henry R. Wagner and Charles L. Camp, compilers (Columbus: Long's College Book Co., third edition, 1953).

1 Abert, James William

Report of an Expedition led by Lieutenant Abert, on the Upper Ar-kansas and Through the Country of the Comanche Indians, in the Fall of the Year 1845 . . . . Journal of Lieutenant J. W. Abert, from Bent's Fort, on the Arkansas River, Saturday, August 9, 1845. U.S. 29th Cong., 1st sess., Vol. 8, Sen. Doc. 438 [Serial 477]. Washington, June 16, 1846.

75 p., 11 plates, two maps, 22.7 cm.

A significant and important document. When Frémont was at Bent's Fort in 1845, on his third expedition, he sent a detachment un-der Abert to examine the country south through Raton Pass and down the Canadian river. Only a portion of the trip was over the SFT. The work has been reprinted twice. Its full text was published in the *Pan-handle-Plains Historical Review*, occupying the entire annual Vol. XIV, 1941, with excellent notes by H. Bailey Carroll who retraced the full route. Some copies were published by the Society in cloth binding, un-der the title *Guadal P'a.* The latest reprint, under the title *Through the Country of the Comanche Indians in the Fall of the Year 1845 . . .* , edited by John Galvin, was issued at San Francisco: John Howell, Books, 1970. Galvin acquired Abert's own watercolor sketches, which are reproduced in this large volume, one of the most handsome ever issued about the Trail. Graff 6; Howes A-10; Wagner-Camp 120.

2 ———

Report of the Secretary of War, communicating . . . a Report and Map of the Examination of New Mexico. . . . U.S. 30th Cong., 1st sess., Sen. Exec. Doc. 23 [Serial 506]. Washington, Feb. 10, 1848.

> Printed wrappers, [ii], [1]-134 p., 1 leaf, 24 leaves plates, fldg. map, 25 cm.

Based on Abert's diary, also published as *Western America in 1846-1847 . . .* (q.v.). Also included in Emory's *Notes of a Military Reconnoissance . . .* (q.v.), pp. 417-546 of the House edition. It describes his trip from Fort Leavenworth over the SFT via Bent's Fort, his survey of the northern part of New Mexico, and his return trip over the Trail. Considered a basic SFT document. Reprinted in facsimile as *Abert's New Mexico Report, 1846-'47*, Albuquerque: Horn and Wallace, 1962. Graff 5; Howes A-11; Wagner-Camp 143.

3 ———

Western America in 1846-1847: The Original Travel Diary of Lieutenant J. W. Abert, Who Mapped New Mexico for the United States Army. Edited by John Galvin. [San Francisco]: John Howell, Books, 1966.

> Cloth, [xiii], 1-116 p., 8 leaves plates incl. frontis., 2 fldg. maps in back, biblio., index, 35.5 cm.

One of the largest and most lavish books about the SFT, edited from the field notebook on which Abert based his official report, . . . *A Report and Map of the Examination of New Mexico* (q.v.). It includes his travel diary from Fort Leavenworth to Santa Fe and return, with Abert's own watercolor sketches. Contains many comments on the SFT found in no other published Abert report.

4   Adams, Blanche V.

"The Second Colorado Cavalry in the Civil War." *The Colorado Magazine*, State Historical Society of Colorado, Vol. VIII, No. 3 (May 1931), pp. 95-106, illus.

This volunteer unit saw much service along the Colorado and Kansas sections of the SFT during the Civil War.

5 Adams, Samuel Hopkins

The Santa Fe Trail. New York: Random House, 1951.

A juvenile.

6 Adams, Zu, 1859-1911

"The Marking of the Santa Fe Trail." In: *Annual Report of the American Historical Association for the Year 1906,* Vol. 1, pp. 152-56. Washington: Government Printing Office, 1908.

A paper read at a conference, describing the problems involved in the first efforts of the Kansas D.A.R. to mark the Trail. Also reprinted in the 15th *Biennial Report of the Kansas State Historical Society,* Topeka, 1907, pp. 74-77.

7 Ainsworth, Newton

Lone Elm Marker: "*Lone Elm Camp Ground, Santa Fe Trail Monument, Erected 1906.* Olathe, Kan.: Olathe Register Print, n.d.

Pamphlet, die cut wrapper, 12 unnumbered p., illus., 21.6 cm.

Lone Elm was a camping place on the SFT in what is now Johnson county, Kansas. This souvenir pamphlet reprints a speech given by Ainsworth when a marker was erected by the D.A.R. on his farm.

8 ———

"The Santa Fe Trail in Johnson County, Kansas." *Kansas Historical Collections,* Vol. XI (1909-1910), pp. 456-63.

Contents are almost identical with previous item by the same author, with the addition of a letter from W. H. Brady, who visited Lone Elm on the SFT in 1854, plus brief comments by other old settlers. Seventeen volumes of *Kansas Historical Collections* were issued, all with that title on the backstrip, although the title pages of Vols. I-X identified them as *Transactions of the Kansas Historical Society.* We have followed the Society's own indexing practice of referring to all as *Collections.* . . .

9 Allison, William H. H.

"John G. Heath." *New Mexico Historical Review*, Vol. VI, No. 4 (Oct. 1931), pp. 360-75.

A biography of Heath, who was a salt manufacturer, businessman, and political figure at Boonville, Missouri. He also figured in the history of Texas and around El Paso. Becknell's journal (q.v.) mentions Heath in a SFT caravan in 1822, and the name *Juan Gid* also appears in Mexican records.

10 Allsopp, Frederick William, 1867-

The Life Story of Albert Pike. Little Rock, Ark.: Parke-Harper News Service, 1920.

[1]-130 p., frontis., illus., 17 cm.

A biography. Of more usefulness is the revised edition, same place and publisher, 1928, titled *Albert Pike; A Biography.* For details of Pike's experiences on the SFT, see entry under Pike, Albert.

11 Arrott, James W.

Arrott's Brief History of Fort Union. Las Vegas, N.M.: Rodgers Library, Highlands University, 1962.

Wrappers, [1]-20 p., map, illus., ltd. 300, 23.5 cm.

Arrott made the largest private collection of documents relating to Fort Union. The material is now at the Rodgers Library.

12 [Ashley, W. H.]

Message from the President . . . Relative to the British Establishments on the Columbia and the State of the Fur Trade, &c. U.S. 21st Cong., 2nd sess., Sen. Doc. 39 [Serial 203]. Washington, Jan. 25, 1831.

36 pp., 22.5 cm.

Although chiefly on the fur trade elsewhere, this contains a letter from W. H. Ashley proposing a unit of 500 mounted riflemen to protect SFT traders. Graff 100; Wagner-Camp 32.

13 Ashton, John

"History of Jack Stock and Mules in Missouri." *The Monthly Bulletin,* Vol. XXII, No. VIII (Aug. 1924). Jefferson City: Missouri State Board of Agriculture, 1924.

> Pamphlet, cover title, saddle stitched, [1]-63 p., port., facsim., scenes, 22.8 cm.

The famed Missouri mules began with stock brought back over the SFT. Ashton locates and cites an extensive array of excerpts from Missouri newspapers, 1823-35, relating to mules and burros.

14 Atherton, Lewis E.

"Business Techniques in the Santa Fe Trade." *Missouri Historical Review,* Vol. XXXIV, No. 3 (April 1940), pp. 335-41.

One of the best detailed short studies on the techniques of merchants and traders on the SFT.

15 ———

"Disorganizing Effects of the Mexican War on the Santa Fe Trade." *Kansas Historical Quarterly,* Vol. VI, No. 2 (May 1937), pp. 115-23.

Traders who were en route when the Mexican War opened continued to Santa Fe and down to Chihuahua with Doniphan's troops. They met an uneasy situation in trying to sell goods in an occupied city. Atherton gives details of the train owned by Samuel Owens and James Aull. Both men were killed.

16 ———

"James and Robert Aull—a Frontier Missouri Mercantile Firm." *Missouri Historical Review,* Vol. XXX, No. 1 (Oct. 1935), pp. 3-27.

A useful study of mercantile methods at the Missouri end of the SFT. James opened his first store in 1825; by 1831 he and his brother Robert operated stores at Lexington, Richmond, Liberty, and Independence, all relying in part on SFT trade. Written from business records; for example: the one big caravan in 1830 bought between $8,000 and $10,000 from the Aulls. Payment was one-fourth cash down and the balance at ten per cent interest after six months. The firm was dissolved in 1836.

17   [Atkinson, Henry]

Expedition up the Missouri. Letter from the Secretary of War, Transmitting the Information . . . Respecting the Movements of the Expedition which Lately Ascended the Missouri River, &c. U.S. 19th Cong., 1st sess., H. R. Doc. 117 [Serial 136]. Washington: Gales & Seaton, Mar. 6, 1826.

> 16 pp., pp. 2 and 4 blank, 22.5 cm.

> Chiefly concerning the upper Missouri, but there is a brief discussion (p. 15) concerning a fort where the SFT crosses the Arkansas river. Gen. Henry Atkinson approves the location but says it would be expensive to supply and would require more troops than the frontier army could spare. Graff 104; Wagner-Camp 32.

18   Balch, C. T.

"The First Graves in La Junta, Colorado." *The Colorado Magazine,* State Historical Society of Colorado, Vol. VIII, No. 6 (Nov. 1931), pp. 223-25, illus.

> As the railroad was built westward, the SFT continued from the end of track. This is one of the few personal memoirs of what life was like in a wild end-of-track town, where wagon freighters mingled with railroad men.

19   Bancroft, Hubert Howe, 1832-

History of Arizona and New Mexico, 1530-1888. The Works of Hubert Howe Bancroft, XVII. San Francisco: The History Company, 1889.

> Full leather, xxxviii, 1-829 p., illus., maps (1 fldg.), index, 22.6 cm.

> A well-recognized standard nineteenth century work on New Mexico, with general SFT material, particularly pp. 291-300, 319-38, 408-16. Reprinted, Albuquerque: Calvin Horn, Publisher, 1962; New York: McGraw-Hill Book Company, 1967. Graff 155; Howes H-91.

20 [Bandel, Eugene]

Frontier Life in the Army, 1854-1861. Edited by Ralph P. Bieber. Southwest Historical Series, II. Glendale: Arthur H. Clark Company, 1932.

> Cloth, [1]-330 p., 9 leaves plates incl. frontis., fldg. map, 24.3 cm.

Letters and journal of Eugene Bandel, a soldier with the 6th Infantry at Fort Leavenworth. His regiment made trips through Nebraska, the Dakotas, and west to California. Of more particular interest is Bandel's material on a survey of the southern Kansas border in 1857. On this march they reached Rabbit Ear creek in New Mexico and often met SFT travelers. Bandel's description of life at Fort Leavenworth is also useful.

21 Barreiro, Antonio

Ojeada sobre Nuevo México, que da una Idea de sus Produciones Naturales, y de Algunas Otras Cosas. . . . Puebla, Mexico: Imprenta del Ciudadano José Maria Campos, 1832.

> Wrappers, [1]-42 plus 3 addl. printed pages and a supplement of [1]-10 p., 20.2 cm.

Translated as *A Glance over New Mexico*, this is one of relatively few works with material on the SFT from the Mexican end. In 1831 the Mexican government sent Barreiro to Santa Fe as a legal advisor. He was asked to prepare a report for his superiors, and this work resulted. It deals with all aspects of New Mexico. It was first published in English in the *New Mexico Historical Review*, Vol. III, No. 1 (Jan. 1928), pp. 73-96, and in No. 2 (April 1928), pp. 145-78; then reprinted in wrappers, Santa Fe: Historical Society of New Mexico, Publications in History, V, 1928. It is also translated in H. Bailey Carroll's *Three New Mexico Chronicles* (q.v.). Graff 194; Howes B-169.

22 Barry, Louise, ed.

"Kansas Before 1854: A Revised Annals." *Kansas Historical Quarterly*, 24 installments: "Part I, 1540-1762," Vol. XXVII, No. 1 (Spring 1961), pp. 67-93; "Part 2, 1763-1803," No. 2 (Summer 1961), pp. 201-

19; "Part 3, 1804-18," No. 3 (Autumn 1961), pp. 353-82; "Part 4, 1819-25," No. 4 (Winter 1961), pp. 497-543; "Part 5, 1826-29," Vol. XXVIII, No. 1 (Spring 1962), pp. 25-29; "Part 6, 1830-32," No. 2 (Summer 1962), pp. 167-204; "Part 7, 1833-34," No. 3 (Autumn 1962), pp. 317-69; "Part 8, 1835," No. 4 (Winter 1962), pp. 497-514; "Part 9, 1836-37," Vol. XXIX, No. 1 (Spring 1963), pp. 41-81; "Part 10, 1838-39," No. 2 (Summer 1963), pp. 143-89; "Part 11, 1840-41," No. 3 (Autumn 1963), pp. 324-59; "Part 12, 1842-43," No. 4 (Winter 1963), pp. 429-86; "Part 13, 1844," Vol. XXX, No. 1 (Spring 1964), pp. 62-91; "Part 14, 1845," No. 2 (Summer 1964), pp. 209-44; "Part 15, 1846," No. 3 (Autumn 1964), pp. 339-412; "Part 16, 1847," No. 4 (Winter 1964), pp. 492-559; "Part 17, 1848," Vol. XXXI, No. 2 (Summer 1965), pp. 138-99; "Part 18, 1849," No. 3 (Autumn 1965), pp. 256-339; "Part 19, 1850," Vol. XXXII, No. 1 (Spring 1966), pp. 33-112; "Part 20, 1851," No. 2 (Summer 1966), pp. 210-82; "Part 21, 1852," No. 4 (Winter 1966), pp. 426-503; "Part 22, 1853," Vol. XXXIII, No. 1 (Spring 1967), pp. 13-64; "Addendum," No. 3 (Autumn 1967), pp. 377-405.

In many ways this is perhaps the single most useful reference source on the SFT since the works of Josiah Gregg and James J. Webb (q.v.). D. W. Wilder published, until 1886, his *Annals of Kansas*. They were historically deficient for the years prior to 1854. As part of a publications program during the Kansas Centennial in 1961, Louise Barry of the staff of the Kansas Historical Society assembled this collection of excerpts, notes, and comments on Kansas history from early and recent sources. While it relates to Kansas as a whole, it includes most major events and personalities on the SFT. Publication in book form is scheduled for 1971 or 1972.

23 Bate, W. N.

Frontier Legend: Texas Finale of Capt. Wm. F. Drannan, Pseudo Frontier Comrade of Kit Carson, Based on Research. New Bern, No. Car.: Owen G. Dunn Company, 1954.

> Wrappers, side stitched, [1]-[69] p., 1 leaf, plus 3 leaves plates, 22.6 cm.

> A history detective builds a case to claim that Drannan's book,

Thirty-one Years on the Plains and in the Mountains, was a fabrication. Graff 206.

24 Baughman, Robert W.

Kansas Post Offices, May 29, 1828—August 3, 1961. [Topeka]: Kansas Postal History Society, [1961].

> Wrappers, viii, 1-256 p., maps, 21.5 cm.

The best source for dates when post offices opened along the SFT in Kansas. The first was at Cantonment Leavenworth in 1828. Also lists first postmasters. Sixteen maps show counties of Kansas at different periods. Available from Kansas State Historical Society, Topeka.

25 Beadle, John Hanson, 1840-1897

The Undeveloped West; or, Five Years in the Territories; Being a Complete History of that Vast Region between the Mississippi and the Pacific, Its Resources, Climate, Inhabitants, Natural Curiosities, etc., etc.; Life and Adventures on Prairies, Mountains, and the Pacific Coast. Philadelphia: National Publishing Company, [c 1873].

> Cloth, [ii], 15-823 p., 8 p. advts., illus., 21 cm.

A personal memoir written in adventurous style, containing an account of a stage ride (pp. 442-49) from Trinidad to Santa Fe. Essentially the same information is contained in his 1881 work, *Western Wilds, and the Men Who Redeem Them* . . . (pp. 215-20). Graff 212; Howes B-269.

26 Beam, D. C.

"Reminiscences of Early Days in Nebraska." *Transactions and Reports of the Nebraska State Historical Society*, Vol. II (1892), pp. 292 ff.

> Beam served in B troop, 1st Dragoons, 1852-57. Most of his service was in the Nebraska area, but he made at least one trip over the SFT to Fort Union. The article had appeared previously in the Omaha *Republican*.

27   Becknell, [William]

"The Journals of Capt. Thomas Becknell from Boone's Lick to Santa Fe and from Santa Cruz to Green River." *Missouri Historical Review*, Vol. 4, No. 2 (Jan. 1910), pp. 65-84.

Becknell's first pack train left Arrow Rock, Missouri, on September 1, 1821, and reached Santa Fe on November 16, 1821. His journal is here reprinted from the *Missouri Intelligencer* of April 22, 1823. His second journal describes a trapping expedition from Santa Fe to Green River in 1824, back to Taos in 1825, thence back to Missouri. The article also has brief items on other SFT expeditions. His first name was William, not Thomas. The work was also published in 1910 by the Society as a separate pamphlet. Graff 225.

28   Beers, Henry Putney

"Military Protection of the Santa Fe Trail to 1843." *New Mexico Historical Review*, Vol. XII, No. 2 (April 1937), pp. 113-33, port., fldg. map.

A brief survey of the subject, drawn from Beers' doctoral dissertation. Not as comprehensive as the later work by Otis E Young (q.v.).

29   ————

The Western Military Frontier, 1815-1846. Upper Darby, Pa.: published by the author, 1935.

Wrappers, vi, 1-227 p., maps, biblio., 23 cm.

A general history of early western forts, with material on Fort Osage and Fort Leavenworth. Also issued, Philadelphia: University of Pennsylvania, 1935.

30   [Bell, John R., ca. 1785-1825]

The Journal of Captain John R. Bell, Official Journalist for the Stephen H. Long Expedition to the Rocky Mountains, 1820. Edited by Harlin M. Fuller and LeRoy R. Hafen. The Far West and the Rockies

Historical Series, 1820-1875, VI. Glendale: Arthur H. Clark Company, 1957.

> Cloth, [1]-349 p., frontis., illus., facsims., fldg. map, index, 24.5 cm.

This expedition returned down the Arkansas in the summer of 1820 along what soon became a portion of the SFT (pp. 180-221). Long's expedition was the first government expedition into the West following those of Lewis and Clark and Pike. The expedition has often been called the Yellowstone Expedition, and until Bell's journal was found in 1932 the only extant account had been that of Edwin James (q.v.).

31   Bell, William Abraham

New Tracks in North America: A Journal of Travel and Adventure whilst Engaged in the Survey for a Southern Railroad to the Pacific Ocean during 1867-8. 2 vols. London: Chapman and Hall, 1869.

> Embossed brown cloth, issued unopened, 22 cm.; Vol. I: [lxvii], [1]-236 p.; Vol. II: ix, [1]-322 p.; 24 leaves plates, 1 fldg. map.

This railroad survey party went through central Kansas and turned south to strike the SFT forty-two miles east of Fort Lyon in 1867. Bell's description is long and thorough in describing the route along the SFT through Fort Lyon, Bent's Fort, Trinidad, Raton Pass, Maxwell's Ranch, Fort Union, and on to the Pecos river. A one-volume edition was issued in 1870; reprinted, facsimile, Albuquerque: Calvin Horn, Publisher, 1965. Graff 246; Howes B-330.

32   Bender, Averam Burton, b. 1891

The March of Empire: Frontier Defense in the Southwest, 1848-1860. Lawrence: University of Kansas Press, 1952.

> Cloth, map endpapers, [x], [1]-323 p., 2 leaves plates, map, biblio., index, 23.5 cm.

A study of military operations, chiefly in the Southwest, during the years mentioned. Includes the author's article, "Military Posts in the Southwest, 1848-1860" (q.v.), as part of a broader discussion of Indian control to protect the SFT and other routes.

33 ———

"Military Posts in the Southwest, 1848-1860." *New Mexico Historical Review*, Vol. XVI, No. 2 (April 1941), pp. 125-47, map.

Minor information on Forts Mann, Marcy, and Union, all located on the SFT.

34 [Bennett, James A.]

Forts and Forays: James A. Bennett, a Dragoon in New Mexico, 1850-1856. Edited by Clinton E. Brooks and Frank D. Reeve. Albuquerque: University of New Mexico Press, 1948.

> Cloth, [iv], 1-85 p., frontis. port., 4 p. plates, index, fldg. map in back pocket, 23.3 cm.

Bennett joined the 1st Dragoons in 1849 and describes his first trip over the SFT that year to Las Vegas. Written after the lapse of several years and the loss of many notes. Most of the text also appeared in the *New Mexico Historical Review*, Vol. XXII, Nos. 1 and 2, 1947.

35 [Bent, Charles]

"The Charles Bent Papers," edited by Frank D. Reeve. *New Mexico Historical Review*, Vol. XXIX, No. 3 (July 1954), pp. 234-39; No. 4 (Oct. 1954), pp. 311-17; Vol. XXX, No. 2 (April 1955), pp. 154-67; No. 3 (July 1955), pp. 252-54; No. 4 (Oct. 1955), pp. 340-52; Vol. XXXI, No. 1 (Jan. 1956), pp. 75-77; No. 2 (April 1956), pp. 157-64; and No. 3 (July 1956), pp. 251-53.

Texts of several letters written between December 1837 and early 1846. Charles and William Bent built Bent's Fort; Charles settled in New Mexico. His letters involved nearly all leading personalities at the New Mexico end of the SFT and furnish useful details on merchants' operations and other aspects of the Trail.

36 ———

Report from the Secretary of War, with an Abstract of Licenses to

Trade with the Indians in 1834, &c. U.S. 23rd Cong., 2nd sess., Sen. Doc. 69 [Serial 268]. Washington, Jan. 21, 1835.

11 p., 22.5 cm.

Useful information on the fur trade, with information on those who were licensed in 1834. Some material on Charles Bent "at Fort William on the north side of the Arkansas" (p. 3).

37 [Bent, William W.]

William W. Bent. U.S. 35th Cong., 2nd sess., H. R. Report 151 [Serial 1018]. Washington, Feb. 1, 1859.

1 p., 22.5 cm.

Bent asks compensation for oxen taken by Indians in the winter of 1854-55. The Committee on Indian Affairs says the claim is valid but feels the amount asked is too high and suggests the claim be adjusted.

38 [Bent, St. Vrain & Co.]

Bent, St. Vrain, & Co. U.S. 28th Cong., 2nd sess., H. R. Report 194 [Serial 468]. Washington: Blair & Rives, printers, Mar. 3, 1845.

9 p., 22.5 cm.

Bent, St. Vrain, & Company asked compensation for loss of goods captured in September 1837 by Pawnee Indians on a branch of the Arkansas. The Committee on Indian Affairs reports adversely, saying the raid occurred in Mexican territory. This well known and useful document contains a complete inventory of goods carried by the pack train, including ten reams of paper and twenty-five pounds of printer's ink.

39 ———

The Committee on Military Affairs, to Whom was Referred the Petition of Bent, St. Vrain, & Co., Praying Compensation for a Quantity of Provisions Collected for a Detachment of U.S. Troops on the Upper Waters of the Arkansas River, in the Year 1843, Report. U.S. 29th

Cong., 1st sess., Sen. Report 115 [Serial 473]. Washington, Ritchie & Heiss, print, Feb. 5, 1846.

> 3 p., 22.5 cm.

The traders stocked $6,500 worth of beef, flour, and onions, under contract for a dragoon expedition. The troops changed their route, and an order cancelling the contract did not reach "Fort William" in time. Committee approves compensation. For another document on the same claim, see U.S. 30th Cong., 1st sess., H. R. Report 37 (Serial 524), Jan. 11, 1848.

40 [Benton, Thomas Hart]

[Report] *Relative to the Establishment of a Military Post for the Protection of the Trade to Santa Fe, in New Mexico.* U.S. 19th Cong., 2nd sess. In: *American State Papers, Military Affairs,* Vol. III, document 359, p. 615. Washington: Gales & Seaton, 1860.

A one-page report dated March 2, 1827. A Senate resolution asks for a fort at the point where the SFT crossed the Arkansas river. General Jacob Brown, then commander in chief of the army, objects to establishment of a post 500 miles from its nearest supply base. Benton submitted the final report, as head of the Senate committee on military affairs.

41 ——————

Report Relative to the Fur Trade. U.S. 20th Cong., 2nd sess., Sen. Doc. 67 [Serial 181]. Washington, Feb. 9, 1829.

> 19 p., 22.5 cm.

Considered one of the basic congressional documents on the fur trade, issued in 1829. Although it does not mention the SFT, the report encouraged trade that involved the Trail. Wagner-Camp 37.

42 ——————

Thirty Years' View; or, a History of the Working of the American Government for Thirty Years, from 1820 to 1850 . . . by a Senator of Thirty Years. 2 vols. New York: D. Appleton and Company, 1854.

Stamped cloth, 24.4 cm. V. I: 1 p.l. adv., ix, [1]-739 p., 8 leaves advts., frontis. port.; V. II: [1]-788 p., 2 leaves advts., frontis.

Senator Benton played the leading political role in developing the SFT. He tells of introducing the first bill for a road west of the Mississippi (Vol. I, pp. 41-44). The work also has material on the conquest of New Mexico in 1846 (Vol. II, pp. 682-88). See also entries under Storrs, Augustus. Reprinted, New York: Greenwood Press, Inc., 1968.

43 [Bent's Fort]

"Letters and Notes from or about Bent's Fort, 1844-45." *The Colorado Magazine*, State Historical Society of Colorado, Vol. XI, No. 6 (Nov. 1934), pp. 223-27.

Nine items reprinted from the *St. Louis Reveille*, describing arrivals or departures of traders over the SFT.

44 ⸻

"More about Bent's Old Fort." *The Colorado Magazine*, State Historical Society of Colorado, Vol. XXXIV, No. 2 (April 1957), pp. 144-49.

Notes and letters about the fort, plus stage line material. One letter by Charles S. Frances, 1867; the other by Miss Mate M. Peck, 1866.

45 Bernard, William R.

"Westport and the Santa Fe Trade." *Kansas Historical Collections*, Vol. IX (1905-1906), pp. 552-65.

Firsthand account; one of the more important memoirs on the SFT. Bernard (b. 1823) reached Westport in 1847, and the firm of Bernard & Kearny became outfitters. Has data on the Chávez killing, Snively expedition, and Aubry.

46 Berry, Erick

When Wagon Trains Rolled to Santa Fe. Champaign, Ill.: Garrard Publishing Co., 1966.

A juvenile; non-fiction.

47   Bieber, Ralph P., ed.

Exploring Southwestern Trails, 1846-1854. By Philip St. George Cooke, William Henry Chase Whiting, François Xavier Aubry. Southwest Historical Series, VII. Glendale: Arthur H. Clark Company, 1938.

> Cloth, t.e.g., [1]-[385] p., 5 leaves plates incl. frontis., fldg. map at back, 24.3 cm.

Contains journals and diaries of three men named, but the work is useful in SFT research chiefly for Bieber's introduction. Cooke's journal of the march of the Mormon Battalion, 1846, opens with their departure from Santa Fe for California. Whiting's journal, 1849, is devoted wholly to a trip across Texas. Aubry's diaries, 1853-54, deal only with his trips between New Mexico and California. Bieber's introduction describes Cooke's earlier years along the SFT (pp. 17-28), and the material on Aubry (pp. 38-62) is probably the best biography of this important trader along the Trail, 1846-52, known for the speed of his caravans. Aubry made a famous horseback ride from Santa Fe to Independence, over 750 miles, in five days and sixteen hours, in September 1848. Bieber cites all sources, many including contemporary newspapers.

48   ———

"Letters of James and Robert Aull." *Missouri Historical Society Collections,* Vol. V (1928), pp. 286-87.

The Aull brothers were prominent SFT outfitters at the eastern end of the Trail.

49   ———

Marching with the Army of the West, 1846-1848. By Abraham Robinson Johnston, Marcellus Ball Edwards, Philip Gooch Ferguson; edited by Ralph P. Bieber. Southwest Historical Series, IV. Glendale: Arthur H. Clark Company, 1936.

> Cloth, [1]-386 p., frontis. port., fldg. map, 24.2 cm.

Journals of three soldiers who marched with the Army of the West in the Mexican War, over the SFT. All three are here published for the first time and describe incidents of the march over the Trail.

50 ———

"The Papers of James J. Webb, Santa Fe Merchant, 1844-1861." *Washington University Studies*, Vol. XI, No. 2 (April 1924), pp. 255-305.

Webb was one of the leading traders along the SFT. This study describes the scope and nature of his business records, which remained with the family: 24 volumes of cash books, ledgers, day books, etc.; 1,100 original letters; 5 letter books with copies of 2,000 letters; and other memoirs. Also issued as a separate pamphlet, in printed green wrappers. Graff 294.

51 ———

"Some Aspects of the Santa Fe Trail, 1848-1880." *Missouri Historical Review*, Vol. XVIII, No. 2 (Jan. 1924), pp. 158-66.

Brief review of the later years of the SFT, with material on stage lines, border troubles, and railroad extension. Gives dates on which AT&SF Ry. reached Trail points: Fort Dodge, 1869; Kit Carson, Colorado, 1870; La Junta, 1875; Trinidad, 1878; Las Vegas, 1879; Santa Fe, 1880. Also published in *Chronicles of Oklahoma*, Vol. 2, No. 1 (March 1924), pp. 1-8.

52 ———

Southern Trails to California. Southwest Historical Series, V. Glendale: Arthur H. Clark Co., 1937.

Cloth, [1]-386 p., fldg. maps, ports., ltd. 1,050, 24.5 cm.

Includes a diary of Dr. Augustus M. Heslep (pp. 353-86), whose party was guided across the SFT by James Kirker as far as Santa Fe.

53 ———

"The Southwestern Trails to California in 1849." *Mississippi Valley Historical Review*, Vol. XII, No. 3 (Dec. 1925), pp. 342-75, map.

Most of the argonauts of '49 who went overland journeyed by the northern route via the Platte river. This article deals with those who went by southern routes across Texas, Oklahoma, and via the SFT. From late April to mid-September 1849 "about 2,500 emigrants" went over the Trail to Santa Fe (pp. 364-66), partly to avoid cholera that was prevalent on the northern trail.

54 [Bigler, Henry W.]

"Extracts from the Journal of Henry W. Bigler." *Utah Historical Quarterly*, Vol. 5, No. 2 (April 1932), pp. 35-64; No. 3 (July 1932), pp. 87-102; No. 4 (Oct. 1932), pp. 134-60.

Bigler was a Mormon who went with the Battalion over the SFT and on to California. A brief section describes the Trail (pp. 37-41). See also entry 261.

55 Binkley, William Campbell, 1889-

"New Mexico and the Texan-Santa Fe Expedition." *Southwestern Historical Quarterly*, Vol. XXVII, No. 2 (Oct. 1923), pp. 85-107.

A documented study of the attitudes in New Mexico before and during the approach of the Texans in their expedition of 1841-42. Much of the information is from letters in archives of Mexico and Texas.

56 Birch, James H.

"The Battle of Coon Creek." *Kansas Historical Collections*, Vol. X (1907-1908), pp. 409-13.

Firsthand account. Birch was with a detachment of recruits in the Mexican War, marching west over the SFT in May 1848. Near present Kinsley, Kansas, they fought off an attack by 800 Indians.

57 Blair, Ed, 1863-

History of Johnson County, Kansas. Lawrence: Standard Publishing Company, 1915.

> Cloth, [1]-469 p., frontis. port., plates, 26.5 cm.

A county history with SFT material (pp. 54-70) taken chiefly from Newton Ainsworth (q.v.). Also includes recollections of a bull-whacker, William Johnson, who was a wagon teamster in the late 1850s. Howes B-497.

58 Blanchard, Leola Howard

Conquest of Southwest Kansas: A History and Thrilling Stories of Frontier Life in the State of Kansas. Wichita: Wichita Eagle Press, 1931.

> Cloth, vi, 7-355 p., illus., 20.5 cm.

A general secondary work useful in any survey study of the area, with frequent mentions of the SFT.

59 [Bliss, Robert S.]

"The Journal of Robert S. Bliss, with the Mormon Battalion." *Utah Historical Quarterly,* Vol. 4, No. 3 (July 1931), pp. 67-96; No. 4 (Oct. 1931), pp. 110-28.

> Bliss was a member of the Battalion and marched across the SFT and to California. Brief section on Trail experiences (pp. 68-74).

60 Bloom, Lansing Bartlett

"The Death of Jacques D'Eglise." *New Mexico Historical Review,* Vol. II, No. 4 (Oct. 1927), pp. 369-79.

> Translates documents concerning D'Eglise, Pedro Vial, and other French adventurers trading into Santa Fe before 1809.

61 ———

"Ledgers of a Santa Fe Trader." *El Palacio,* Vol. XIV, No. 9 (May 1, 1923), pp. 133-36.

A brief paper on Manuel Alvarez. Born in Spain, Alvarez left there in 1818, spent a few years in Havana, and went to New York. In 1824 he secured a passport in Missouri and went over the SFT to Santa Fe. Although not a U.S. citizen, he served in a consular capacity to the U.S. in the 1830s and 1840s. He was also a merchant. His ledgers offer information on business practices at the far end of the Trail. Alvarez still awaits full treatment in a major paper or book; much archival material is available. Bloom's paper was also reprinted in *New Mexico Historical Review*, Vol. XXI, No. 2 (April 1946), pp. 135-39.

62 ———

"New Mexico under Mexican Administration, 1821-1846." *Old Santa Fe*, Vol. I, No. 1 (July 1913), pp. 3-49, through Vol. II, No. 4 (April 1915), pp. 351-80.

A general study of the years when New Mexico was part of the Republic of Mexico. Material on the SFT in Chapter III of Part III (Vol. II, No. 2, Oct. 1914, pp. 119-28), with data on costs of wagon trains; in this same section there is a chapter on the Texan-Santa Fe and Snively expeditions.

63 Boggs, William M.

"Reminiscences of Wm. M. Boggs, Son of Governor Lilburn W. Boggs." *Missouri Historical Review*, Vol. 6, No. 2 (Jan. 1912), pp. 86-90.

William was about nineteen when he and his family moved to California. He recalls a meeting with Kit Carson on the SFT in 1844. William's brother Tom was a close friend of Carson.

64 ———

"A Short Biographical Sketch of Lilburn W. Boggs, by His Son." *Missouri Historical Review*, Vol. 4, No. 2 (Jan. 1910), pp. 106-10.

Lilburn W. Boggs (1792-1860) was a Santa Fe trader in the 1830s. He was governor of Missouri during the Mormon incidents, then moved to California in 1846 and died there.

65 ————

"The W. M. Boggs Manuscript about Bent's Fort, Kit Carson, the Far West and Life among the Indians," edited by LeRoy R. Hafen. *The Colorado Magazine*, State Historical Society of Colorado, Vol. VII, No. 2 (Mar. 1930), pp. 45-69, port.

Boggs wrote this manuscript in 1905, giving descriptions of the SFT fort and the Indians and traders who frequented it. Data on duties levied by Mexicans on SFT wagon trains; also the tale of a wagonload of contraband tobacco. A separate pamphlet edition, privately printed, has been reported.

66   Bolton, Herbert Eugene, 1870-

Athanaze de Mézières and the Louisiana-Texas Frontier, 1768-1780. 2 vols. Spain in the West Series, I, II. Cleveland: Arthur H. Clark Co., 1914.

> Cloth, 24.3 cm.; Vol. I: [1]-351 p., fldg. map as frontis.; Vol. II: [1]-392 p., frontis., index, 24.5 cm.

An excellent historical introduction of more than 100 pp., with the balance devoted to translations of documents. Contains little on the SFT (pp. 58-60), but the brief material is highly important: data on De Bourgmont's trip in 1724, the Mallet brothers in 1739-40, French traders at El Quartelejo in Kansas in 1748, mention of Jean Chapuis, and Felipe Sandoval's trip west along the Arkansas to Santa Fe in 1750. Reprinted in one volume, New York: Kraus Reprint Co. Howes B-584.

67 ————

Coronado on the Turquoise Trail: Knight of Pueblos and Plains. Coronado Cuarto Centennial Publications, I. Albuquerque: University of New Mexico Press, 1949.

> Cloth, xvi, 1-491 p., frontis., 3 fldg. maps, biblio., index, 26.5 cm.

Considered to be the best work on Coronado since the original documents. Coronado's men were the first Europeans on the Arkansas, crossing it in the area of the SFT (pp. 288-89). Also available in reprint and in paperback.

68 ―――――

"New Light on Manuel Lisa and the Spanish Fur Trade." *Quarterly of the Texas State Historical Association*, Vol. XVII, No. 1 (1903), pp. 61-66.

First publication of a letter by Manuel Lisa, written at Fort Manuel on the Missouri in 1812. He offers to open trade with New Mexico and to supply any goods needed. Spanish text, with English translation, indicating an early interest in trade between Missouri and Santa Fe before the Trail was opened. Also issued as a separate.

69 ―――――

"Papers of Zebulon M. Pike." *American Historical Review*, Vol. XIII, No. 4 (July 1908), pp. 798-827.

Reprints fifteen letters, notes, and other documents taken from Pike by the Mexicans. Bolton found them in Mexico at the Secretariat of Foreign Relations. They include some letters from James Biddle Wilkinson to his father, the general, describing scenes along the Arkansas.

70 ―――――

Texas in the Middle Eighteenth Century: Studies in Spanish Colonial History and Administration. University of California Publications in History, III. Berkeley: University of California Press, 1915.

Wrappers, x, [1]-501 p., frontis., 12 maps, facsims., biblio., index, 25 cm.

The middle third of the eighteenth century was a period of French ventures from Louisiana toward New Mexico. Bolton cites archival sources and documents in describing several such expeditions (pp. 66-69): the Mallet brothers in 1739; Fabry de la Bruyère in 1741; Febre, Satren, and Raballo's trip to Taos in 1749 by way of the Arkansas river; and Chapuis and Feulli in 1752. There is also material on Pedro Vial's trip from Santa Fe to Missouri (pp. 127-33). Reprinted, New York: Russell & Russell, Publishers, 1962, ltd. 400; New York: Kraus Reprint Co.; also in paperback, Austin: University of Texas Press, 1970. Howes B-589.

71   Bolton, Herbert Eugene, and Thomas Maitland Marshall

The Colonization of North America, 1492-1783. New York: The Mac-millan Company, 1920.

Cloth, [xvii], 1-609 p., maps, index, 21 cm.

Written essentially as a college text, this contains (pp. 282-97) one of the best summaries of the French advance toward New Mexico, 1703-53. Bolton mentions twenty Canadians going to New Mexico around 1703 to trade.

72   Bonner, T. D.

The Life and Adventures of James P. Beckwourth, Mountaineer, Scout, and Pioneer, and Chief of the Crow Nation of Indians. New York: Harper & Brothers, 1856.

Cloth, xii, [13]-537 p., illus., 19.5 cm.

A noted trapper and Mountain Man, Beckwourth was active along the upper Missouri in the 1820s and later in California. He was at Bent's Fort and in New Mexico but apparently did not travel the eastern section of the SFT until in the 1850s (see entry 265). Other reported editions include London 1856, Paris 1860, and an abridged version at London 1892; reprinted New York: A. A. Knopf, Inc., 1931, with useful introduction and notes by Bernard DeVoto. Graff 347; Howes B-601; Wagner-Camp 272. N.

73   Bork, Albert William

Nuevos Aspectos del Comercio entre México y Misuri, 1822-46. México: National University of Mexico, 1944.

Unpublished doctoral dissertation, 134 p.

This is the only unpublished manuscript listed in this bibliography, the exception being made because of its importance. It is, however, "published" on microfilm, Reel 67-8074, University of California at Berkeley. Bork, currently director of the Latin American Institute at Southern Illinois University, Carbondale, did this in Mexico City on the hundredth anniversary of the publication of Gregg's *Commerce of the Prairies.* Almost entirely in Spanish, it presents to Mexicans a

55

summary of the SFT taken from U.S. sources; for those north of the border it contains the texts of many Mexican archival documents: reports from the customs house at Santa Fe, manifests of caravan freight, lists of caravan members, etc., 1830-34. Much of it should be translated and reissued in English.

74 Bosch Garcia, Carlos

Historía de las Relaciones entre México y los Estados Unidos, 1819-1848. México: Universidad Nacional Autónoma de México, Escucla Nacional de Ciencias Politicas y Sociales, 1961.

Wrappers, sewn, [1]-295 p., ltd. 2000, 21.6 cm.

Text in Spanish only, dealing principally with the Texas revolution and the Mexican war, but with one chapter dealing with early commerce. The U.S. viewed the SFT as an extended artery of commerce; many Mexicans viewed it as an approaching military highway. These attitudes affected all negotiations, beginning with U.S. Ambassador Poinsett's first discussions in 1825 regarding the proposed survey of the Trail.

75 ———

Material para la Historía Diplomática de México (México y los Estados Unidos, 1820-1848). Mexico: Universidad Nacional Autónoma de México, Escuela Nacional de Ciencias Politicas y Sociales, 1957.

Wrappers, sewn, [1]-655 p., ltd. 2000, 22 cm.

A chronological catalog or calendar of diplomatic documents from both the Mexican and U.S. national archives, with a synopsis of the contents of each document. It deals with a broad range of topics; items relating to the SFT include Poinsett's reports on discussions concerning the SFT survey, 1825; and Waddy Thompson's efforts to free the Texan-Santa Fe expedition prisoners, 1842. Text in Spanish only.

76 Bott, Emily Ann O'Neil

"Joseph Murphy's Contribution to the Development of the West." *Missouri Historical Review*, Vol. XLVII, No. 1 (Oct. 1952), pp. 18-28.

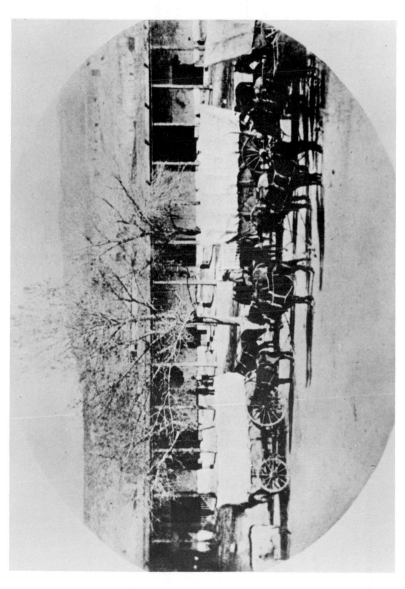

At the end of the Santa Fe Trail: Elsberg & Amberg wagon train in front of the Palace of the Governors in Santa Fe Plaza, 1861. (Courtesy Museum of New Mexico)

Old Santa Fe Trail ruts seen from the air as dark streaks, starting at lower left and cut by a winding irrigation ditch, about nine miles west of Dodge City, 1962. White line at left is U.S. 50. (Courtesy Kansas Dept. of Economic Development)

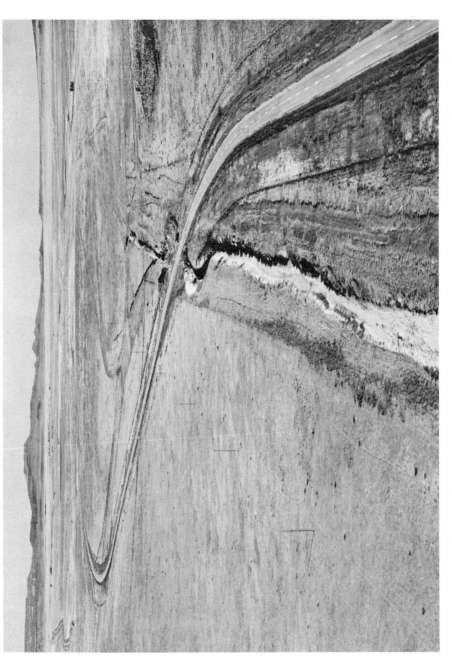

Santa Fe Trail ruts, lower right, are crossed by a modern highway south of Fort Union near Watrous, N.M., in this aerial view taken in 1962. (Photo by Laura Gilpin for National Park Service)

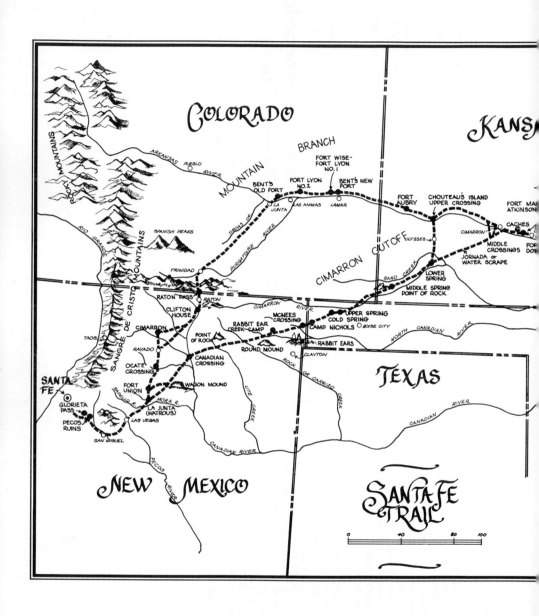

SANTA FE TRAIL

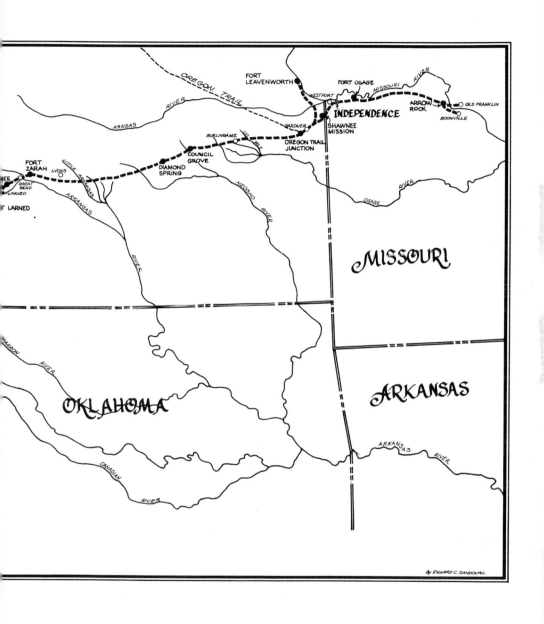

OREGON TRAIL

FORT
LEAVENWORTH

FORT OSAGE

MISSOURI   RIVER

WESTPORT

ARROW
ROCK

OLD FRANKLIN

KANSAS   RIVER

GARDNER

INDEPENDENCE

BOONVILLE

SHAWNEE
MISSION

BURLINGAME

100 MILE

OREGON TRAIL
JUNCTION

FORT
ZARAH

LYONS

LITTLE ARKANSAS

COUNCIL
GROVE

DIAMOND
SPRING

NEOSHO   RIVER

RIVER

OSAGE

NEE

GREAT
BEND

LARNED

ARKANSAS

RIVER

T LARNED

MISSOURI

RIVER

CIMARRON   RIVER

OKLAHOMA

ARKANSAS

ARKANSAS   RIVER

CANADIAN

RIVER

By RICHARD C. SANDOVAL

Along the Trail in Kansas: light wagons at the Shamleffer & James trading post at Council Grove in the 1860s. (Courtesy Kansas State Historical Society)

Bent's Old Fort National Historic Site near La Junta, Colo., as seen from the air in 1970. (Courtesy National Park Service, U.S. Dept. of the Interior)

Last days of the Trail: yoked oxen at Pigeon's Ranch station in Glorieta Pass, New Mexico, photographed by Ben Wittick in 1880, just after the railroad reached Santa Fe. (Museum of New Mexico)

An excellent paper on a great SFT wagonmaker. Murphy opened his shop in St. Louis in 1825; altogether he built over 200,000 wagons for Western trail use. By 1840 he was building big wagons for Trail use, carrying a bigger payload with no increase in Mexican taxes. The wheels were seven feet high, the bed was so deep that a man inside barely exposed the top of his head, and the wagon tongue was fifty feet long. Wheel rims were eight inches wide, and the load was 4,000 to 5,000 lbs.

77 Boyd, Le Roy

Fort Lyon, Colorado: One Hundred Years of Service. [Printed by H & H Printing Co., Colorado Springs, Colo., 1967].

Pamphlet, [ii], [1]-30 p., illus., map, 22.5 cm.

A souvenir history distributed at the 100th anniversary of Fort Lyon, now a hospital. The text is a good, brief history of this fort.

78 Brackett, Albert G.

History of the United States Cavalry, from the Formation of the Federal Government to the 1st of June, 1863. . . . New York: Harper & Brothers, 1865.

Cloth, xii, [13]-337 p., 1 leaf advts., maps, illus., 18.7 cm.

History of the organization of the Dragoons and their operations in the West, including the SFT; cavalry operations along the Trail; data on arms, uniforms, and horse care. Reprinted, New York: Argonaut Press, Ltd., 1965; also Westport, Conn.: Greenwood Press, Inc. Graff 381; Howes B-692, Wagner-Camp 411.

79 Bradley, Glenn Danford, 1884-

Winning the Southwest: A Story of Conquest. Chicago: A. C. Mc-Clurg & Co., 1912.

Cloth, [xii], 13-225 p., frontis. port., ports., 18.6 cm.

Seven biographical sketches that first appeared separately in the *Santa Fe Employees Magazine.* Written for a general audience, from standard sources, they include sketches of Richens Wootton, Kit Carson, Stephen W. Kearny, and others.

80 Brake, Hezekiah, b. 1814

On Two Continents: A Long Life's Experience. Topeka: Crane & Company, 1896.

> Cloth, frontis. port., [viii], [9]-240 p., port., 19.7 cm.

Brake was born in England in 1814, went to Canada in 1847, then made a trip over the SFT to Fort Union in 1858-59. He settled at Council Grove in 1861. Pp. 118-81 detail his memoirs of the Trail. Graff 389 mentions an edition, same date and place, published by the author. Howes B-718. KSH.

81 Brandon, William

The Men and the Mountain: Frémont's Fourth Expedition. New York: William Morrow & Company, 1955.

> Cloth, map endpapers, xiii, [1]-337 p., map, notes, index, 21.8 cm.

A readable history of John C. Frémont's expedition in 1848-49, which became stalled in the snows of the Rocky Mountains in lower central Colorado. Part of their journey (pp. 107-17) was along the SFT just below Bent's Fort. For documents written by members of the party, see LeRoy R. Hafen's *Frémont's Fourth Expedition*. . . .

82 Brewerton, George Douglas, 1820-1901

Overland with Kit Carson: A Narrative of the Old Spanish Trail in '48. Introduction by Stallo Vinton. New York: Coward-McCann, Inc., 1930.

> Cloth, [x], [1]-301 p., frontis. port., illus. woodcuts, fldg. map, 21.5 cm.

The last two chapters deal with the SFT (pp. 219-87) and were first published as an article by Brewerton in *Harper's New Monthly Magazine*, Vol. XXV, No. CXLVIII (Sept. 1862), pp. 447-66, entitled "In the Buffalo Country." A long, careful firsthand account of a trip over the SFT in 1848, going east from Mora, New

Mexico, to Independence. Illustrated with line drawings by Brewerton. The earlier part of the book describes a trip with Carson, heading west from Santa Fe; the latter part has been reprinted as *In the Buffalo Country*, Corvallis: Oregon State University Press, 1970. The complete 1930 edition was reprinted, New York: A. L. Burt Co., n.d.

83 Brice, James

Reminiscences of Ten Years Experience on the Western Plains: How the United States Mails Were Carried Before Railroads Reached the Santa Fe Trail. Kansas City, Mo., [1906?].

> Pamphlet, cover title, saddle stitched, 1-24 p., drawings, 20.5 cm.

Brice began in 1858 as a helper on the mail route of Hall & Porter, operating from Independence to Santa Fe. He spent ten years on the SFT, working for this firm and others, including Barlow & Sanderson. Howes B-759.

84 Brigham, Lalla Maloy

The Story of Council Grove on the Santa Fe Trail. N.p., 1921.

> Cloth, [1]-168 p., ports., scenes, 19.2 cm.

When George Sibley and other treaty commissioners met with the Osage chiefs in 1825, the location became known as Council Grove. It was not settled until 1847. A local history with some SFT material (pp. 5-39). Part of the material was used in a later work, *The Centennial, Council Grove, Kansas, 1825-1925 . . . ,* 1925, a pamphlet of 64 pp.

85 Broadhead, Garland C.

"The Santa Fe Trail." *Missouri Historical Review,* Vol. 4, No. 4 (July 1910), pp. 309-19.

Broadhead, a professor at the University of Missouri, here gives a general review of the SFT. It is useful chiefly for citations from the *Missouri Intelligencer,* issues of 1822-30.

86 Brown, D. Alexander

The Galvanized Yankees. [Urbana: University of Illinois Press, 1963.]

> Cloth, map endpapers, [v], [1]-243 p., notes, sources, index, 23.4 cm.

"Galvanized Yankees" were former Confederate soldiers, taken prisoner and freed on condition they join the Union Army and serve on the Western frontier. An excellent study of military activity from September 1864 to November 1866 along the Trail, with descriptions of Forts Larned, Leavenworth, and Zarah.

87 Brown, Everett

A History of Fort Larned National Historic Site. N.p., n.d. [ca. 1964].

> Wrappers, 14 p., illus., map.
> A brief history of the fort.

88 [Brown, James]

Message from the President of the United States to the Two Houses of Congress at the Commencement of the First Session of the Thirty-second Congress. U.S. 32nd Cong., 1st sess., Sen. Exec. Doc. 1, Part 1 [Serial 612]. Washington: A. Boyd Hamilton, printer, Dec. 2, 1851.

> Part 1: 469 p., 22.5 cm.

Includes data on wagon freighters hauling from Fort Leavenworth to Santa Fe (p. 295): David Waldo; Brown, Russell & Co.; Joseph Clymer; Jones & Russell; and others, with quantity hauled and rates, July 1850 to June 1851. Also has the report of Thomas Swords' trip over the SFT in August 1851 (pp. 238-41). He describes a mule-drawn train moving thirty miles a day and making its third trip in one season.

89 ———

Report of the Secretary of War, Showing the Contracts Made . . . During the Year Ending 30th June, 1849. U.S. 31st Cong., 1st sess., Sen. Exec. Doc. 26 [Serial 554]. Washington, Feb. 24, 1850.

> 52 p., 22.5 cm.

Among many contracts are some relating to the SFT: James Brown received the first civilian contract to haul supplies. On May 17, 1848, he contracted to haul 200,000 lbs. of supplies from Fort Leavenworth to Santa Fe. Jabez Smith & Co. contracted to haul military supplies from Independence to Las Vegas, 1848; James Brown and William II. Russell, April 1849, hauling from Leavenworth to Santa Fe; St. Vrain and McCarty, Jan. 31, 1849, carrying mail from Santa Fe to Leavenworth and return, at $800 a round trip; see pp. 12-13.

90 [Brown, Joseph C.]

"Report of Committee Appointed to Prepare a Correct Map of the old Santa Fe Trail across the State of Kansas." In: *Eighteenth Biennial Report of the Board of Directors of the Kansas State Historical Society for the Biennial Period July 1, 1910, to June 30, 1912.* Topeka: State Printing Office, 1913.

> Cloth, folding map. See pp. 107-25.

One of the most essential documents on the Trail, containing the field notes of Joseph C. Brown, civil engineer with the government survey expedition along the SFT in 1825-27. The folding map shows Kansas portion of the Trail, drawn for the committee which included William E. Connelley, George A. Root, and Charles S. Gleed. The full biennial report was also issued in paper wrappers; the article on the Trail was also issued as a pamphlet, 21 pages, with map, by the Society.

91 [Brown, William E.]

[The Santa Fe Trail.] The National Survey of Historic Sites and Buildings Series, Theme XV: Westward Expansion and Extension of the National Boundaries, 1830-1898; the Santa Fe Trail (Subtheme). N.p., United States Department of the Interior, National Park Service, 1963.

> Plastic comb binding, clear acetate cover, [iv], i-vii, 2 parts in 1 vol.: Pt. I: 91 leaves text, 21 leaves plates; 2 fldg. maps; Pt. II: 106 leaves text, 54 leaves plates, 5 leaves local maps; 3 fldg. maps; 1 large map of SFT in pocket; all duplicator processed from typewritten original and photos on one side only, 26.8 cm. Issued for limited distribution.

William E. Brown was the coordinating historian of this work. Major contributions were made by Ray H. Mattison, Roy E. Appleman, and Robert M. Utley. Indisputably one of the most important and useful works on the SFT, especially in regard to the remaining terrain features and structures still visible in 1962. Sections give details and photos of all remaining major landmarks, including aerial photo of Raton Pass.

92   Bryant, Edwin

What I Saw in California: Being the Journal of a Tour, by the Emigrant Route and South Pass of the Rocky Mountains, across the Continent of North America, the Great Desert Basin, and through California, in the Years 1846, 1847. . . . New York: D. Appleton & Company, MDCCCXLVIII.

Cloth, [1]-455 p., 18.3 cm.

Bryant left Independence in May 1846, and his journal (pp. 13-35) describes the first portion of his trip, which was forty-one miles over the SFT to the point where it forked with the Oregon Trail. He met eastbound Mexican trains. This work went through several editions, the handsomest at Santa Ana, Calif., 1936, and the poorest being cheap editions under the title *Rocky Mountain Adventures*. Recent good reprints include: Ashland, Ore.: Lewis Osborne; Minneapolis: Ross & Haines, Inc., 1967; New York: Johnson Reprint Corp. Graff 457; Howes B-903; Wagner-Camp 146.

93   Burnap, Willard A.

What Happened in One Man's Lifetime, 1840-1920: A Review of Some Great, Near Great and Little Events. Fergus Falls, Minn.: Burnap Estate, 1923.

Cloth, [viii], [11]-461 p., scenes, map, index, 20.2 cm.

Burnap spent part of his youth in the Southwest and describes a trip over the SFT in 1860 from Santa Fe to Bent's New Fort (pp. 11-64).

94 Burns, Thomas F.

"The Town of Wilmington and the Santa Fe Trail." *Kansas Historical Collections*, Vol. XI (1909-1910), pp. 597-99.

Firsthand account. Memoirs of 1859 and later in a small stage stop on the SFT. Descriptions of wagon trains, including Mexican trains headed east.

95 Burton, E. B.

"Texas Raiders in New Mexico in 1843." *Old Santa Fe*, Vol. II, No. 4 (April 1915), pp. 407-29.

Material on the expedition led by Snively, whose men were disarmed on the SFT by Capt. Philip St. George Cooke. Part of the material is taken from John Henry Brown's *Indian Wars and Pioneers of Texas*, from J. W. Wilbarger's *Indian Depredations in Texas*, and from Cooke's own account in *Army and Navy Journal* for May 25, 1882.

96 [Calhoun, James S.]

The Official Correspondence of James S. Calhoun, while Indian Agent at Santa Fe and Superintendent of Indian Affairs in New Mexico. Collected and edited by Annie Heloise Abel, Office of Indian Affairs. Washington: Government Printing Office, 1915.

> Buckram, xiv, port. leaf, 1-554 p., 4 fldg. maps in back pocket, 23.4 cm.

Calhoun was also the first territorial governor of New Mexico. He left Fort Leavenworth in May 1849, via the SFT to Santa Fe. His letters include material on massacre of the White family near Point of Rocks, 1849, and killing of mail carriers near Wagon Mound, 1850. In 1852 he was ill and went east over the Trail, with a coffin among his baggage. He died en route. Howes C-28.

97 Callon, Milton W.

Las Vegas, New Mexico: The Town that Wouldn't Gamble. Las Vegas: Las Vegas Daily Optic, 1962.

Cloth, [xvi], 1-352, plus 2 leaves (one with map), illus., index, ltd. 1500 numbered copies, 23.2 cm.

A local history of an important town on the SFT. Devoted chiefly to the post-railroad years but it has some material on the earlier SFT period: local freight rates and teamsters; a chapter on Giovanni de Augustino, the hermit of the Trail, with a daguerreotype portrait; and the construction of nearby Fort Union.

98 ———

"The Merchant-colonists of New Mexico." In: *Brand Book of the Denver Westerners*, Vol. XXI. [Denver: The Denver Westerners, Inc., c 1966], pp. 3-26.

A general review of those merchants who built the commercial world at the western end of the SFT: Gustave Elsberg, Jacob Amberg, the Bibo brothers, Henry Connelly, Franz Huning, and others—all of whom went over the SFT, many as traders before they became settled.

99 Campbell, Harriet P.

"Moving Pictures on the Santa Fe Trail." *The Trail*, Vol. I, No. 8 (Jan. 1909), pp. 6-12.

Has nothing to do with cinema; describes more than 30 markers erected along SFT in Colorado. KHS.

100 [Campbell, Hugh]

"The Southern Kansas Boundary Survey: From the Journal of Hugh Campbell, Astronomical Computer," edited by Martha B. Campbell. *Kansas Historical Quarterly*, Vol. VI, No. 4 (Nov. 1937), pp. 339-77.

An account of a survey made in 1857, parts of which involved travel along the SFT. See also entries 20 and 330.

101 Carpenter, A. L.

"A Fight on the Old Trail." *Santa Fe Employees Magazine*, Vol. I, No. 5 (April 1907), pp. 145-46.

Firsthand account by a Kansas City man who was a stage driver in 1862. He describes repulse of an Indian attack.

102 Carroll, Horace Bailey

"Steward A. Miller and the Snively Expedition of 1843." *Southwestern Historical Quarterly*, Vol. LIV, No. 3 (Jan. 1951), pp. 261-86, ports., map.

Miller kept a diary when with the Snively Expedition of Texans en route to attack Mexican caravans on the SFT. Carroll takes the position that the Texans were laudable privateers, and that Philip St. George Cooke, who disarmed them, was arbitrary and harsh. Miller's diary also takes this view.

103 ———

"The Texan Santa Fe Trail." *Panhandle Plains Historical Review*, Vol. XXIV (1951), pp. 1-201, index.

This *Review* was an annual and Carroll's article comprised the entire 1951 issue. A limited number of copies were bound in cloth for sale separately. This expedition from Texas toward Santa Fe went over a short portion of the SFT, from San Miguel, New Mexico, to Santa Fe in October 1841, and its men were prisoners at the time. Another unit of the expedition went by another route to the Rio Grande. This incursion caused alarm and wariness for many months along the western part of the SFT.

104 ———and J. Villasana Haggard

Three New Mexico Chronicles: the Exposición of Don Pedro Bautista Pino, 1812; the Ojeada of Lic. Antonio Barreiro, 1832; and the Additions by Don José Augustín de Escudero, 1849. Translated, with introduction and notes, by H. Bailey Carroll and J. Villasana Haggard. Quivira Society Publications, XI. Albuquerque: The Quivira Society, 1942.

Half cloth and paper over boards, colored endpapers, [xxxii], 1-342 p., 2 fldg. maps inside back, frontis., facsims., index, ltd. 557, 25.3 cm.

One of the relatively few documents from the Mexican end of the Trail, here translated from the Spanish. In 1812 there was published in Cadiz a work by Don Pedro Bautista Pino entitled *Exposición Sucinta y Sencilla de la Provincia del Nuevo México*, giving a general description of New Mexico but with no mention of any trade with the U.S., although there was mention of trade with Chihuahua. In Puebla, Mexico, 1832, there was published a work by Antonio Barreiro (q.v.), entitled *Ojeada sobre Nuevo México . . .*, containing brief material regarding the SFT. In 1849, at Mexico City, appeared a work by Don José Agustín de Escudero, entitled *Noticias Históricas y Estadisticas de la Antigua Provincia del Nuevo-México, Presentadas por su Diputado en Córtes, D. Pedro Bautista Pino, en Cadiz el año de 1812, Adicionadas por el Lic. D. Antonio Barreiro en 1839; y Ultimamente Anotadas por el Lic. Don José Agustín de Escudero*. Agustín de Escudero combined the earlier works of Pino and Barreiro, adding new material of his own, much of it taken from Gregg with proper acknowledgments. Complete facsimiles of the Pino and Barreiro works are included. Reprinted, New York: Arno Press, 1967. Howes B-169, E-178, and P-383.

105 Carter, Harvey Lewis

'Dear Old Kit:' The Historical Christopher Carson, with a New Edition of the Carson Memoirs. [Norman: University of Oklahoma Press, 1968].

> Cloth, colored endpapers, [xx], [1]-250 p., frontis. port., ports., appendixes, index, 26 cm.

One of the most careful studies ever done on Kit Carson, with a scrupulously annotated edition of the Carson memoirs, 1809-1856. Carson went over the SFT, in whole or part, in 1826, 1827, 1842, 1843, 1847, 1851, and 1865, at least. His main activities were not along the Trail, of course, except for the region around Bent's Fort and west of there. The literature on Carson is immense; for students of the SFT this work and those of Estergreen and Sabin (q.v.) will suffice in regard to the Trail and will guide the reader to other works if any are needed.

106   Carteret, John Dunloe

A Fortune Hunter; or, the Old Stone Corral: a Tale of the Santa Fe Trail. Cincinnati: printed for the author, 1888.

Fiction; historically valueless.

107   Carvalho, Solomon N.

Incidents of Travel and Adventure in the Far West; with Col. Frémont's Last Expedition across the Rocky Mountains: Including Three Months' Residence in Utah, and a Perilous Trip across the Great American Desert to the Pacific. New York: Derby & Jackson, 1856.

Cloth, issued uncut, [xv], [17]-380 p., 19.5 cm.

Carvalho was an artist and daguerreotypist who accompanied Frémont's fifth expedition in 1853. His journal is perhaps the best account of that trip, part of which was along the SFT to Bent's Fort. This first edition appeared in both New York and London; there were other New York editions in each of the next four years. Graff 618; Howes C-213; Wagner-Camp 273. N, UNM.

108   Chapman, W. A.

"Santa Fe Trail and Clifton House." *New Mexico Historical Review,* Vol. II, No. 4 (Oct. 1927), pp. 398-400.

Memoirs of experiences on the SFT between Raton and Las Vegas, reprinted from the Raton *Reporter* issues of 1927.

109   Chappell, Phillip E.

"A History of the Missouri River." *Kansas Historical Collections,* Vol. IX, (1905-1906), pp. 237-316, illus.

Much SFT traffic came first up the Missouri river to various landings at the eastern end of the Trail. Therefore the history of the river relates in part to the Trail. This work deals with the Missouri from the time of Joliet in 1673 to the coming of the railroads around 1873. Descriptions of steamers, pilots, and details of 700 river steamers. The work has also been reported issued in pamphlet form in two editions: 1904 and 1905. Howes C-301.

110   Chase, Charles Monroe, 1829-1902

"An Editor Looks at Early Day Kansas: the Letters of Charles Monroe Chase," edited by Lela Barnes. *Kansas Historical Quarterly*, Vol. XXVI, No. 2 (Summer 1960), pp. 113-51; and No. 3 (Autumn 1960), pp. 267-301.

Chase was an editor and in 1863 wrote letters back to the *True Republican and Sentinel*, Sycamore, Ill., reprinted here. A short section (pp. 116-17) tells briefly about stage lines to New Mexico and describes Independence, Mo.

111   ————

The Editor's Run in New Mexico and Colorado, Embracing Twenty-eight Letters on Stock Raising, Agriculture, Territorial History. . . . Lyndon, Vermont, 1882.

> Wrappers, [1]-233 p., 3 p. advts., illus. dwgs., 22.5 cm.

Chase had visited eastern Kansas briefly in the 1860s. Here he describes a long trip by rail in 1881. This was so soon after the railroad was built that his descriptions of people and places in Trinidad, Raton, Cimarron, Las Vegas, and Santa Fe reflect the latter days of the Trail and include many Trail narratives. Reprinted, facsimile, Fort Davis, Texas: Frontier Book Co., 1968. Graff 652; Howes C-315. N.

112   Chittenden, Hiram Martin

The American Fur Trade of the Far West: A History of the Pioneer Trading Posts and Early Fur Companies of the Missouri Valley and the Rocky Mountains and of the Overland Commerce with Santa Fe. 3 vols. New York: Frances P. Harper, 1902.

> Cloth, 24.3 cm. Vol. I: xxii, [1]-482 p., 1 p. adv., frontis., illus.; Vol. II: [x], [483]-892 p., illus.; Vol. III: [iv], [893]-1029 p., index, large fldg. map in back pocket.

Among early works on the fur trade, Ray Allen Billington says this is "the most useful work. . . ." The SFT material (pp. 483-533) is general, taken from Gregg, Inman, Cooke, and Waldo. Reprinted,

New York, 1935, with omissions; a better reprint, from the 1902 original, is a 2-vol. set, without map, Stanford, Calif.: Academic Reprints, 1954, in facsimile. Graff 696; Howes C-390.

113 Christy, Charles

"The Personal Memoirs of Capt. Christy." *The Trail*, Vol. I, No. 8 (Jan. 1909), pp. 13-19.

This article, comprising the twelfth chapter of Christy's memoirs, describes his experiences as a government scout at Fort Zarah on the Arkansas river. From there in 1867 he went to the scene of an ambush where relatives of Franz Huning, a prominent Albuquerque merchant, had been killed by Indians on the SFT. There have been comments that Christy often exaggerated, but the Huning account is close to other known versions of the episode. *The Trail*, published in Denver, 1908-28, was the official magazine of the Society of Sons of Colorado.

114 Clark, Calvin Perry

Two Diaries: the Diary & Journal of Calvin Perry Clark, who Journeyed by Wagon Train from Plano, Illinois, to Denver and Vicinity over the Santa Fe Trail in the Year 1859, together with the Diary of His Sister, Helen E. Clark, Who Made a Similar Journey by the Northern Route in the Year 1860. Denver: Denver Public Library, [c 1962].

> Dec. cloth, label on spine, bound dos-a-dos, xviii, 1-91 p.; and xiv, 1-44 p., illus. dwgs., dec. endpapers, printed from handset type by John R. Evans at his Little Press of Este Es at Parker, Colorado.

Clark arrived at St. Joseph, Mo., in March 1859 and reached Pike's Peak May 31. Personal SFT impressions (pp. 1-9) in C. P. Clark diary only.

115 Clarke, Dwight L., ed.

The Original Journals of Henry Smith Turner, with Stephen Watts Kearny in New Mexico and California, 1846-1847. American Exploration and Travel Series, 51. Norman: University of Oklahoma Press, [1966].

Cloth, xii, [1]-[174] p., ports., scenes, map, index, 23.5 cm.

Turner was adjutant to Stephen Watts Kearny in the march over the SFT with the Army of the West in 1846. His diary entries (pp. 58-72) and letters (pp. 136-42) describe their journey over the Trail.

116 ————

Stephen Watts Kearny: Soldier of the West. Norman: University of Oklahoma Press, [1961].

Cloth, xv, [1]-448 p., ports., scenes, map, biblio., index, 23.5 cm.

Probably the best biography of Kearny (1794-1848), who was at Fort Leavenworth by 1830, served with the 1st Dragoons, and led his Army of the West along the SFT in 1846.

117 Cleland, Robert Glass

This Reckless Breed of Men: the Trappers and Fur Traders of the Southwest. New York: Alfred A. Knopf, 1950.

Cloth, title in gilt on spine, 1 leaf, xv, [1]-361 p., xx p. index, colophon leaf, colored frontis., 16 p. plates, 4 maps in text, biblio., index, 21.7 cm.

A recognized work on the Mountain Men, with a chapter on the SFT, starting with the La Lande trip of 1804.

118 Clum, John P.

"Santa Fe in the '70s." *New Mexico Historical Review,* Vol. II, No. 4 (Oct. 1927), pp. 380-86, port.

Firsthand account of a stage trip over the SFT from end of the railroad at Kit Carson, Colorado, to Santa Fe in 1871.

119 [Clymer, Joseph]

Report: The Committee on Military Affairs, to Whom was Referred the Memorial of Joseph Clymer, Praying Indemnity for Damages Incurred by Him, Owing to the Violation by Agents of the Government, for the Transportation of Army Supplies to Various Military Posts, in the *Territory of New Mexico*. U.S. 33rd Cong., 2nd sess., H.R. Report 110 [Serial 808]. Washington, Feb. 23, 1855.

9 p., 22.5 cm.

Clymer was a freighter who won a two-year contract in 1851 to haul freight to Santa Fe and beyond. He bought thirty wagons and 192 yoke of oxen, then was told there would be little freight in 1852. A useful report with details on freighting. This claim was brought up many times before settlement; see: U.S. 35th Cong., 1st sess., Sen. Report 305, 1858, 5 pp.; U.S. 35th Cong., 1st sess., Sen. Misc. Doc. 218, 1858, 36 pp.; U.S. 35th Cong., 1st sess., H.R. Court of Claims 161, 1858, 70 pp.; U.S. 45th Cong., 2nd sess., H.R. Report 425, 1878, 4 pp.; U.S. 46th Cong., 2nd sess., H.R. Report 200, 1880, 4 pp.; and U.S. 46th Cong., 3rd sess., Sen. Report 877, 1881, 4 pp.

120   Collins, James L.

"Perils of the Santa Fe Trail in Its Early Days, 1822-1852," edited by Benjamin M. Read. *El Palacio*, Vol. XIX, No. 10 (Nov. 15, 1925), pp. 206-11.

A letter from Collins to William Carr Lane, then governor of New Mexico, dated December 10, 1852, detailing the extreme hardships that faced anyone attempting a trip over the SFT in winter.

121   Conard, Howard Louis

"Uncle Dick" Wootton, the Pioneer Frontiersman of the Rocky Mountain Region: an Account of the Adventures and Thrilling Experiences of the Most Noted American Hunter, Trapper, Guide, Scout, and Indian Fighter Now Living. Chicago: W. E. Dibble & Co., 1890.

Cloth, [1]-472 p., plus frontis., adv. p., and plates, 23.3 cm.

Richens Lacy "Uncle Dick" Wootton, b. 1816, made his first trip over the SFT in 1836 and spent years in the Far West. In 1856 he hauled government freight on the Trail. In 1866 he secured a charter and built a toll road through Raton Pass, operating it until the railroad came in 1878. His account contains many tales of the Trail and descriptions of wagons, techniques, and personalities. Reprinted,

Columbus: Long's College Book Co., 1950, ltd. 500. Graff 846; Howes C-659.

122 Connelley, William Elsey

"Characters and Incidents of the Plains." *Kansas Historical Collections*, Vol. X (1907-1908), pp. 111-19.

Includes extracts from War Dept. records giving details of Gilpin's Santa Fe Trace Battalion, Missouri Mounted Volunteers, in the Mexican War.

123 ———

Quantrill and the Border Wars. Cedar Rapids, Iowa: The Torch Press, 1910.

> Cloth, [1]-539 p., frontis., port., maps, ports., scenes, index, errata leaf, 24.5 cm.

Quantrill's guerrillas during the Civil War were active at times along the eastern end of the SFT. In October 1862 some of his men were en route to burn Shawneetown when they came upon a wagon train on the Trail, guarded by an infantry escort. Quantrill's men killed fifteen soldiers and scattered the rest (p. 274). Reprinted, New York: Cooper Square Publishers, 1956. Graff 850; Howes C-689.

124 ———

A Standard History of Kansas and Kansans. 5 vols. Chicago: Lewis Publishing Company, 1918.

See Vol. I, pp. 84-144. Of all general Kansas histories, this has one of the best sections on the SFT. Includes text of the Osage treaty of 1825; field notes of surveyor Joseph C. Brown, 1825-27; county by county summary of the SFT in Kansas; table of distances from Wetmore's 1837 gazetteer; roster of Gilpin's Santa Fe Battalion, 1848; and data on Jedediah Smith, the Chávez killing, and the Snively raid.

125 ———

War with Mexico, 1846-1847: Doniphan's Expedition and the Con-

quest of *New Mexico and California*. Topeka: published by the author, 1907.

> Cloth, xiv, errata sheet, [1]-670 p., frontis. port., illus., appendixes, 2 fldg. maps, index, 22.5 cm.

The central part of this work is a reprint of John T. Hughes' (q.v.) report on the Doniphan expedition, to which Connelley has added a long introduction, rosters of all companies, and eleven appended interviews or similar special reports. Of importance for a study of the SFT are "Personal Recollections of Charles R. Morehead" (pp. 600-24), with data on William H. Russell, the freighter; trailing cattle over the SFT in 1861; a stage trip on the Trail in 1863; Michael McEnnis' trip east on the Trail in the winter of 1846-47; a biographical sketch of F. X. Aubry; and Edward James Glasgow's experiences on the SFT. Graff 851; Howes C-688.

126 [Conner, Daniel Ellis]

A Confederate in the Colorado Gold Fields. Edited by Donald J. Berthrong and Odessa Davenport. Norman: University of Oklahoma Press, [1970].

> Cloth, colored endpapers, [xiv], [1]-186 p., 6 leaves of plates, 2 maps in text, biblio., index, 23.5 cm.

Daniel Ellis Conner was not yet twenty-two when he joined a party of gold-seekers journeying over the SFT to Bent's Fort and on to Colorado in 1859. His account of the Trail (pp. 13-61) contains superior accounts of landscapes, Indians, and camp life on the Trail. The book is a continuation of Conner's earlier journals published under the title of *Joseph Reddeford Walker and the Arizona Adventure*.

127 Conway, Jay T.

A Brief Community History of Raton, New Mexico, 1880-1930. N.p. [Raton]: Colfax County Pioneers Assn., 1930.

> Pamphlet, printed paper wrappers, saddle stitched, 20 unnumbered p., 23 cm.

Raton really began as a town at the New Mexico end of Raton Pass when the railroad arrived in 1879. Some information on the nearby Clifton House stage station and on Willow Springs government forage station that is now within the city.

128   Cook, John R.

The Border and the Buffalo: an Untold Story of the Southwest Plains; the Bloody Border of Missouri and Kansas; the Story of the Slaughter of the Buffalo; Westward among the Big Game and Wild Tribes; a Story of Mountain and Plain. Topeka: Crane & Company, 1907.

> Yellow pict. cloth, xii, [1]-352 p., frontis., illus., 22.8 cm.

Cook describes an experience of selling oxen to a Trail trader during the Kansas border troubles in 1862. He also rode the Trail from the end of the railroad at Granada to Santa Fe in 1874 and was in business at Raton after 1880, but these accounts are brief. Reprinted from new type, Chicago: R. R. Donnelley, 1938; the 1938 edition later reprinted in facsimile, New York: Citadel Press, 1967. Graff 864; Howes C-730.

129   Cooke, Philip St. George, 1809-1895

The Conquest of New Mexico and California, an Historical and Personal Narrative. New York: G. P. Putnam's Sons, 1878.

> Cloth, v, 1-307 p., fldg. map, 18.5 cm.

A companion volume to his earlier *Scenes and Adventures in the Army*, Cooke writes here of the march of the Army of the West over the SFT to Santa Fe in 1846. There Cooke took command of the Mormon Battalion and led it to California. Reprinted, Oakland, Calif., 1952, ltd. 600; also Albuquerque: Horn & Wallace, Publishers, 1964, with new introduction by Philip St. George Cooke III; and Chicago: Rio Grande Press, Inc., 1964. Graff 869; Howes C-738.

130   ————

"A Journal of the Santa Fe Trail," edited by William E. Connelley. *Mississippi Valley Historical Review*, Vol. XII, No. 1 (June 1925), pp. 72-98; No. 2 (Sept. 1925), pp. 227-55.

A detachment of the Dragoons was assigned to accompany the

annual caravan of traders' wagons over the SFT in 1843. Captain
Cooke's men left Council Grove with the wagons on June 3, con-
voyed them to their crossing of the Arkansas on July 4, and were back
at Fort Leavenworth on October 25. Cooke's journal is important not
only for details of the caravan and the Trail but because it was on this
trip that Cooke disarmed a large party of Texans under Jacob Snively.

131 ———

"One Day's Work of a Captain of Dragoons, and Some of Its Con-
sequences." *Magazine of American History, with Notes and Queries,*
Vol. XVIII, No. 1 (July 1887), pp. 35-44.

Cooke's own version of his detachment's seizure of the Snively
expedition along the SFT in 1843, rewritten in narrative form from
his official report. This account also appeared in *Army and Navy Journal,* Summer 1882, and the text is included in William R. Bernard's
"Westport and the Santa Fe Trade" (see entry 45).

132 ———

Scenes and Adventures in the Army; or, Romance of Military Life.
Philadelphia: Lindsay & Blakiston, 1857.

Cloth, xii, [13]-432 p., 23 cm. Presentation copies were gilt edged.

Cooke's first book about his Western experiences, describing his
service with the 2nd Dragoons along the SFT. Wagner-Camp, 288,
says that much of the material was issued earlier in installments in the
Southern Literary Messenger, beginning in 1842. It was reissued in
1859. Graff 871; Howes C-740.

133 Coombs, Franklin S.

"Santa Fe Prisoners: Narrative of Franklin Combs." *New Mexico Historical Review,* Vol. V, No. 3 (July 1930), pp. 305-14.

Coombs was with the Texan-Santa Fe expedition in 1841-42.
His account was printed in *Niles National Register,* March 5, 1842,
and also in Thomas Falconer's book (N.Y., 1930), entry 198.

134 Copeland, Fayette

Kendall of the Picayune: Being His Adventures in New Orleans, on the Texan-Santa Fe Expedition, in the Mexican War, and in the Colonization of the Texas Frontier. Norman: University of Oklahoma Press, [1943].

> Cloth, [xi], [1]-351 p., colophon leaf, fldg. facsim., 8 leaves plates, biblio., index, 22 cm.

The best biography to date of this noted newspaperman who was with the Texan-Santa Fe Expedition in 1841-42, with comments on related events that preceded and followed that venture.

135 Cordry, [Mrs.] T. A.

The Story of the Marking of the Santa Fe Trail by the Daughters of the American Revolution in Kansas and the State of Kansas. Topeka: Crane & Company, 1915.

> Cloth, [1]-164 p., frontis. port., fldg. map, ports., scenes, 20 cm.

Contains list of 96 markers placed in Kansas, with pictures of many monuments and the story of the program of work to mark the SFT. W. A. Madaris, an old wagon freighter, wrote a letter (pp. 56-57) describing the precise type of teams to be shown on any marker.

136 Covington, James W.

"Correspondence between Mexican Officials at Santa Fe and Officials in Missouri, 1823-1825." *Bulletin of the Missouri Historical Society,* Vol. XVI, No. 1 (Oct. 1959), pp. 20-32.

A useful set of letters gathered by a professional historian, concerning the correspondence between officials at Santa Fe and the Saint Louis superintendency of Indian affairs. Content deals with mutual problems relating to Indians along the SFT. Archival sources are cited.

137 ———

"A Robbery on the Santa Fe Trail." *Kansas Historical Quarterly,* Vol. XXI, No. 7 (Autumn 1955), pp. 560-63.

Reprints a petition of traders for compensation in their loss of 100 mules and asses. On October 12, 1827, the Pawnee attacked a party of traders returning east over the SFT, probably in present Edwards county, Kansas. Names of signers include William Wolfskill, James Collins, Solomon Houck, and four others.

138 ⸺

"Thomas James, Traveler to Santa Fe." *Bulletin of the Missouri Historical Society* Vol. X, No. 1 (Oct. 1953), pp. 86-89.

Text of a letter from James, author of *Three Years Among the Indians and Mexicans*, to President Andrew Jackson. The letter, written in 1834, gives a summary of James' trip to Santa Fe in 1821, but the dates and other facts are at variance with James' book, published in 1846. Scholars have long questioned many details in the book.

139 Cox, Isaac Joslin

The Early Exploration of Louisiana. University of Cincinnati Studies, Series 2, Vol. 2, No. 1. Cincinnati: University of Cincinnati Press, 1906.

> Wrappers, 160 p., frontis., maps, biblio., 23 cm.

One short chapter (pp. 116-23) deals with the SFT region before the Trail opened. Cox mentions La Lande, Purcell, and others, based on archival research. He later expanded on this material in the *Quarterly of the Texas State Historical Association*, Vol. X, Nos. 4-6.

140 ⸺

"Opening the Santa Fe Trail." *Missouri Historical Review*, Vol. XXV, No. 1 (Oct. 1930), pp. 30-66.

A useful general review of the earliest period of the adventures over the Trail, by a competent historian. Expanded from a chapter in his earlier work (see entry 139); this article in the *Review* is more useful.

141 Coy, Owen Cochran

The Great Trek. Los Angeles: Powell Publishing Company, [c 1931].

Cloth, illus. endpapers, [xvi], 1-349 p., maps, illus. dwgs., biblio., index, 24 cm.

A very general secondary work on the trails that led to California. The chapter on the SFT (pp. 19-41) is drawn almost entirely from Josiah Gregg's work.

142   Coyner, David Holmes

The Lost Trappers: a Collection of Interesting Scenes and Events in the Rocky Mountains; together with a Short Description of California: also, Some Account of the Fur Trade. . . . Cincinnati: J. A. & U. P. James, 1847.

Cloth, xv, 17-255 p., 7 p. advts., 18.7 cm.

Contains a generous amount of fiction, but it was written by a man who lived for a time in frontier Missouri. The essential SFT material concerns Ezekiel Williams, a trapper who came down the Arkansas river in 1809 and went back up the river in 1814. Reprinted, facsimile, Glorieta, N.M.: Rio Grande Press, Inc., 1969; also reprinted from new type with extensive notes by David J. Weber, Albuquerque: University of New Mexico Press, 1969. Graff 897; Howes C-836; Wagner-Camp 130.

143   Crichton, Kyle S.

"Zeb Pike." *Scribner's Magazine*, Vol. LXXXII, No. 4 (Oct. 1927), pp. 462-67, illus.

A brief general article, written in journalistic style, with emphasis on Pike's connections with General James Wilkinson.

144   Culmer, Frederic A.

"Marking the Santa Fe Trail." *New Mexico Historical Review*, Vol. IX, No. 1 (Jan. 1934), pp. 78-93.

Culmer deals with the first survey of the SFT, made by George C. Sibley's party. Included are several letters from archival sources. In editorial comment immediately following the article, Lansing B. Bloom discusses the official Mexican point of view regarding the SFT; opinion was not always favorable.

145 Curtis, William E.

A Summer Scamper along the Old Santa Fe Trail and through the Gorges of Colorado to Zion. Chicago: The Inter-Ocean Publishing Company, 1883.

¾ leather and marbled paper over boards, [3]-113 p., 7 p. advts., 16.8 cm. Also issued in pict. wrappers.

In spite of its title, this is a general roundup of information that is not only secondary but tertiary. It is not an account of a journey. KSH.

146 [Customs Duties]

Documents Relating to the Bill (S. 347) "to Establish Ports of Entry in the States of Arkansas and Missouri, and to Allow Debenture on Foreign Goods Conveyed Overland from such Ports to Mexico. U.S. 26th Cong., 1st sess., Sen. Doc. 472 [Serial 360]. Washington, May 18, 1840.

11 p., 22.5 cm.

Contains a memorial dated Dec. 27, 1838, from the Missouri Legislature reviewing the advantages of the SFT trade and proposing an arrangement by which customs duties will be refunded by "drawback" on goods imported from abroad for the Santa Fe trade and cleared through proposed Western ports of entry in original containers.

147 ————

Report on H.R. Bill 441: To Establish Ports of Entry in Arkansas and Missouri and to Allow Debenture, &c. U.S. 26th Cong., 1st sess., H.R. Report 540 [Serial 372]. Washington, May 12, 1840.

17 p., 22.5 cm.

The Committee on Commerce approves the proposal. Contains a general review of the Santa Fe trade. Arkansas hopes to establish a direct trade route to Chihuahua, competing with Missouri's direct route to Santa Fe.

148   Darton, N. H.

Guidebook of the Western United States; Part C: the Santa Fe Route, with a Side Trip to the Grand Canyon of the Colorado. Department of the Interior, United States Geological Survey, Bulletin 613. Washington: Government Printing Office, 1915.

> Wrappers, sewn, iv, 1-194 p., illus., 42 plates, 40 figures in text, 25 fldg. maps, index of stations, 23 cm.

A historical and geological guidebook along the route of the Atchison, Topeka & Santa Fe Railway from Kansas City to Los Angeles. The detailed maps show many points of historic SFT interest; text frequently mentions points on the Trail.

149   [Daughters of the American Revolution]

Souvenir Program: Dedication of Monument Marking the Starting Point of the Santa Fe Trail. New Franklin, Missouri, May 17, 1913.

> Pamphlet; 8 unnumbered pages in heavy wrappers tied with blue ribbon; 19.5 cm.

Useful for text of marker, shown in closeup photograph: "Captain William Becknell of Franklin, 'Father of the Santa Fe Trail,' with four companions, led the first organized trade expedition to Santa Fe, September 1st, 1821. Franklin, 'Cradle of the Santa Fe Trail,' 1821. This Trail, one of the great highways of the world, stretched nearly one thousand miles from Franklin, Missouri, to Santa Fe, New Mexico, 'from civilization to sundown.' Marked by The Daughters of the American Revolution and the State of Missouri, 1909." Otherwise the work has no text except list of speakers and officials. Sketch map in centerfold. KHS.

150   Davis, Clyde Brion

The Arkansas. New York: Farrar & Rinehart, Inc., [1940].

> Cloth, pict. endpapers, x, [1]-340 p., drawings, map, index, 20.8 cm.

The title of this, and the fact that it is in the *Rivers of America* series, may mislead a researcher into considering it a useful source. However, the author almost completely ignores the SFT traffic along the river, although he does have a chapter on Coronado's expedition, with much invented dialogue.

151 [Davis, Sylvester]

"Diary of Sylvester Davis," edited by Paul A. F. Walter. *New Mexico Historical Review*, Vol. VI, No. 4 (Oct. 1931), pp. 383-416.

Describes Davis' trip to Colorado in 1859, via Iowa; one section (pp. 409-15) describes a trip over Raton Pass on the SFT and along the Trail to Cañoncito near Santa Fe in August and September, 1859.

152 [Davis, Willard]

In the Supreme Court of Kansas. Archie O'Laughlin, and William Furguson, Appellants, vs. the State of Kansas, Appellee. Case no. 1230. Brief for Appellee, by Willard Davis, Attorney General. N.p., n.d.

Pamphlet, title on wrapper, [1]-14 pp., 1 leaf, 22.7 cm.

O'Laughlin and Furguson were found guilty in 1877 of building a fence across part of the SFT in Johnson county, Kansas. This legal brief, filed opposing their appeal, cites various surveys, state acts, and private testimony to prove existence of the Trail at the point concerned.

153 Davis, William Watts Hart

El Gringo; or, New Mexico and Her People. New York: Harper & Brothers, Publishers, 1857.

Cloth, xii, [13]-432 p., illus., 19.8 cm.

Davis left Independence in November 1853 and went over the Trail to Santa Fe. He relates personal experiences along the Trail and names individuals met. Davis was quite literate; he was U.S. district attorney in New Mexico and served for several months as acting governor in the 1850s. Reprinted, Santa Fe: Rydal Press, 1938; Chicago: Rio Grande Press, 1963. Graff 1021; Howes D-139; Wagner-Camp 289.

154 Dawson, John S.

"The Legislature of 1868." *Kansas Historical Collections*, Vol. X (1907-1908), pp. 254-79.

Biographies of Kansas legislators, of whom at least two were significant on the SFT: Atlantic Abraham Moore (p. 267), who went over the Trail in 1858 and later owned the station at Cottonwood Crossing, and Charles O. Fuller (p. 271), who was a stage driver on the Overland line from Missouri to New Mexico and established Fuller's Ranche on the SFT in 1855.

155 Deatherage, Charles P.

Early History of Greater Kansas City, Missouri and Kansas: the Prophetic City at the Mouth of the Kaw; Diamond Jubilee Edition, 1928, Volume I: Early History, from October 12, 1492, to 1870. Kansas City, Mo.: Charles P. Deatherage, 1927.

Cloth, [1]-[702] p., fldg. map of city at back, ports., scenes, maps, drawings, tables, 26 cm.

Deatherage planned to issue three volumes but published only this one. Has material on the founding of Westport and Independence; general data on the SFT; much of the information is general, but there is occasional original material. The number of illustrations is greater than in most books up to its time. Howes D-178.

156 [De Bourgmont, Etienne Veniard]

"Etienne Veniard de Bourgmont's 'Exact Description of Louisiana'," edited by Marcel Giraud, translated by Mrs. Max W. Myers. *Bulletin of the Missouri Historical Society*, Vol. XV, No. 1 (Oct. 1958), pp. 3-19.

First English translation of a French document. In 1714, De Bourgmont reported on an exploration up the Missouri. He commented that "by way of the Missouris one can also find opportunity to trade with the Spanish, who are very rich in mines in this region" and noted that the route did not appear to be difficult because Indians traded with the Spanish.

157 Deming, Elizabeth Mary

"Personal Recollections of the Santa Fe Trail." *The Club Member*, Vol. 5, No. 5 (Aug. 1907), pp. 10ff.

As personal recollections, these have little value. This magazine served several Kansas women's clubs. The recollections are concerned chiefly with activities in placing markers along the Trail. KHS.

158 [De Mun, Jules]

Message from the President . . . on the Subject of Depredations by the Mexicans on the Property of Messrs. Chouteau and Demun. U.S. 24th Cong., 1st sess., Sen. Doc. 400 [Serial 283]. Washington, June 15, 1836.

3 p., 22.5 cm.

Chouteau and De Mun ask for $50,000 for loss and damages, claiming they were seized by Mexicans on U.S. soil near the Arkansas in 1817, sent to Santa Fe and imprisoned for six weeks before release, and their goods confiscated.

159 ———

Report: The Committee on Foreign Relations . . . in Regard to Depredations Committed upon Persons and Property of Messrs. Chouteau and Demun. . . . U.S. 24th Cong., 1st sess., Sen. Doc. 424 [Serial 284]. Washington, July 2, 1836.

1 p., 22.5 cm.

A committee report recommending that the U.S. demand redress from Mexico for the arrest and imprisonment of Jules de Mun and A. P. Chouteau and the confiscation of their goods in 1817.

160 ———

United States and Mexico. Report of the Committee on Foreign Affairs. . . . U.S. 25th Cong., 2nd sess., H.R. Report 1056 [Serial 336]. Washington, July 7, 1838.

17 p., 22.5 cm.

Discusses various claims against Mexico, reporting (p. 6) that Mexico has paid part of the claim of A. P. Chouteau and Jules de Mun and is considering payment of the remainder of that claim.

161 DeVoto, Bernard

The Year of Decision. Boston: Little, Brown and Company, 1943.

> Cloth, map endpapers, [xix], [1]-524 p., notes, biblio., index, 22 cm.

Together with Lavender's work on Bent's Fort, this is among the most readable of all recent works relating to the SFT. It deals only in part with the Trail, with material on Susan Magoffin, the Mormon Battalion, Kearny, and Doniphan. Also issued in paperback, 1961.

162 Dick, Charles Howard

Territory Aflame and the Santa Fe Trail. [Lawrence, Lawrence Outlook, 1954].

> Pamphlet, yellow printed wrappers, saddle stitched, [1]-34 p., illus., 22.5 cm.

A short work of only general interest.

163 Dick, Everett

Vanguards of the Frontier: A Social History of the Northern Plains and Rocky Mountains from the Earliest White Contacts to the Coming of the Homemaker. New York: D. Appleton-Century Company, 1941.

> Cloth, map endpapers, [xviii], 1-574 p., frontis. and 31 leaves of plates, biblio., index, 23.1 cm.

One of the most widely accepted general survey works, whose field is defined in its title. It has good chapters on the fur trade, Mountain Men, SFT traders, stagecoaching, and wagon freighting. The bibliography is far more extensive than in most such books. Reprinted, paperback, Lincoln: University of Nebraska Press, 1965.

164 Dick, Herbert W.

"The Excavation of Bent's Fort, Otero County, Colorado." *The*

Colorado Magazine, State Historical Society of Colorado, Vol. XXXIII, No. 3 (July 1956), pp. 181-96.

An anthropologist describes excavations made in 1954, with aerial view and plan of the fort.

165   Dike, Sheldon

The Territorial Post Offices of New Mexico [Albuquerque: published by the author], c 1958.

Wrappers, 2 p. text, 54 unnumbered leaves of tables, errata slip, 28 cm.

Useful in locating first postoffices in New Mexico along the SFT. The material was also published in the *New Mexico Historical Review:* Vol. XXXIII, No. 4 (Oct. 1958), pp. 322-27, illus.; Vol. XXXIV, No. 1 (Jan. 1959), pp. 55-69; No. 2 (April 1959), pp. 145-52; No. 3 (July 1959), pp. 203-26; No. 4 (Oct. 1959), pp. 308-09.

166   Dimick, Howard T.

"Ancestry and Some Descendants of William Gregg I." *New Mexico Historical Review*, Vol. XXIII, No. 1 (Jan. 1948), pp. 32-39.

Genealogical information on Josiah Gregg.

167   ———

"Reconsideration of the Death of Josiah Gregg." *New Mexico Historical Review*, Vol. XXII, No. 3 (July 1947), pp. 274-85.

Josiah Gregg died in California, February 25, 1850. In 1856 Lewis K. Wood published a hearsay account of Gregg's death, giving the cause as starvation or malnutrition. Dimick disputes this and says the cause was probably an organic attack. He also hints at the possibility of homicide.

168   ———

"Visits of Dr. Josiah Gregg to Louisiana, 1841-1847." *Louisiana Historical Review*, Vol. XXIX, No. 1 (Jan. 1946), pp. 5-13.

General biographical data on Gregg, whose visits to Louisiana occurred after he had ceased to be active along the SFT.

169 [Dodge, Henry]

Report on the Expedition of Dragoons, under Colonel Henry Dodge, to the Rocky Mountains in 1835. 24th Congress, 1st Session. In: *American State Papers, Military Affairs,* Vol. VI, document 654, pp. 130-46, large fldg. map. Washington: Gales & Seaton, 1861.

The detachment left Leavenworth May 29, 1835, and went northwest to the Platte, along that river and its south fork, past the site of present Denver, down to Bent's Fort, then back along the SFT and to Fort Leavenworth. Text deals chiefly with peace councils with the Indians; some description of Bent's Fort and the terrain along the SFT. See also entries under Lemuel Ford and Gaines P. Kingsbury.

170 Doran, Thomas F.

"Kansas Sixty Years Ago." *Kansas Historical Collections,* Vol. XV (1919-1922), pp. 482-501.

Firsthand memoirs, Doran's family moved to Council Grove, Kansas, in 1859. Contains data on prairie fires, Indian troubles, and Dick Yeager raid.

171 Doster, Frank

"Eleventh Indiana Cavalry in Kansas in 1865." *Kansas Historical Collections,* Vol. XV (1919-1922), pp. 524-29.

Firsthand memoirs. Doster served with the cavalry along the SFT in the summer of 1865. He claims that many newspaper stories of the time concerning Indian troubles were "fanciful exaggerations founded on little fact."

172 Douglas, Walter B.

Manuel Lisa, by Walter B. Douglas, with Hitherto Unpublished Material. Annotated and edited by Abraham P. Nasatir; New York: Argosy-Antiquarian Ltd., 1964.

Cloth, [iv] 1-207 p., ports., scenes, notes, index, ltd. 750, 22.2 cm.
Lisa was one of the early fur traders on the Missouri river who

suspected the possibilities of rich trade with New Mexico. This work has material on other figures who were involved in early Santa Fe trade: Chouteau, St. Vrain, and James Wilkinson—whose policies affected the first ventures. Nasatir's notes are a good guide to manuscript material before 1820 and indicate that the U.S. drive toward New Mexico had its genesis in the Missouri river fur trade. Douglas' material first appeared in *Missouri Historical Collections*, Vol. III, Nos. 3 and 4, 1911.

173 [Dragoons]

Remounting the Second Regiment Dragoons. U.S. 28th Cong., 1st sess., H.R. Report 77 [Serial 445]. Washington, Jan. 27, 1844.

11 p., 22.5 cm.

Report from the Committee on Military Affairs urging that the 2nd Dragoons be restored to mounted duty. The unit had been converted to a regiment of riflemen, and the committee feels that the First Dragoons do not afford enough strength to handle the added duty of SFT escort work.

174 Drannan, William F.

Thirty-one Years on the Plains and in the Mountains; or, The Last Voice from the Plains; an Authentic Record of a Lifetime of Hunting, Trapping, Scouting and Indian Fighting in the Far West. Chicago: Rhodes & McClure Publishing Co., 1899.

Cloth, [5]-596 p., 9 p. advts., illus., 19.5 cm.

Although Drannan claimed to have known the SFT, this item is included here only as a curiosity. Wright Howes describes Drannan as "a senile braggart" and "this hoary-headed father of liars." See also entries under W. E. Bate and Kenneth Englert. This work had several editions, followed by an equally dubious sequel, *Capt. Wm. F. Drannan, Chief of Scouts.* . . . Graff 1147; Howes D-482.

175 Driggs, Howard Roscoe, 1873-

Westward America. New York: Somerset Books, Inc., [c 1942].

Cloth, [x], 1-312 p., 16 leaves of full color paintings by Wm. H. Jackson, biblio., index, 28.3 cm. Also author's autographed edition.

A general secondary work on the western trails, chiefly to Oregon. The chapter on the SFT (pp. 20-28) is a good elementary account but of no new usefulness to scholars.

176 Drum, H. C.

"Motoring on the Santa Fe Trail." *Santa Fe Employees Magazine*, Vol. 5, No. 12 (Nov. 1912), pp. 35-45.

Firsthand account of an early motor trip from New York to San Francisco, partly over the SFT via Raton Pass. Several photographs of the primitive auto roads of the time. Reprinted from *The World Today* magazine.

177 Duffus, Robert L.

The Santa Fe Trail. New York: Longmans, Green and Co., 1930.

Cloth, map endpapers, [xiii], 1-283 p., frontis., 15 leaves plates, biblio., index, 23.9 cm.

A standard work about the SFT, for the general reader. It was the first such major work to follow that of Inman (1897) and is still used widely. Reprinted, New York: Tudor Publishing Co., 1936; also, New York: Reprint House International.

178 Dufouri, James H.

Historical Sketch of the Catholic Church in New Mexico. San Francisco: McCormick Bros., 1887.

[1]-164 p., 18 cm.; from photocopy at Univ. of N.M.

Contains an account of a trip by a group of nuns who went over the SFT in 1852 with Archbishop Lamy, written from a record by Mother Magdalene Hayden kept in the Mother House in Kentucky. The group suffered from cholera, storms, and other difficulties.

179 Dunbar, Seymour

A History of Travel in America: Being an Outline of the Development in *Modes of Travel from Archaic Vehicles of Colonial Times to the Completion of the First Transcontinental Railroad. . . .* 4 vols. Indianapolis: Bobbs-Merrill Company, 1915.

> Cloth, liv, 1-1531 p., 12 leaves colored plates incl. frontis., 2 fldg. maps, illus., appendixes, biblio., index, 23 cm. Also large paper edition, ltd. 250.

A general history of transportation in the U.S., useful for understanding the broad pattern but with limited specific information on the SFT. It does show how the Trail was an extension of the Boon's Lick Road that ran across Missouri. The overland narrative of Stanislaus Lasselle in Appendix M is not a Santa Fe Trail narrative, as claimed; Lasselle was going by the Fort Smith to Albuquerque trail, not the SFT. Reprinted in one vol., same pagination, New York, 1937. Also reprinted, Westport, Conn.: Greenwood Press, Inc., 1968, 4 vols. Howes D-557.

180   Duncan, Robert Lipscomb

Reluctant General: the Life and Times of Albert Pike. New York: E. P. Dutton & Co., Inc., 1961.

> Cloth, [1]-289 p., notes, index, 21.5 cm.

Biography of Albert Pike (1809-1891), a young New England schoolteacher who went over the SFT first in 1831 and wrote a book about his experiences (*see also* entry under Pike, Albert). He became a lawyer and in 1861 was made a Confederate major general with powers to make treaties with Indians.

181   Dunham, Harold H.

"Lucien B. Maxwell: Frontiersman and Businessman." In: *1949 Brand Book . . . of the Denver Posse of the Westerners,* Denver, 1950, pp. 269-95, illus., ports.

One of the best brief biographies of Maxwell, whose baronial estate in northeastern New Mexico was a noted stopping point on one branch of the SFT.

182   ———

"Sidelights on Santa Fe Traders, 1839-1846." In: *1950 Brand Book,*

Volume VI, The Westerners. Denver: The University of Denver Press, [c 1951], pp. 263-82.

A reprint of several letters of Manuel Alvarez, who served as acting U.S. consul at Santa Fe and who was often involved with transactions concerning the Santa Fe trade. The originals are in the National Archives: *Consular Despatches, Santa Fe, New Mexico,* General Records of the Department of State, Record Group No. 59, Aug. 28, 1830—Sept. 4, 1846, Vol. I.

183   Dunlop, Eugene

The Trail to Santa Fe. Chicago: Encyclopedia Britannica Press, [1963].

A children's book.

184   Edwards, Frank S.

A Campaign in New Mexico with Colonel Doniphan. Philadelphia: Carey and Hart, 1847.

> Cloth, xvi, [17]-184 p., 22 p. advts., fldg. map, 18.5 cm. Also issued in wrappers.

A personal account of the march over the SFT with Doniphan's men during the Mexican War. Henry R. Wagner says, "This is the most entertaining account of the expedition." Edwards was in an artillery battery of St. Louis men, commanded by Richard H. Weightman and attached to the 1st Missouri Mounted Volunteers. There was also an English edition in 1848 and American editions in 1848 and 1849. Reprinted, Ann Arbor, Mich.: University Microfilms, 1966. Graff 1210; Howes E-52; Wagner-Camp 132.

185   Einsel, Mary

Stagecoach West to Kansas: True Stories of the Kansas Plains. Boulder, Colo.: Pruett Publishing Company, 1970.

> Cloth, [1]-108 p., illus. photos, 22 cm. Also issued in wrappers.

A general work, for the broadest possible audience. It contains brief material on forts and incidents along the SFT.

186 Elliott, Richard Smith, 1817-

Notes Taken in Sixty Years. St. Louis: R. P. Studley & Co., 1883.

Cloth, title *Elliott's Notes* in gilt on spine, viii, [1]-336 p., port., 23.5 cm.
Elliott spent many years in Saint Louis and also went up the Missouri. He describes his trip over the SFT with Doniphan's column during the Mexican War (pp. 221-38) and his return east over the Trail in 1847. Graff 1236; Howes E-111.

187 Emmett, Chris

Fort Union and the Winning of the Southwest. Norman: University of Oklahoma Press, [1965].

Cloth, xvi, [1]-436 p., ports., maps, diagr., scenes, biblio., index, 24 cm.

The best book to date on this famous SFT fort, with an introduction by William S. Wallace. The late James W. Arrott gathered a remarkable collection of documents on Fort Union. Emmett was the first writer allowed full access to the collection, which is now at New Mexico Highlands University. An understanding of the role of Fort Union is essential for any appreciation of the military importance of the Trail.

188 Emory, William Hemsley

Notes of a Military Reconnoissance, from Fort Leavenworth, in Missouri, to San Diego, in California, including Part of the Arkansas, Del Norte, and Gila Rivers. U.S. 30th Cong., 1st sess., H. R. Exec. Doc. 41 [Serial 517]. Washington: Wendell and Van Benthuysen, Printers, Feb. 9, 1848.

Full leather, [1]-614 p., 64 plates, 5 maps and plans, large fldg. map, 23 cm.

A basic document on the SFT (see pp. 7-32, 198-247, 386-405, 419-47, and 512-46). This edition includes reports of Emory and Lt. J. W. Abert on their trip over the Trail with the Army of the West in 1846; the Abert section is his *Report . . . of the Examination of New Mexico*, which was also issued separately (q.v.). Also included is P.S.G. Cooke's report on his march from Santa Fe to California, and Capt. A. R. Johnston's journal when he accompanied Cooke. This document also appeared as Sen. Exec. Doc. 7 (Serial 505) in the same session but without some of the appended reports. Variations in plates, dates, military ranks, etc., still cause disputes over which is definitely the first edition, but the House edition is usually preferred. The Emory report section was reprinted, Albuquerque: University of New Mexico Press, 1951, as *Lieutenant Emory Reports*, also available in paperback from the same publisher. Graff 1249; Howes E-145; Wagner-Camp 148.

189 Englert, Kenneth, and Lorene Englert

Oliver Perry Wiggins: Fantastic, Bombastic Frontiersman. Palmer Lake, Colo.: The Filter Press, 1968.

Wrappers, iv, 1-60 p., illus., 18.5 cm.

Wiggins, who died in 1913, claimed to have been a companion of Carson. He also claimed to have journeyed west over the SFT with a wagon train that, in various interviews, he said had 52, 130, and 180 wagons. Englert builds a strong, professionally documented case that classifies Wiggins with William Drannan (q.v.), as a writer of dubious accuracy to say the least.

190 Espenscheid, Lloyd

"Louis Espenscheid and His Family." *Bulletin of the Missouri Historical Society*, Vol. XVIII, No. 2 (Jan. 1962), pp. 87-103.

One of the best articles about wagons used on the SFT and other trails from Saint Louis. Louis Espenscheid opened his own wagonmaking firm in Saint Louis in 1843. He died in 1887, but the business continued until 1934. In some overland accounts the wagons were called "esponshays."

191 Estep, Hugh

The Santa Fe Trail: An Essay. Logan, Kansas: The Logan Democrat, Publishers, [c 1906].

Pamphlet, 12 unnumbered p. in overhung wrapper, 16.2 cm.

A general work of little value. Apparently published first as a newspaper article with type held for reprinting as a pamphlet to be used in connection with a meeting to raise funds for marking the SFT in Kansas.

192   Estep, Raymond

"The Le Grand Survey of the High Plains—Fact or Fancy." *New Mexico Historical Review*, Vol. XXIX, No. 2 (April 1954), pp. 81-96, 141-53.

Alexander Le Grand was an interesting, often important, and generally elusive figure in the Southwest. This article questions the accuracy of a statement that he surveyed a certain large tract in Texas. Of SFT interest is the material on Le Grand's first trip over the Trail: he captained the caravan that left Franklin, Missouri, in April, 1824. It reached Santa Fe on July 31.

193   Estergreen, Marion Morgan

Kit Carson: a Portrait in Courage. Norman: University of Oklahoma, [c 1962].

Cloth, [xxiv], [1]-320 p., 9 leaves plates incl. frontis., map, notes, biblio., index, 23.5 cm.

A recent biography of Carson based partly on notes taken by Blanche Grant, a Taos local historian who interviewed several of Carson's relatives. Carson's SFT experiences remain essentially the same here as in works by Harvey Carter and Edwin Sabin (q.v.).

194   [Evans, Hugh]

"Hugh Evans' Journal of Colonel Henry Dodge's Expedition to the Rocky Mountains in 1835," edited by Fred S. Perrine. *Mississippi Valley Historical Review*, Vol. XIV, No. 2 (Sept. 1927), pp. 192-214.

Evans was a sergeant with Co. G, 1st Dragoons, when they went, under the command of Col. Dodge, up the Platte river to the Rockies, south to the Arkansas river, and back east along the SFT. The first part of his journal, also edited by Perrine, was published in

93

Chronicles of Oklahoma, Vol. III, 1925, pp. 175-215. Only this second part mentions the SFT route (pp. 211-14), from Bent's Fort to a point near Chouteau's Island, where the journal ends.

195 [Evans, N. G.]

N. G. Evans. Mr. Sapp, for the Committee on Military Affairs, Made the Following Report. U.S. 34th Cong., 3rd sess., II.R. Report 244 [Serial 914]. Washington, Mar. 3, 1857.

1 p., 22.5 cm.

Lt. Evans claims compensation for loss of personal baggage, carried on the Brown, Russell & Co. wagon train that was attacked by Indians and burned on Sept. 30, 1850, en route from Fort Leavenworth to New Mexico. Payment denied.

196 Ewing, Floyd F., Jr.

"The Mule as a Factor in the Development of the Southwest." *Arizona and the West*, Vol. 5, No. 4 (Winter 1963), pp. 315-26.

The SFT created the first big demand for mules and also provided a major source. See also entry under John Ashton.

197 [Expulsion of Traders]

Message from the President of the United States Communicating . . . Correspondence with the Government of Mexico, in Relation to the Expulsion of Citizens of the United States from Upper California. U.S. 28th Cong., 1st sess., Sen. Doc. 390 [Serial 436]. Washington, June 14, 1844.

19 p., 22.5 cm.

Contains a letter from the Mexican government to the U.S. explaining that the departments of New Mexico, Chihuahua, Sonora, and Sinaloa (all served by the SFT trade) are not affected by the order expelling Americans from California.

198 Falconer, Thomas

Expedition to Santa Fe. An Account of Its Journey from Texas through Mexico, with Particulars of Its Capture. New Orleans: Office of the Picayune, 1842.

Pamphlet, 12 p. (This first edition not examined personally.)

Falconer was with the Texan-Santa Fe Expedition. An Englishman, he was soon released when his government exerted influence. He read an enlarged paper on the subject in London, published there in 1844 as Notes of a Journey through Texas and New Mexico in the Years 1841 and 1842. The most useful edition was edited by Hodge, published at New York: Dauber & Pine Bookshops, 1930, as Letters and Notes on the Texan Santa Fe Expedition, 1841-1842. This 1930 edition was reprinted, Glorieta, N.M.: Rio Grande Press, Inc., 1963. Howes F-14; Wagner-Camp 90 and 106a.

199   Faris, John T.

On the Trail of the Pioneers: Romance, Tragedy and Triumph on the Path of Empire. New York: George H. Doran Company, [c 1920].

Cloth, [1]-319 p., frontis., illus., biblio., index, 20.9 cm.

A secondary work with a chapter on the SFT (pp. 181-201).

200   [Farmer, James E.]

My Life with the Army in the West: the Memoirs of James E. Farmer, 1858-1898. Edited by Dale F. Giese. Santa Fe: Stagecoach Press, [1967].

Cloth, [1]-[84] p., 1 leaf, frontis., port., notes, index, ltd. 750, 17.8 cm.

During the Civil War, Farmer was at the battle of Glorieta and shortly afterward went to work for the sutler at Fort Union.

201   Farnham, Thomas Jefferson

Travels in the Great Western Prairies, the Anahuac and Rocky Mountains, and in the Oregon Territory. Poughkeepsie: Killey & Lossing, Printers, 1841.

Cloth, [1]-197 p., 17.9 cm.

Farnham left Independence on May 30, 1839, and was at Bent's Fort on July 11, having traveled the SFT. Henry Wagner says Farnham may have been a U.S. agent bound for Oregon, which would account for his careful description of the route and comments on Indian tribes met. Reprinted, New York: Plenum Publishing Corp., 1968; also (and best) in *Early Western Travels Series*, Vols. 28, 29, Cleveland: Arthur H. Clark Co., 1906, with SFT material on pp. 45-173, Vol. 28. Graff 1294; Howes F-50; Wagner-Camp 85.

202   [Farrar, Horatio Russ]

"Tales of New Mexico Territory, 1868-1876," edited by Harold R. Farrar. *New Mexico Historical Review*, Vol. XLIII, No. 2 (April 1968), pp. 137-52.

Horatio Farrar was a wagon freighter in the last days of the Trail, driving from the end of the railroad at Sargent, Kansas, on to New Mexico. He also helped lay out the variant route through the Raton mountains known as the Tollgate Road. His pertinent letters and tales are here edited by his son.

203   Farrell, Cliff

Santa Fe Wagon Boss. Garden City, N.Y., 1958.

Fiction.

204   Favour, Alpheus H.

Old Bill Williams, Mountain Man. Chapel Hill: University of North Carolina Press, [c 1936].

Buckram, map endpapers, colored frontis., [xii], [1]-229 p., 6 leaves plates, fldg. map, notes, biblio., index, 23.7 cm.

William Sherley Williams (1787-1849) was a hunter, trapper, and guide who left his mark in many parts of the Southwest. George C. Sibley hired Bill Williams as interpreter during the first survey of the Trail in 1825 (pp. 56-63). Reprinted, with new introduction by William Brandon, Norman: University of Oklahoma Press, 1962.

205   Field, Matthew C.

"Sketches of Big Timber, Bent's Fort and Milk Fort in 1839." *The*

Colorado Magazine, State Historical Society of Colorado, Vol. XIV, No. 3 (May 1937), pp. 102-08.

The same text appears in the book *Matt Field on the Santa Fe Trail* (pp. 140-46, 149-53), entry 470.

206   Fierman, Floyd S.

"The Triangle and the Tetragrammaton: a Note on the Cathedral at Santa Fe." *New Mexico Historical Review*, Vol. XXXVII, No. 4 (Oct. 1962), pp. 310-21, illus.

Church history, generally not related to the SFT, but pp. 313-14 describe a trip by Bishop Lamy over the Trail in 1852 (see also entry 178), during a time when cholera was frequent. This small item originally appeared in *The Southwestern Jewish Chronicle*, Oklahoma City, 1933. The notes carry information on Jewish merchants who ventured over the Trail, such as Staab and Spiegelberg.

207   [Fitzpatrick, Thomas]

Message from the President of the United States to the Two Houses of Congress, at the Commencement of the First Session of the Thirtieth Congress. U.S. 30th Cong., 1st sess., Sen. Exec. Doc. 1 [Serial 503]. Washington: Wendell and Van Benthuysen, Dec. 7, 1847.

1369 & 249 p., 17 fldg. maps, 22.5 cm.

The appendix (pp. 238-49) contains a letter from Thomas Fitzpatrick, dated at Bent's Ford (sic), 18 Sept., 1847, describing his trip over the SFT, May-Aug., 1847, and urging the Trail be guarded by mounted riflemen, dragoons, and a hundred Mexicans armed with lances. Also issued as H.R. Exec. Doc. 8 [Serial 515], same session. Graff 1344; Wagner-Camp 133.

208   ———

"Robbery on the Santa Fe Trail in 1842." *Kansas Historical Quarterly*, Vol. XIX, No. 1 (Feb. 1951), pp. 50-51.

Thomas Fitzpatrick (1799-1854), the Mountain Man, was

robbed on the SFT in 1842. This article reprints his letter and a claim against the government, listing personal possessions taken.

209 Folmer, Henri

"Contraband Trade Between Louisiana and New Mexico in the Eighteenth Century." *New Mexico Historical Review*, Vol. XVI, No. 3 (July 1941), pp. 249-74.

Accounts of early French ventures toward New Mexico, including the Mallet brothers' trip to Santa Fe in 1739 and Jean Chapuis' trip to Pecos in 1752. Also issued in pamphlet form, as Historical Society of New Mexico *Review* Reprint No. 50.

210 ———

Franco-Spanish Rivalry in North America, 1524-1763. Spain in the West series, VII. Glendale: Arthur H. Clark Company, 1953.

Cloth, [1]-346 p., fldg. map frontis., biblio., index, 24.5 cm.

An essential and scholarly work, with material on the French ventures toward New Mexico (pp. 277-289, 297-303). Contains details on the trips by the Mallet brothers, De Bourgmont, Fabry de la Bruyère, and others; also material about El Quartelejo outpost.

211 ———

"The Mallet Expedition of 1739 through Nebraska, Kansas and Colorado to Santa Fe." *The Colorado Magazine*, State Historical Society of Colorado, Vol. XVI, No. 5 (Sept. 1939), pp. 161-73, map.

Lansing Bloom judged this article to be "worth more than a fat book." The Mallet brothers have been credited with being the first traders to reach New Mexico by land. They apparently left the Missouri from the site of present Kansas City and rode almost due west, not via the later SFT route. Part of the material is translated from Margry (q.v.) and some portions are from Charles W. Hackett's *Historical Documents Relating to New Mexico, Nueva Vizcaya, and Approaches Thereto* (Washington: Carnegie Institution of Washington, 1937, Vol. III). The French seem to have made other attempts many years earlier, but the Mallet men were successful. The paper was also issued as a separate pamphlet.

212 Fonda, John H.

"Early Wisconsin." *Collections of Wisconsin Historical Society*, Vol. V, 1868, pp. 205-84.

Reminiscences of a Wisconsin newspaper editor. A brief section (pp. 210-11) describes his trip east over the SFT with a caravan. This volume was reissued by the Society in 1907.

213 Ford, Lemuel

"Captain Ford's Journal of an Expedition to the Rocky Mountains," edited by Louis Pelzer. *Mississippi Valley Historical Review*, Vol. XII, No. 4 (March 1926), pp. 550-79.

This journal describes the march by the Dragoons in 1835. The regiment went northwest and then west along the Platte, then south to the Arkansas, and returned east over a long portion of the SFT. The expedition encountered little activity on the Trail because the main caravan had already passed, heading west.

214 ————

March of the First Dragoons to the Rocky Mountains in 1835: the Diaries and Maps of Lemuel Ford; a Biography of Ford, with a History of the Dragoons, the Expedition, and a Map of the Route. Edited by Nolie Mumey. Denver: The Eames Brothers Press, 1957.

> Half cloth and marbled paper over boards, marbled endpapers, [1]-[116] p., frontis. port., facsims., errata slip, fldg. map in back, issued unopened, ltd. 350 numbered and signed, 34 cm.

The diaries of Ford written on his march with the Dragoons. Part of the trip was along the SFT. See also other entries under Henry Dodge, James Hildreth, and G. P. Kingsbury.

215 ————

"A Summer Upon the Prairie," by "F" [Captain Lemuel Ford]. In: *The Call of the Columbia: Iron Men and Saints Take the Oregon*

Trail. Edited by Archer Butler Hulbert. Overland to the Pacific series, Vol. 4. Denver: Stewart Commission of Colorado College and Denver Public Library, 1934, pp. 228-305.

Ford was with Col. Henry Dodge's U.S. Dragoons on their march during 1835. He wrote a skeleton journal (see adjoining entry under Ford) and later expanded his entries into an article entitled "A Summer Upon the Prairie," published first in the *Army and Navy Chronicle,* Vols. II and III (see Wagner-Camp 63), and reprinted here with notes.

216 Foreman, Carolyn Thomas

"General Philip St. George Cooke." *Chronicles of Oklahoma,* Vol. XXXII, No. 2 (Summer 1954), pp. 195-213, port.

A careful biographical sketch of the noted commander.

217 Foreman, Grant

"Antoine Leroux, New Mexico Guide." *New Mexico Historical Review,* Vol. XVI, No. 4 (Oct. 1941), pp. 367-78.

Leroux was a famous guide, but he was most active beyond the end of the SFT. On some occasions, as in 1853, he served as a Trail guide.

218 [Fort Atkinson]

Fort Atkinson. Memorial of the Legislative Council of New Mexico, Asking the Re-establishment of Fort Atkinson. U.S. 33rd Cong., 1st sess., H.R. Misc. Doc. 47 [Serial 741]. Washington, April 4, 1854.

> 2 p., 22.5 cm.

New Mexico asks that the fort be reestablished as a "halfway house" on the SFT, not only to guard against Indian attacks but also to provide a place where wagons may be repaired en route.

219 [Fort Atkinson]

Fort Atkinson. U.S. 33rd Cong., 1st sess., H.R. Report 223 [Serial 743]. Washington, June 23, 1854.

1 p., 22.5 cm.

The House Committee on Military Affairs declines New Mexico's request for re-establishment of the fort, saying the post is no longer tenable.

220 [Fort Larned]

Fort Larned Centennial Celebration: 100, 1859-1959, Larned, Kansas, "Along the Santa Fe Trail." N.p., n.d.

Wrappers, side stitched, 31 unnumbered leaves, illus., 28 cm.

A local souvenir booklet with old and new photographs and historical information on Fort Larned, Pawnee Rock, and adjacent sections of the SFT.

221 [Fort Union]

Guide to Fort Union; Fort Union National Monument, New Mexico. [Globe, Arizona: Southwestern Monuments Association, 1962].

Pamphlet, cover title, saddle stitched, 1-[13] p., scenes, 22.6 cm.

A self-guiding tour, with legends for each of 30 view points.

222 [Forts]

Military Post. Memorial of the General Assembly of Missouri Asking the Establishment of an Additional Military Post. U.S. 28th Cong., 1st sess., H.R. Doc. 30 [Serial 441]. Washington: Blair & Rives, printers, Dec. 22, 1843.

2 p., 22.5 cm.

Indirectly referring to the SFT trade, the memorial asks that another fort be established "midway between Forts Scott and Leavenworth."

223 ———

Military Posts on the Road from Missouri to New Mexico. U.S. 35th Cong., 2nd sess., H.R. Report 154 [Serial 1018]. Washington, Feb. 3, 1859.

3 p., 22.5 cm.

An adverse report on a bill proposing to establish certain military posts. Only one fort is related to the SFT: proposed at Rabbit Ear Creek. The road was one that lay below the SFT, along a line surveyed by J. E. Johnston.

224   Fowler, Jacob, 1765-1850

The Journal of Jacob Fowler, Narrating an Adventure from Arkansas through the Indian Territory, Oklahoma, Kansas, Colorado, and New Mexico, to the Sources of Rio Grande del Norte, 1821-22. Edited by Elliott Coues. New York: Francis P. Harper, 1898.

> Cloth, xxiv, [1]-183 p., 1 leaf adv., fldg. facsim. at front, ltd. 950 numbered copies, 23.4 cm.

An important early journal; Fowler was second in command in a party of twenty men under Hugh Glenn. They left Fort Smith in September, 1821, and went along the Arkansas river, following approximately the route that later became the SFT in that region, to the site of present Pueblo, Colorado. They went on to Taos and returned east in 1822, following the SFT in part and mentioning seeing the tracks of Becknell's wagons. Reprinted, Minneapolis: Ross & Haines; reprinted from new type with added notes by Raymond W. and Mary Lund Settle and Harry R. Stevens, Lincoln: University of Nebraska Press, 1970. Howes F-298.

225   Frazer, Robert W.

Forts of the West: Military Posts and Presidios and Posts Commonly Called Forts West of the Mississippi River to 1898. Norman: University of Oklahoma Press, [c 1965].

> Cloth, xxxvii, [1]-246 p., 4 leaves plates, maps, biblio., index, 23.5 cm.

Contains a brief and authoritative history of every fort connected with the Santa Fe Trail.

226   [Frémont, John Charles]

Central Railroad Route to the Pacific. Letter of J. C. Frémont to the Editors of the National Intelligencer, *Communicating Some General*

Results of a Recent Winter Expedition across the Rocky Mountains, for the Survey of a Route for a Railroad to the Pacific. U.S. 33d Cong., 1st sess., Sen. Misc. Doc. 67 [Serial 705]. Washington, June 15, 1854.

> 7 p., 22.5 cm.

Also issued as House Misc. Doc. 8, (Serial 807), U.S. 33rd Cong., 2d sess., 1854. Describes Frémont's Fifth Expedition, privately financed. It followed much of the SFT route along the Arkansas to Bent's Fort. Wagner-Camp 239.

227 ————

Geographical Memoir upon Upper California, in Illustration of his Map of Oregon and California. 30th Cong., 1st sess., Senate Misc. Doc. 148 [Serial 511]. Washington: Wendell and Van Benthuysen, 1848.

> 67 p., map.

Also issued as House Misc. Doc. 5 (Serial 544), U.S. 30th Cong., 2nd sess., 1849. A report of Frémont's Third Expedition in 1845-1846, which went along the SFT as far as Bent's Fort before continuing west. Graff 1429; Howes F-366; Wagner-Camp 150.

228 ————

Memoirs of My Life, by John Charles Frémont. Including in the Narrative Five Journeys of Western Exploration, During the Years 1842, 1843-4, 1845-6-7, 1848-9, 1853-4. . . . Vol. I. Chicago and New York: Belford, Clarke & Co., 1887.

> Cloth, xix, [1]-654 p., 82 leaves of plates incl. frontis., 7 maps (4 fldg.), 27 cm.

Only Vol. I was issued, and it ends with 1847, thus describing only the first three expeditions and the California events. Brief material on the SFT (pp. 170, 425-28) and personal comments on the men who accompanied him. Howes F-367.

229 ————

Report of the Exploring Expedition to the Rocky Mountains in the

Year 1842, and to Oregon and North California in the Years 1843-'44.
28th Cong., 2nd sess., Sen. Doc. 174 [Serial 461]. Washington: Gales
and Seaton, 1845.

> 1-693 p., 4 maps in text, 1 fldg. map in pocket.

Also issued as House Doc. 166, same session (Serial 467), 583
p. The 1842 trip is usually called Frémont's First Expedition, in which
he left Westport and went a short distance along the SFT before
turning north toward the Platte. On his Second Expedition he returned along part of the SFT below Bent's Fort. There were several
reprints by commercial publishers; for details see Graff 1433; Howes
F-370; Wagner-Camp 115.

230 ——————

*Report on the Expediency of Publishing the Results of the Late Ex-
ploring Expedition of Capt. J. C. Frémont's to California and Oregon,
as a National Work.* 30th Cong., 1st sess., Senate Report 226 [Serial
512]. Washington, Aug. 1, 1848.

A report approving publication of this account of Frémont's
Third Expedition, which went along the SFT for part of the journey
west. See also entry 227.

231 Froebel, Julius

*Seven Years' Travel in Central America, Northern Mexico, and the
Far West of the United States.* London: Richard Bentley, MDCCC-
LIX.

> Cloth, [xix], [1]-587 p., 8 engraved views, 23 cm.

Books I-III in one vol.; Book II deals with the SFT, especially
pp. 203-93. In the spring of 1852 Froebel went over the SFT with the
wagon train of Mayer & Co. and then on down to Chihuahua. The
first edition was in German: *Aus Amerika. Erfahrungen, Reisen und
Studien;* 2 vols., Leipzig, 1857. There was also an edition in French:
A travers l'Amerique, Brussels, 1861, in 3 vols. Graff 1448; Howes F-
390; Wagner-Camp 292. KHS, N.

232   Gardner, Hamilton

"Captain Philip St. George Cooke and the March of the 1st Dragoons to the Rocky Mountains in 1845." *The Colorado Magazine*, State Historical Society of Colorado, Vol. XXX, No. 4 (Oct. 1953), pp. 246-69.

Both Cooke and Kearny were on this march, which went from Fort Leavenworth up the Platte and into Wyoming, then back and down the eastern flank of the Rockies to the Arkansas and along the SFT east to their base. Pp. 266-69 refer to the return trip from Bent's Fort.

233   ————

"The Command Staff of the Mormon Battalion in the Mexican War." *Utah Historical Quarterly*, Vol. 20, No. 4 (Oct. 1952), pp. 331-51.

A military writer describes the officers of the Mormon Battalion, with biographical sketches of James Allen, Philip St. George Cooke, Andrew Jackson Smith, and George Stoneman.

234   ————

"Romance at Old Cantonment Leavenworth: the Marriage of 2d Lt. Philip St. George Cooke in 1830." *Kansas Historical Quarterly*, Vol. XXII, No. 2 (Summer 1956), pp. 97-113, illus.

General brief biography of Cooke, with emphasis on his marriage. Cooke made many trips over the SFT, 1829 to 1852 and later.

235   Garfield, Marvin H.

"The Military Post as a Factor in the Frontier Defense of Kansas, 1865-1869." *Kansas Historical Quarterly*, Vol. I, No. 1 (Spring 1931), pp. 50-62.

Condensed information on all Kansas military posts of the period, several of which had been established to guard the SFT.

236 Garrard, Lewis Hector, 1829-1887

Wah-to-yah, and the Taos Trail; or Prairie Travel and Scalp Dances, with a Look at Los Rancheros from Muleback, and the Rocky Mountains Campfire. Cincinnati: H. W. Derby & Co., 1850.

> Cloth, [viii], [1]-349 p., 20 cm.
>
> Garrard, whose name was really Hector Lewis Garrard although he usually changed the arrangement, was only seventeen when he went to the West. He describes his trip over the SFT in the fall of 1846 with Ceran St. Vrain's train, via Bent's Fort. After a winter in Taos, he returned over the SFT in 1847. Garrard captured the sound of the trapper's language with a skill equal to Ruxton's, and this work remains one of the great classics not only on the Trail but of the entire Southwest. Available in many reprint editions. Graff 1513; Howes G-70; Wagner-Camp 182.

237 Ghent, William J.

"The Centenary of the Santa Fe Trail." *The Outlook,* Vol. CXL (Aug. 12, 1925), pp. 517-19.

> A general review of the Trail.

238 ⸻

The Early Far West: A Narrative Outline, 1540-1850. New York: Longmans, Green & Co., 1931.

> Cloth, [xi], 1-412 p., plates, ports., maps, biblio., index, 23.7 cm.
>
> Written for the general reader and for classroom use. SFT material (pp. 186-98) is general; there are occasional details on other pages about troops on the Trail. The work should not be dismissed lightly. Reprinted, New York: Tudor Publishing Co., 1936.

239 Gianini, Charles A.

"Manuel Lisa: One of the Earliest Traders on the Missouri River." *New Mexico Historical Review,* Vol. II, No. 4 (Oct. 1927), pp. 323-33.

Chiefly from standard sources, with slight material on the SFT. Repeats that Lisa "cast his eyes towards Santa Fe (trade, but) . . . General Wilkinson . . . thwarted his plans." See index for better works on Lisa.

240 Gibson, George Rutledge, ca. 1810-1885

Journal of a Soldier under Kearny and Doniphan, 1846-1847. Edited by Ralph P. Bieber. Southwest Historical Series, III. Glendale: Arthur H. Clark Co., 1935.

> Cloth, [1]-371 p., 4 leaves plates incl. frontis., fldg. map at back, appendix, 24.2 cm.

Gibson was publisher of the *Independence Journal* at Independence, Mo., in 1844; he later moved to Weston, Mo. In 1846 he enlisted in the Army of the West under Kearny and marched over the SFT (pp. 111-204). In Santa Fe he was editor of the Santa Fe *Republican* in 1847 and returned east over the Trail in 1848. The length of his journal and Bieber's careful notes make this a valuable work.

241 [Gibson, William D.]

William D. Gibson. U.S. 30th Cong., 1st sess., H.R. Report 421 [Serial 535]. Washington, March 28, 1848.

> 3 p., 22.5 cm.

A sad, human incident. Gibson was a wagon-master from Missouri who served with the Army in 1846 over the SFT to Santa Fe. When he returned home in the spring of 1847 he was given three yoke of miserable oxen and a wagon for the trip. Some died, and he bought poor replacements, only to lose all in an Indian attack. The claims committee disapproves his request for compensation.

242 Gilbert, Edmund W.

The Exploration of Western America, 1800-1850: An Historical Geography. New York: Cambridge University Press, 1933.

> Cloth, [xx], [1]-233 p., 8 leaves plates, maps (3 fldg. in back pocket), biblio., index.

A general history of Western exploration, with a geographical essay. SFT material includes James L. Collins' letter in 1852 regarding the dangers of winter traffic over the Trail; also Zebulon Pike's description of the Arkansas river. Gilbert credits Pike's report with being a major influence on opening a trail to Santa Fe. Reprinted, New York: Cooper Square Publishers, Inc., 1966.

243 [Gilpin, William]

Message from the President of the United States to the Two Houses of Congress, at the Commencement of the Second Session of the Thirtieth Congress. U.S. 30th Cong., 2nd sess., H.R. Exec. Doc. 1 [Serial 537]. Washington: Wendell and Van Benthuysen, 1848.

> 1275 p., 22.5 cm.

Military action along the SFT (pp. 136-51). Report of Lt. Col. Wm. Gilpin on operations of the Missouri Volunteer Battalion, Oct. 1847-Aug. 1848, with reports of junior officers on a fight with Comanches along the Cimarron cutoff; also a report of Lt. W. B. Royall concerning an attack on a government train by Indians on the Arkansas in June 1848.

244 Goetzmann, William H.

Army Exploration in the American West, 1803-1863. Yale Publications in American Studies, 4. New Haven: Yale University Press, 1959.

> Cloth and paper over boards, xx, [1]-509 p., 8 leaves plates, appendixes, biblio., index, 5 fldg. maps in back pocket, 23.8 cm.

An important study that describes and evaluates the role of the U.S. Army in exploring the trans-Mississippi West, with particular emphasis on the role of the Topographical Engineers, 1838-63. It unifies the work of such government men as Abert, Cooke, Emory, Frémont, Heap, Kearny, Long, Marcy, and Pike—whose books are all described separately in this bibliography. Available also in paperback from the same publisher.

245 Golder, Frank Alfred, with Bailey, Thomas A., and J. Lyman Smith, eds.

The March of the Mormon Battalion from Council Bluffs to Califor-

nia, Taken from the Journal of Henry Standage. New York: The Century Co., [1928].

> Cloth, map endpapers, xiii, 1-295 p., frontis. port., ports., scenes, biblio., roster, index, 20.5 cm.

During the war with Mexico in 1846, the Mormons were moving west but halted at Council Bluffs, without funds. 500 of their men enlisted under Kearny in what became the Mormon Battalion and marched over the SFT and on to California. Their pay helped the Mormon trek continue. Pp. 145-74 here present a day-by-day account of the march to Santa Fe. Standage was a private in Co. E. A complete roster is included (pp. 281-88).

246   [Gold Rush]

"The Emigrants by the Santa Fe Route." *Kansas Historical Quarterly,* Vol. XVIII, No. 3 (Aug. 1950), pp. 324-25.

Reprints an article from the New York *Weekly Tribune* of July 21, 1849, which had in turn taken it from the *Cincinnati Dispatch,* as a letter written from Council Grove, Kansas, on June 7 by one of a party heading for California via the SFT. The group hoped to reach California by pack train from Santa Fe in thirty-five days. Mention of Kaw Indians, wagon equipment, and trail conditions.

247   Golley, Frank B.

"James Baird, Early Santa Fe Trader." *Bulletin of the Missouri Historical Society,* Vol. XV, No. 3 (April 1959), pp. 171-93.

A descendant of Baird writes a well-documented biography of an early Santa Fe trader. James Baird (1767-1826) was one of a party of men who reached Santa Fe in 1812. They were promptly imprisoned and not all freed until 1820. Included are an inventory of goods confiscated and the text of official letters exchanged between governments regarding release of the prisoners.

248   [Goodman, Julia Cody]

"Julia Cody Goodman's Memoirs of Buffalo Bill," edited by Don Russell. *Kansas Historical Quarterly*, Vol. XXVIII, No. 4 (Winter 1962), pp. 442-96.

Memoirs by the elder sister of William F. Cody. Brief mention of SFT: Cody served as a scout for the 9th Kansas Cavalry under Lieut. Col. Charles S. Clark over the Trail to Santa Fe in 1861.

249 Gracy, David B., II, and Helen J. H. Rugeley

"From the Mississippi to Pacific: an Englishman in the Mormon Battalion." *Arizona and the West*, Vol. 7, No. 2 (Summer 1965), pp. 127-60, map, illus.

An anonymous diary, presumably written by Robert W. Whitworth, describing the march of the Mormon Battalion over the SFT, August-October 1846 (pp. 135-43).

250 Grant, Blanche Chloe

When Old Trails Were New: the Story of Taos. New York: The Press of the Pioneers, Inc., 1934.

> Cloth, [xi], [1]-344 p., front., 23 leaves plates, notes, biblio., index, 23.4 cm.

History and legends of the region around Taos, New Mexico, by a local historian. Most useful for its reprint of the diary of artist Richard H. Kern, who was with the Frémont expedition of 1848-1849, in part along the SFT. Reprinted facsimile, with negligible omission of plates, Chicago: The Rio Grande Press, Inc., 1963.

251 Green, Charles R.

Early Days in Kansas: Along the Santa Fe Trail. Green's Historical Series, 5 vols. Olathe: C. R. Green, 1912-14.

These crudely printed thin volumes, edited in homespun fashion, are the work of one amateur's devotion. Among the haphazard contents are verbatim memoirs not readily available elsewhere. Vol. I refers to the counties of Douglas, Franklin, Shawnee, Osage, and Lyon. Vol. II contains memoirs about Council City, Superior, and Burlingame, with reminiscences of men who settled there in 1854-60.

Vol. IV is devoted principally to the Lawrence and Ridgeway vicinities. Vols. III and V have been reported but not examined. These newsprint volumes are worth the search if one seeks completeness in a collection on the Trail. Graff 1636.

252   Greene, J. Evarts

"The Santa Fe Trade: Its Route and Character." *Proceedings of the American Antiquarian Society*, New Series, Vol. VIII, Part 3 (April 26, 1893), pp. 324-41.

Greene rode the SFT in 1857. The work is quite general, with useful statistics for the period 1845-60 (p. 15) and mention of the wagons built by the Murphy firm in St. Louis. Also issued as a separate pamphlet, folios 1-20, from the Press of Charles Hamilton, Worcester, Mass. Later reprinted in *Journal of the United States Cavalry Association*, Vol. X, No. 38 (Sept. 1897), pp. 264-77.

253   Greene, Max

The Kanzas Region: Forest, Prairie, Desert, Mountain, Vale, and River. . . . New York: Fowler and Wells, Publishers, 1856.

¾ leather and marbled paper over boards, map frontis., viii, [9]-192 p., 12 p. advts. at back (some copies have only 6 or 8), 18.8 cm.

Contains some general information on the SFT, pp. 73-99, but should not be considered a major work. Has a useful table of distances from Independence to Santa Fe, compiled by Greene on a trip in 1850. Graff 1650; Howes G-383; Wagner-Camp 276. KHS.

254   Gregg, Jacob Ray

A History of the Oregon Trail, Santa Fe Trail, and Other Trails. Portland, Oregon: Binfords & Mort, Publishers, [c 1955].

Cloth, map endpapers, [viii], [1]-313, 3 leaves, 22.2 cm.

A misleading title. The book is devoted almost entirely to the Oregon Trail, with only a page or two of general information on the SFT.

255   Gregg, Josiah, 1806-1850

Commerce of the Prairies: or the Journal of a Santa Fe Trader, during Eight Expeditions across the Great Western Prairies, and a Residence of nearly Nine Years in Northern Mexico. 2 vols. New York: Henry G. Langley, 1844.

> Embossed cloth, 18.8 cm.; Vol. I: xvi, 17-320 p.; Vol. II: viii, 9-318 p., 2 leaves; 6 plates, 2 maps (1 fldg.).

If you can read only two books about the Trail, read Gregg and Lewis Garrard. Gregg made his first trip over the SFT in 1831; his last trip to Santa Fe was in 1839. The work stands as a cornerstone of all studies on the SFT in the early period, describing the origin and development of the trade, Gregg's own experiences, and useful statistics for 1822-43. Gregg was aided by John Bigelow, who apparently did only minor polishing. From 1844 to 1933 there were fourteen printings. The most useful edition for modern scholars is that edited by Max Moorhead, Norman: University of Oklahoma Press, 1954; also available in paperback, Lincoln: University of Nebraska Press, 1967; although a new edition is in press, Indianapolis: Bobbs-Merrill Co., scheduled for 1971, with an introduction by David F. Hawke. Graff 1659; Howes G-401; Wagner-Camp 108.

256   ———

Diary and Letters of Josiah Gregg. Edited by Maurice Garland Fulton; introduction by Paul Horgan. Norman: University of Oklahoma Press, 1941 (Vol. I), 1944 (Vol. II).

> Cloth; Vol. I: xvii, [1]-413 p., frontis. port., facsims., ports., scenes, maps (2 fldg.), index; Vol. II: xvii, [1]-396 p., colophon leaf, frontis. port., facsims., map, index; 23.5 cm.

Unlike Gregg's Commerce of the Prairies, these volumes contain little on the SFT, but they provide a useful supplement to the earlier work. Vol. I deals with his Southwestern enterprises, 1840-47; Vol. II deals with his excursions to Mexico and California, 1847-50.

257   Gregg, Kate Leila, ed., 1883-1954

The Road to Santa Fe: the Journal and Diaries of George Champlin

Sibley and Others Pertaining to the Surveying and Marking of a Road from the Missouri Frontier to the Settlements of New Mexico, 1825-1827. [Albuquerque: University of New Mexico Press, c 1952].

> Cloth, map endpapers, viii, 1-280 p., frontis. port., appendix, notes, biblio., index, 23.6 cm.

One of the basic works on SFT history, with documents relating to the first survey of the Trail: George C. Sibley's journal and diary, 1825-26; Joseph Davis' diary, 1825; Benjamin Reeves' diary, 1825; Sibley's journal, 1827; the report of the survey commissioners, and correspondence relating to the survey. Also available, same publisher, in paperback. The Newberry Library has papers of Thomas Mather, one of the Trail commissioners; see Graff 2707.

258   Grinnell, George Bird, 1849-

"Bent's Old Fort and Its Builders." *Kansas Historical Collections,* Vol. XV, 1919-1922, pp. 28-91, illus., ports., fldg. map.

The earliest really comprehensive work on the history of Bent's Fort and on William Bent and Ceran St. Vrain; cited as a source by nearly every subsequent writer on the subject. Map shows details of the upper Arkansas river. Also issued as a separate pamphlet and in boards, 1923. Howes G-431.

259   ———

Beyond the Old Frontier: Adventures of Indian-fighters, Hunters, and Fur-traders. New York: Charles Scribner's Sons, 1913.

> Cloth, [xiv], [1]-374 p., 8 leaves plates incl. frontis., map, index, 20 cm.

Rewritten for the general reader, not for the scholar, with chapters taken from George Ruxton and Lewis Garrard, dealing chiefly with the region between Santa Fe and Bent's Fort. Reprinted, same publisher, 1930.

260   [Guadalupe Hidalgo, Treaty of]

Treaty of Guadalupe Hidalgo—Indian Incursions. U.S. 31st Cong., 1st sess., H.R. Report 280 [Serial 584]. Washington, April 24, 1850.

> 3 p., 22.5 cm.

The House Committee on Indian Affairs recommends adding a regiment of cavalry, to be stationed in the West, because "Indians constantly waylay the road from Missouri to Santa Fe," and under the Treaty of Guadalupe Hidalgo the U.S. was obligated to control the Indians.

261 Gudde, Erwin G., ed.

Bigler's Chronicle of the West: The Conquest of California, Discovery of Gold, and Mormon Settlement as Reflected in Henry William Bigler's Diaries. Berkeley: University of California Press, 1962.

> Cloth, [xiv], 1-145 p., frontis., 6 leaves plates, biblio., index, 22 cm.

Bigler recorded information about the discovery of gold in California and became noted as a contemporary authority. It is less known that he marched with the Mormon Battalion, and this book (pp. 19-26) contains Bigler's diary for the march over the SFT from Fort Leavenworth to Santa Fe in 1846. See also entry 54.

262 Hackett, Charles Wilson

"New Light on Don Diego de Peñalosa: Proof that He Never Made an Expedition from Santa Fe to Quivira and the Mississippi River in 1662." *Mississippi Valley Historical Review*, Vol. VI, No. 3 (Dec. 1919), pp. 313-35.

Don Diego Dionisio de Peñalosa Briceño y Verdugo, a discredited one-time Spanish governor of New Mexico, tried to interest the French (especially La Salle) in conquering the Southwest. Peñalosa wrote a report in 1682, published in French by Margry (q.v.) and by Shea in English in 1882. Had it not been for proof by Hackett and others that the reported journey was entirely fictitious, Peñalosa's report might have become truly the first Santa Fe Trail item.

263 Hadley, James Albert

"The Nineteenth Kansas Cavalry and the Conquest of the Plains Indians." *Kansas Historical Collections*, Vol. X (1907-1908), pp. 428-56, 657-65.

Indian fighting along the SFT in 1868, with brief details on the captivity of Clara Blinn (pp. 657-59) and on the killing of George Peacock at Allison's Ranch by Satanta in 1860 (pp. 664-65).

264   Hafen, LeRoy R., 1893-

Frémont's Fourth Expedition: a Documentary Account of the Disaster of 1848-1849, with Diaries, Letters, and Reports by the Participants in the Tragedy. Far West and the Rockies Historical Series, XI. Glendale: Arthur H. Clark Co., 1960.

> Cloth, [1]-319 p., illus., fldg. map, appendixes, index, 24.5 cm. Title on spine: *The Frémont Disaster, 1848-1849.*

In October 1848 John C. Frémont's Fourth Expedition left Westport and headed across central Kansas. They struck the SFT near Chouteau's Island and followed the Trail to Bent's Fort, then headed west and met disaster in the snows of the Rockies. This collection of diaries and letters includes entries describing the Trail, by Benjamin Kern, Richard Kern, Edward M. Kern, Thomas S. Martin, and Thomas E. Breckenridge (pp. 88-90, 114-17, 136, 176, 294-95). For a general work on this expedition, see William Brandon's *The Men and the Mountain,* entry 81.

265   ───────

"The Last Years of James P. Beckwourth." *The Colorado Magazine,* State Historical Society of Colorado, Vol. V, No. 4 (Aug. 1928), pp. 134-39.

Bonner's book on Beckwourth (q.v.) described the life of this Mountain Man only to 1855. Beckwourth then went back to Westport and in 1859 took a wagon train over the SFT for Louis Vasquez, a Westport trader, and remained for the rest of his life near Denver.

266   ───────

The Mountain Men and the Fur Trade of the Far West: Biographical Sketches of the Participants. . . . 8+ vols. Glendale: Arthur H. Clark Company, 1965-.

Cloth, map, ports., facsims. Vol. I: 397 p.; Vol. II: 401 p.; Vol. III: 411 p.; Vol. IV: 397 p.; Vol. V: 401 p.; Vol. VI: 407 p.; Vol. VII: 392 p.; 24.5 cm.

In this series, "a project estimated to run to eight or nine volumes," seven volumes had been issued through 1969. The final volume will be an index to the series. This massive work presents biographies of scores of important Mountain Men by a galaxy of scholars, each an expert on his subject. Among those connected most significantly with the history of the SFT are Manuel Alvarez (Vol. I, pp. 181-98), Charles Bent (Vol. II, pp. 27-48), Jacques Clamorgan (Vol. II, pp. 81-94); Albert Pike (Vol. I, pp. 265-74), Ewing Young (Vol. II, pp. 379-401), James Baird (Vol. III, pp. 27-38), Jacob Fowler (Vol. III, pp. 119-30), Rufus B. Sage (Vol. III, pp. 263-72), Richens Wootton (Vol. III, pp. 397-411), George and Robert Bent (Vol. IV, pp. 39-48), Antoine Leroux (Vol. IV, pp. 173-84), James Ohio Pattie (Vol. IV, pp. 231-50), James Kirker (Vol. V, pp. 125-44), Ceran St. Vrain (Vol. V, pp. 297-316), William W. Bent (Vol. VI, pp. 61-84), Kit Carson (Vol. VI, pp. 105-32), Baptiste La Lande (Vol. VI, pp. 219-22), Sylvestre Pratte (Vol. VI, pp. 359-70), Thomas Fitzpatrick (Vol. VII, pp. 75-86), Alexander Le Grand (Vol. VII, pp. 201-16), Charles A. Warfield (Vol. VII, pp. 353-70), and William Workman (Vol. VII, pp. 381-92).

267 ——————

The Overland Mail, 1849-1869: Promoter of Settlement, Precursor of Railroads. Cleveland: Arthur H. Clark Co., 1926.

Cloth, [1]-361 p., fldg. map, index, 24.5 cm.

Devoted primarily to the route through central Kansas rather than the Santa Fe routes, but there is some mention of the line from Independence via Bent's Fort to Santa Fe. Howes H-11.

268 ——————

Overland Routes to the Gold Fields, 1859, from Contemporary Diaries: Arkansas River Route, Platte River Route, Leavenworth and Pike's Peak Express Route, Smoky Hill Trail, etc. Southwest Historical Series, XI. Glendale: Arthur H. Clark Co., 1942.

Cloth, [1]-320 p., colophon leaf, 6 plates incl. frontis., fldg. map in back, 24.2 cm.

During the Colorado gold rush in 1859 travellers at first went by the SFT along the Arkansas river; soon they found other and shorter routes. Here are diaries of five travellers, plus other documents. Only Charles C. Post's diary (pp. 19-55) describes the Arkansas route, and there are two letters (pp. 317-20) describing this trail.

269 ——————

Pike's Peak Gold Rush Guidebooks of 1859, by Luke Tierney, William B. Parsons, and Summaries of the Other Fifteen. Southwest Historical Series, IX. Glendale: Arthur H. Clark Company, 1941.

Cloth, [1]-[347] p., frontis., illus., fldg. map, 24.3 cm.

Reprints the complete text of two important guidebooks, by Luke Tierney and William B. Parsons (see separate entry on latter), with comments on others. Most of these had brief data about the SFT. An appendix (pp. 322-27) reprints a letter by Parsons describing a trip over the Trail in 1858 and a diary of Augustus Voorhees (pp. 336-43) who went over the Trail with same group.

270 ——————

"Raton Pass, an Historic Highway." *The Colorado Magazine,* State Historical Society of Colorado, Vol. VII, No. 6 (Nov. 1930), pp. 219-21.

A brief general history of the famous pass.

271 ——————

Relations with the Indians of the Plains, 1857-1861: A Documentary Account of the Military Campaigns, and Negotiations of Indian Agents—with Reports and Journals of P. G. Lowe, R. M. Peck, J. E. B. Stuart, S. D. Sturgis, and Other Official Papers. The Far West and the Rockies Historical Series, IX. Glendale: Arthur H. Clark Co., 1959.

Cloth, [1]-310 p., 5 leaves plates, fldg. map, 24.5 cm.

A well-researched work on the Indian campaigns that preceded the Sand Creek massacre. Although much of the action was along the upper Platte, there were many troop movements along the SFT. Lowe's journal is taken from his *Five Years a Dragoon* (q.v.); Peck's account is from *Transactions of the Kansas State Historical Society, 1903-04;* Stuart's journal is from the original at Yale University Library. Included are Indian agents' reports from Bent's Fort: Robert C. Miller, 1859, and William Bent, 1859, with other documents dealing with the establishment of Fort Wise and the Fort Wise treaty in 1861.

272 ———

"Thomas Fitzpatrick and the First Indian Agency in Colorado." *The Colorado Magazine,* State Historical Society of Colorado, Vol. VI, No. 1 (Jan. 1929), pp. 63-62.

Fitzpatrick was one of the best scouts and guides ranging the West. This article deals with the years 1847-54, describing several trips over the SFT in connection with his work as an Indian agent.

273 ———

To the Rockies and Oregon, 1839-1842, with Diaries and Accounts by *Sidney Smith, Amos Cook, Joseph Holman, E. Willard Smith, Francis Fletcher, Joseph Williams, Obadiah Oakley, Robert Shortess, T. J. Farnham.* The Far West and the Rockies Historical Series, III. Glendale: Arthur H. Clark Company, 1955.

Cloth, [1]-315 p., 11 leaves plates incl. frontis., fldg. map, index, 24.5 cm.

Accounts of caravans to Oregon, of which two went along part of the SFT. The "Peoria Party," 1839, was headed by Thomas J. Farnham; the firsthand accounts with page references to SFT material include records of Obadiah Oakley (pp. 26-49), Sidney Smith (pp. 68-72), Robert Shortess (pp. 95-103), and Joseph Holman (pp. 125-26). Also included is the diary of E. Willard Smith (pp. 154-63) on another caravan in 1839. Appendixes include letters by Farnham and others.

274 ————

"The Voorhees Diary of the Lawrence Party's Trip to Pike's Peak, 1858." *The Colorado Magazine*, State Historical Society of Colorado, Vol. XII, No. 2 (Mar. 1935), pp. 41-54, map, port.

This party from Lawrence, Kansas, was one of the first groups to journey to Colorado in search of gold. Augustus Voorhees kept a diary of the trip, which followed the SFT from Council Grove to the ruins of Bent's Fort.

275 ————

"When was Bent's Fort Built?" *The Colorado Magazine*, State Historical Society of Colorado, Vol. XXXI, No. 2 (April 1954), pp. 105-19.

Hafen produces evidence indicating that the old fort was built in 1833 and refutes other versions. There is also material on the Bent brothers and on Ceran St. Vrain.

276 ————

"Zebulon Montgomery Pike." *The Colorado Magazine*, State Historical Society of Colorado, Vol. VIII, No. 4 (July 1931), pp. 132-42.

A biographical sketch, with emphasis on Pike's explorations in the Southwest.

277 ————

Broken Hand: the Life Story of Thomas Fitzpatrick, Chief of the Mountain Men. Denver: The Old West Publishing Company, 1931.

Cloth, [xiv], [15]-316 p., 9 leaves of plates incl. frontis. port., notes, index, 24.3 cm. Also a signed edition, ltd. 100.

Fitzpatrick (1799-1854) ranks with Jedediah Smith, Bridger, and Carson as the four greatest Mountain Men. His first trip over the SFT was in 1831, with the caravan on which Jedediah Smith lost his life. Fitzpatrick was later a guide for such men as Frémont, Abert, and Kearny; in 1846 he was agent for the tribes on the Arkansas, Platte, and Kansas rivers. Howes H-10.

278 ———————

"The Mormon Settlement at Pueblo, Colorado, during the Mexican War." *The Colorado Magazine*, State Historical Society of Colorado, Vol. IX, No. 4 (July 1932), pp. 121-36, port.

Data on members of the Mormon Battalion who went west only to Santa Fe and left the Battalion to return north. They wintered at Pueblo. Much of the information is from a journal kept by Elder John Brown.

279   [Hall, Jacob]

The Committee on the Post Office and Post Roads, to Whom was Referred the Petition of Jacob Hall, make the Following Report. U.S. 34th Cong., 1st sess., Sen. Report 252 [Serial 837]. Washington, July 30, 1856.

1 p., 22.5 cm.

In 1854 Hall secured a four-year contract to carry the mail from Independence to Santa Fe for $10,990 a year. Indian troubles increased his expenses for guards. Committee approves paying Hall $22,000 a year in 1856 and had approved the same for 1855. For another report on the same claim, see: U.S. 34th Cong., 1st sess., H.R. Report 299 [Serial 870], Washington, 1856.

280 ———————

Report: The Committee on Indian Affairs, to Whom was Referred the Memorial of Jacob Hall . . . Report. U.S. 36th Cong., 1st sess., H.R. Report 344 [Serial 1069]. Washington, April 6, 1860.

3 p., 22.5 cm.

Committee can report favorably only if damages were caused by an Indian tribe with whom the U.S. has a treaty.

281   Hall, James C.

"Personal Recollections of the Santa Fe Trail." *Kansas Magazine*, Vol. V, No. 1 (Jan. 1911), pp. [49]-55.

A firsthand account, written later from a journal kept at the time. In 1863 Hall was a young man "run down in health." He went to Fort Leavenworth and hired out with Irwin & Jackman, freighters leaving with a train of supplies for Fort Union.

282   Hall, Thomas B.

History of the Memorial Presbyterian Church and the Experiment Farm of Napton, Missouri. . . . [N.p., n.d.].

> Pamphlet, printed wrappers, [1]-36 p., frontis. port., map, scenes, ports., 22.8 cm.

Material on Josiah Gregg, M. M. Marmaduke, and others who went over the SFT.

283   Hamilton, Jean Tyree

Arrow Rock, Where Wheels Started West. Columbia, Mo.: American Press, Inc., 1963.

> Pamphlet, colored wrappers, saddle stitched, 52 unnumbered p., illus., biblio., 23.5 cm.

On the west bank of the Missouri river, a few miles above Boonville, the settlement of Arrow Rock was an early terminus of the SFT. This pamphlet is most useful for the many photographs of old buildings, portraits, and scenes. It contains brief biographical data on M. M. Marmaduke, John Sappington, and others. Available through Doyle Stationery Co., Marshall, Mo.

284   Hammond, George P., and Agapito Rey, eds.

The Rediscovery of New Mexico, 1580-1594: The Explorations of Chamuscado, Espejo, Castaño de Sosa, Morlete, and Leyva de Bonilla and Humaña. Coronado Cuarto Centennial Publications, III. Albuquerque: University of New Mexico Press, 1966.

> Cloth, map endpapers, xiv [1]-341 p., frontis., index, errata slip, 26.5 cm.

Between the entry of Coronado in 1540 and Oñate's settlement of New Mexico in 1598, five other lesser-known expeditions entered New Mexico. One of these went into Kansas along the approximate route of the western part of the SFT. This was the trip in 1593 by Francisco Leyva de Bonilla, who was killed in Kansas by Antonio Gutiérrez de Humaña (pp. 323-26). Vicente de Zaldivar, an Oñate captain, also visited the Kansas site in 1598, described in Hammond's *Oñate, Colonizer of New Mexico, 1595-1628* (Albuquerque: University of New Mexico Press, 1953, 2 vols.).

285 Hardeman, Nicholas P., ed.

"Camp Sites on the Santa Fe Trail in 1848, as Reported by John A Bingham." *Arizona and the West*, Vol. 6, No. 4 (Winter 1964), pp. 313-19, map.

In a letter written back East in 1849, Bingham gave a long and detailed list of campsites along the SFT with distance between the stops, from his trip taken the previous year.

286 Harding, Samuel Bannister

Life of George R. Smith, Founder of Sedalia, Mo., in Its Relation to the Political, Economic, and Social Life of Southwestern Missouri. Sedalia: Printed for the author, 1904.

391 p., illus., photos, fldg. map, index.

Contains some references to wagon freighting over the SFT in 1849.

287 [Harmony, Manuel X.]

[Report on petition of . . .] in: 30th Cong., 1st sess., H.R. Report 458, [Serial 525]. Washington, March 30, 1848.

Harmony was a trader headed with goods over the SFT when overtaken by Kearny's men. Subsequently most of his good were commandeered. His detailed inventory describes a typical wagon train of the time. Many other traders are named in the document, including Solomon Houck, Francisco Elguea, Owens & Aull, and Samuel Magoffin. The committee is adverse to payment of $182,000. For other documents on the same claim, see U.S. 30th Cong., 1st sess., Sen. Misc. Doc. 11 (Serial 511). Washington, Jan. 5, 1848.

288 Harvey, Charles M.

"The Story of the Santa Fe Trail." *Atlantic Monthly*, Vol. CIV, No. 6 (Dec. 1909), pp. 774-85.

An adequate general article, summarizing the history of the SFT as it was known in 1909.

289 Hayes, Augustus A., Jr.

New Colorado and the Santa Fe Trail. New York: Harper & Brothers, 1880.

Cloth, colored endpapers, [1]-200 p., frontis., map, illus.

Contains two chapters (pp. 133-59) repeating general descriptions and tales of the SFT. The book consists of five articles which originally appeared in *Harper's Monthly* and one from the *International Review*. Graff 1831.

290 Heap, Gwinn Harris

Central Route to the Pacific, from the Valley of the Mississippi to California: Journal of the Expedition of E. F. Beale, Superintendent of Indian Affairs in California, and Gwinn Harris Heap, from Missouri to California. Philadelphia: Lippincott, Grambo, and Co., 1854.

Cloth, [1]-136 p., plus 16 to 46 p. advts. (varies), 13 leaves plates, map, 22.7 cm.

This expedition went over the SFT from Westport to Bent's Fort in May and June, 1853. A long report by Antoine Leroux is included. Reprinted, Glendale, Calif.: Arthur H. Clark Co., 1957, with several added useful documents, in The Far West and Rockies Historical Series, VII. Graff 1837; Howes H-378; Wagner-Camp 235.

291 Heaston, Michael D.

Trails of Kansas: A Bibliography. Dodge City: Cultural Heritage and Arts Center, [c 1969].

Cloth, [1]-64 p., maps, 21.5 cm.

The largest and most recent title list of books and articles relating to all of the historic trails in Kansas. Contains references, without annotations, on the Chisholm Trail, Oregon Trail, and scores of other lesser trails that fed or crossed the SFT. Also issued in wrappers.

292   [Hess, John W.]

"John W. Hess, with the Mormon Battalion," edited by Wanda Wood. *Utah Historical Quarterly*, Vol. 4, No. 2 (April 1931), pp. 47-55.

Hess' own account. He was a private with the Battalion and marched over the SFT to Santa Fe. There he was detailed to the detachment of men who were to return to the Mormons. From Santa Fe they returned over the SFT to Fort Bent and then went north. The narrative has only a short account of SFT incidents.

293   Hicks, Virginia Pierce, ed.

History of Kearny County, Kansas. Vol. I. Dodge City: printed by Rollie Jack, Inc., [for Kearny County Historical Society, c 1964].

> Heavy buckram, map endpapers, [1]-457 p., ports., scenes, index, 28.7 cm.

This county is west of Garden City, on the mountain branch of the SFT. Its chief SFT landmark is Chouteau's Island, exact location of which was a matter of controversy. Auguste Pierre Chouteau, a trapper returning down the Arkansas, was attacked by the Pawnee and took refuge on this island. The book also has material on ranching along the SFT in the 1860s and data on Wagon Bed Springs. On his famous long ride, F. X. Aubry swung north through this county. Only one volume of the work has been issued to date.

294   [Hildreth, James]

Dragoon Campaigns to the Rocky Mountains; Being a History of the Enlistment, Organization, and First Campaigns of the Regiment of United States Dragoons. New York: Wiley & Long, 1836.

> Cloth, [1]-288 p., 19 cm.

A firsthand account of the march of the 1st Dragoons to the Rocky Mountains in 1835, returning along the SFT. See our entry under Thoburn, Joseph B. He gives strong arguments that Hildreth personally did not write this work but that it was written by a British officer who had joined the Dragoons. Graff 1885; Howes H-471; Wagner-Camp 59.

295 Hill, Joseph J.
"Ewing Young in the Fur Trade of the Far Southwest, 1822-1834." *Quarterly of the Oregon Historical Society*, Vol. XXIV, No. 1 (March 1923), pp. 1-35, fldg. facsimile document.

Young is said to have been with William Becknell on the first pack-train trip in 1821 and also on the 1822 wagon caravan over the SFT. A general review of Young's subsequent career in the Southwest.

296 ———
"An Unknown Expedition to Santa Fe in 1807." *Mississippi Valley Historical Review*, Vol. VI, No. 4 (March 1920), pp. 560-62.

Spanish text, translation, and commentary on a letter from Joachin del Real Alencaster, Spanish governor of New Mexico, dated at Santa Fe, December 12, 1807. It reports that the St. Louis trader, Jacques Clamorgan, was proceeding from Santa Fe southward to Chihuahua, with a small pack train of trade goods.

297 Hine, Robert V.
Edward Kern and American Expansion. New Haven: Yale University Press, 1962.

Cloth, [1]-180 p., 18 leaves plates, 21 cm.

A biography of Edward Kern, an artist with Frémont. It contains a description of Kern's first visit to Westport, Mo., in 1845 (pp. 8-21).

298 Hine, Robert V., and Bingham, Edward R., eds.
The Frontier Experience: Readings in the Trans-Mississippi West. Belmont, Calif.: Wadsworth Publishing Co., 1963.

Cloth, map endpapers, xiv, 1-418 p., index, 23.2 cm.

One chapter devoted to the SFT; also a very good selection of extracts from such writers as Gregg, Garrard, Pattie, Ruxton, Frémont, Leonard Arrington, and W. Turrentine Jackson.

299   Hobbs, James, 1819-

Wild Life in the Far West: Personal Adventures of a Border Moun-tain Man, Comprising Hunting and Trapping Adventures with Kit Carson and Others; Captivity and Life among the Comanches; Ser-vices under Doniphan in the War with Mexico. . . . Hartford: Wiley, Waterman & Eaton, 1872.

Cloth, [1]-488 p., 21 leaves plates incl. colored frontis., 21.5 cm.

Hobbs knew James Kirker, Albert Speyer, and Kit Carson. In 1835 he joined a wagon train going over the SFT via Bent's Fort. Contains material (pp. 59-61) on the Speyer caravan caught in snow, and on other Trail caravans in 1843-45. Other editions appeared in 1873-75. Reprinted, Glorieta, N.M.: Rio Grande Press, 1969. Graff 1914; Howes H-550. UNM.

300   Hobbs, Wilson, M.D.

"The Friends' Establishment in Kansas Territory." *Kansas Historical Collections,* Vol. VIII (1903-1904), pp. 250-71.

A Quaker physician's firsthand account of experiences on the SFT west to "110" creek in 1852. Most of the article refers to Kansas points other than the Trail.

301   Hodge, Frederick Webb

"French Intrusion toward New Mexico in 1695." *New Mexico His-torical Review,* Vol. IV, No. 1 (Jan. 1929), pp. 72-76.

Translations of three Spanish documents, dated 1695, report-ing French explorers venturing toward "the plains of Cibola" east of Picuris, New Mexico.

302   Hoffhaus, Charles E.

"Fort du Cavagnial: Imperial France in Kansas, 1744-1764." *Kansas Historical Quarterly,* Vol. XXX, No. 4 (Winter 1964), pp. 425-54.

This French fort existed from about 1744 to 1764, near present Kansas City. Contains mention of the Mallet brothers' trip in 1739 (p. 429) and the Chapuis expedition in 1752 (p. 437). Later authorities (Frazer, Loomis, Nasatir) spell it Cavagnolle.

303 Holbrook, James

Ten Years among the Mail Bags; or, Notes from the Diary of a Special Agent of the Post-Office Department. Philadelphia: H. Cowperthwait & Co., 1855.

Cloth, xxiv, (25)-432 p., ports., illus., drawings, 19.5 cm.

Pages 192-200 deal with mail service in New Mexico over the SFT, with some useful details on vehicles used.

304 Hollister, Ovando James, 1834-1892

History of the First Regiment of Colorado Volunteers. Denver: Thos. Gibson & Co., 1863.

Cloth, [1]-178 p., 19 cm. Also issued in wrappers.

Said to be Colorado's rarest book. Hollister was a private in the regiment, which marched from Fort Wise on the Arkansas via Raton Pass and the SFT to take part in the Civil War battle in Glorieta Pass. Well written and one of the most entertaining accounts of that event. Reprinted, Lakewood, Colo.: The Golden Bell Press, Publishers, 1949, under the title *Boldly They Rode.* Graff 1937; Howes H-601; Wagner-Camp 392.

305 Hollon, W. Eugene

The Lost Pathfinder: Zebulon Montgomery Pike. American Exploration and Travel Series, 12. Norman: University of Oklahoma Press, 1949.

Cloth, [xvi], [1]-240 p., 8 leaves of plates, map in text, biblio., index, 23.5 cm.

A study of Pike's two expeditions, up the Mississippi and up the Arkansas, in 1805-07, together with essential biographical information. The thorough annotation and good bibliographical essay make this a valuable guide.

306 Holmes, Kenneth L.

"The Benjamin Cooper Expeditions to Santa Fe in 1822 and 1823." *New Mexico Historical Review*, Vol. XXXVII, No. 2 (April 1963), pp. 139-50, fldg. map.

A detailed and documented paper on the important Benjamin Cooper expeditions over the Trail. The first left in May 1822 with a pack train, going to Taos and then to Santa Fe. A second caravan of thirty men with pack animals left Missouri in May 1823 and was the first train out that year. The party almost met disaster during an Indian attack.

307 Honig, Louis C.

Westport, Gateway to the Early West. It Happened in America Series. N.p., n.d. [c 1950].

Cloth, [viii], 1-149 p., tinted deckle edges, illus., subscribers' edition, ltd. to 525 autographed copies.

Useful data on firms and families at Westport, an eastern terminus of the SFT in its earliest years. Foreword by Paul I. Wellman.

308 Horgan, Paul

"The Prairies Revisited: A Re-estimation of Josiah Gregg." *Southwest Review*, Vol. XXVI, No. 2 (Winter 1941), pp. 145-66.

A critical analysis of Gregg's *Commerce of the Prairies* as a literary work.

309 Houck, Louis

A History of Missouri, from the Earliest Explorations and Settlement until the Admission of the State into the Union. 3 vols. Chicago: R. R. Donnelley & Sons Company, 1908.

Buckram, leather label on spine, top edge gilt, 24.1 cm. Vol. I: xviii, 1-404 p., frontis., 6 leaves plates, illus., appendix; Vol. II: viii, 1-418 p., illus.; Vol. III: x, 1-380 p., illus., index.

Ends with the admission of Missouri as a state in 1821. Of all

Missouri state histories, this one is cited most often by writers about the SFT. It contains a number of documents on early exploration and fur trade (see Wagner-Camp, 3). Reprinted, Cape Girardeau, Mo.: College Co-operative Store. Howes H-671.

310 Hubbard, David
"Reminiscences of the Yeager Raid, on the Santa Fe Trail, in 1863." *Kansas Historical Collections*, Vol. VIII (1903-1904), pp. 168-71.

Personal memoirs. In May 1863 a detachment of Quantrill's guerrillas under Dick Yeager robbed and raided along a short stretch of the SFT, including Hubbard's home. The area was between Council Grove and Gardner in Kansas.

311 Hughes, John T.
Doniphan's Expedition; Containing an Account of the Conquest of New Mexico; General Kearney's Overland Expedition to California; Doniphan's Campaign against the Navajos; His Unparalleled March upon Chihuahua and Durango; and the Operations of General Price at Santa Fe: with a Sketch of the Life of Col. Doniphan. Cincinnati: Published by J. A. & U. P. James, 1848.

Cloth, xii, 13-407 p., frontis. port., fldg. map, 19.3 cm.

This edition is usually considered the best, although there was an 1847 edition of 144 pp., reprinted in 1848 with same pagination. A classic work on the expedition along the SFT during the Mexican War. The units left Fort Leavenworth in late June 1846 and reached Santa Fe on August 18, 1846 (pp. 21-78). They went via Bent's Fort and Raton Pass. For specifications of the first edition, see Wagner-Camp 134 and Howes H-769. Reprinted from new type as a government document in 1916: 63rd Cong., 2nd sess., Sen. Exec. Doc. 608. The 1848 edition (described) was also reprinted, Chicago: The Rio Grande Press, Inc., 1963. Graff 2004.

312 Hulbert, Archer Butler, ed.
The Crown Collection of Photographs of American Maps. 5 series, 19 vols. V.p., v.d.

Approximately 1150 photographs of maps on the history of America. Series I, 5 vols., 239 maps of eastern and southern states, was published at Cleveland: Arthur H. Clark Co., 1904-09. Series II, 5 vols., 250 maps, of northeastern states, Canada, and the Carolinas and Georgia, was published at Harrow, England, 1909-12. Series III, 1 vol., 250 maps of the Carolinas, Florida, Georgia, New England, New York, and Louisiana, was published at London, 1914-1916. Series IV, 6 vols., 302 maps, is generally entitled "The Great American Transcontinental Trails." It includes Santa Fe Trail maps. Series V, 1 vol., 59 maps, contains Western stage route maps. Reissued, Glendale: The Arthur H. Clark Co., in 10 by 12 inch facsimiles of the photographs, each series boxed, with index to Series I. Howes H-772.

313 ———

Southwest on the Turquoise Trail: The First Diaries on the Road to Santa Fe. Overland to the Pacific Series, 2. [Stewart Commission of Colorado College and the Denver Public Library, c 1933].

> Cloth, [xv], [1]-301 p., frontis., 3 leaves illus., index, 24.6 cm.

A group of essential source documents about the SFT: Pedro Vial's Santa Fe to St. Louis diary; William Becknell's journals of expeditions in 1821-22; M. M. Marmaduke's journal, 1824; Augustus Storrs' replies to Thomas H. Benton; Richard Graham's report to Benton; treaty with the Kanzas, 1825; Joseph C. Brown's field notes while surveying the Trail, 1825-27; George C. Sibley's diary on the SFT, 1825-26; Alphonso Wetmore's diary, 1828; and appended journals of expeditions related to branches or extensions of the SFT: Zebulon Pike's diary after his capture north of Taos in 1805, and Antonio Armijo's account of a trip westward from Santa Fe to California in 1829-30. The source of each document is given.

314 Hunt, Aurora

Major General James Henry Carleton, 1814-1873: Western Frontier Dragoon. Frontier Military Series, II. Glendale: Arthur H. Clark Company, 1958.

> Cloth, [1]-390 p., frontis. port., illus., maps, biblio., index, 24.8 cm.

A biography of Carleton, who became an officer in the 1st Dragoons in 1839. Details of a trip over the SFT from Fort Leavenworth in 1851; maintaining order along the Trail between Santa Fe and Fort Union; and service at Fort Union.

315 Hurd, Charles W.

Bent's Stockade, Hidden in the Hills. Las Animas, Colo.: Bent County Democrat, 1960.

Wrappers, 88 p., illus. photos, biblio.

A history of the trading post, with biographical material on William Bent.

316 Hyde, George E.

Life of George Bent: Written from His Letters. Edited by Savoie Lottinville. Norman: University of Oklahoma Press, [1968].

Cloth, xxv, [1]-[390] p., 12 leaves plates, maps, biblio., index, 23.5 cm.

George Bent was the son of William Bent, of Bent's Fort. Born in 1843, he wrote the story of his life to 1875 in a series of letters to George E. Hyde. Extensive details on Bent's Fort, Sand Creek events, wagon trains, and Indian affairs.

317 [Indians]

Condition of the Indian Tribes. Report of the Joint Special Committee, Appointed Under Joint Resolution of March 3, 1865, with an Appendix. U.S. 39th Cong., 2nd sess., Sen. Report 156 [Serial 1279]. Washington, Jan. 26, 1867.

532 p., 22.5 cm.

One of the most generally useful Congressional documents on Indian affairs along the SFT. Although much of the material relates to the Sand Creek affair and to the military reservation at Bosque Redondo, there are long biographical depositions, including opinions by "Kit" Carson, William Bent, and others. Also included are tables of supplies purchased from sutlers and SFT traders for the Indians at Bosque Redondo and an account of the killing of Mrs. White by Indians.

318 ———————

*Documents in Relation to a Treaty Proposed to be Negotiated with
the Indians of the Prairie South and West of the Missouri River to
the Northern Line of the State of Texas, Embracing the Indians of
the Mountains, and Including Those of New Mexico.* U.S. 31st Cong.,
1st sess., Sen. Misc. Doc. 70 [Serial 563]. Washington, Mar. 18, 1850.

> 5 p., 22.5 cm.

The Committee on Indian Affairs approves the proposed treaty
and lists probable expense of $200,000 for gifts, annuity, and purchase
of Mexicans taken prisoner by the Indians. The report lists Indian
tribes concerned, including 8,000 Comanche.

319 ———————

*Letter from the Secretary of War . . . Relative to the Plan Proposed
for the Defence of the Western Frontier; also what Tribes of Indians
Inhabit the Country Immediately West of Arkansas and Missouri.*
U.S. 26th Cong., 1st sess., Sen. Doc. 379 [Serial 359]. Washington,
April 13, 1840.

> 14 p., 22.5 cm.

Includes an estimate of the number of warriors of various
tribes such as the Pawnee and Comanche in the vicinity of the SFT.
The defense line discussed is not that of the Trail but lies chiefly inside Arkansas and Missouri.

320 ———————

*Regulating the Indian Department. To Accompany Bills H.R. Nos.
488, 489, & 490. Mr. H. R. Everett, from the Committee on Indian
Affairs, Made the Following Report.* U.S. 23rd Cong., 1st sess., H.R.
Report 474 [Serial 263]. Washington: Gales & Seaton, May 20, 1834.

> 131 p., fldg. map, 22.5 cm.

This important set of bills established the Department of Indian Affairs. Contains general information on Indian tribes of the
West. Map shows the SFT. Wagner-Camp 49.

321 ————————

Report of the Commissioner of Indian Affairs, Submitting, In Compliance with a Resolution of the Senate, an Estimate of the Amounts That Will be Required to Hold Councils with Certain Indians of the Plains and in the State of Minnesota. U.S. 35th Cong., 1st sess., Sen. Exec. Doc. 35 [Serial 924]. Washington, April 16, 1860.

19 p., 22.5 cm.

Includes letters from William Bent concerning Indian attacks led by Buffalo Hump along the SFT in 1860.

322 Inman, Henry, 1837-1899

In the Van of Empire: Sketches and Anecdotes of Western Adventure. Midland Library, series 1, number 1. Kansas City, Mo.: Inter-State Publishing Co., 1889.

Paperback, dec. wrappers, side stitched, [1]-122 p. plus prospectus, 15.8 cm.

The sort of cheap paperback that newsbutchers hawked on early railroad trains, reprinting five of Inman's tales of the Trail. Howes I-56. KSH.

323 ————————

The Old Santa Fe Trail: The Story of a Great Highway. New York: The Macmillan Company, 1897.

Cloth, [xvii], 1-493 p., 3 p. advts., 9 leaves plates incl. frontis., fldg. map, 22 cm.

The first book to follow Gregg's devoted entirely to the SFT. One of the most popular works on the route, with emphasis on unusual characters, stirring events, and adventures. Inman was a colorful writer, but his historical sources were not always reliable. He covers the entire life of the Trail, from early trips to the coming of the railroad. Other editions appeared in New York and Topeka in 1898, 1899, 1909, and 1916—all apparently from the same plates and with illustrations by Frederic Remington. Reprinted, Minneapolis: Ross & Haines. Howes I-57.

324 ———————

Stories of the Old Santa Fe Trail. Kansas City, Mo.: Book Publishing House of Ramsey, Millett & Hudson, 1881.

> Cloth, [viii], [1]-287 p. illus. dwgs.

Fifteen tales of the SFT. There was also another edition, undated, with 281 pp., of undetermined priority. This work is partially the same as Inman's *Tales of the Trail* (q.v.), issued later. Graff 2115; Howes I-58. KSN, N.

325 ———————

Tales of the Trail: Short Stories of Western Life. Topeka: Crane & Company, 1898.

> Cloth, viii, 1-280 p., illus. dwgs., 19.4 cm.

Thirteen episodes along the SFT, more entertaining than historical, but with material on the hermit priest (whom Inman identifies as Matteo Boccalini) and Pawnee Rock. Howes (I-58) identifies this work as a reprint of *Stories of the Old Santa Fe Trail* (q.v.), but only four chapters of that work were reprinted in the present book. Graff 2116.

326 [Jackson County, Missouri]

The History of Jackson County, Missouri, Containing a History of the County, its Cities, Towns, etc. Kansas City, Mo.: Union Historical Company; Birdsall, Williams & Co., 1881.

> Cloth, xi, [9]-1006 p., 23.4 cm.

SFT material on pp. 170-78 and 389-401. Much of it is general information of little new value, except for good data on the early firms who supplied SFT travelers leaving from Franklin, Westport, and Independence prior to 1848. Reprinted in facsimile with new index added, Cape Girardeau, Mo.: Ramfre Press, 1966.

327 James, Edwin

Account of an Expedition from Pittsburgh to the Rocky Mountains, Performed in the Years 1819 and '20, . . . Under the Command of

Major Stephen H. Long. 2 vols., atlas. Philadelphia: H. C. Carey and I. Lea, 1823.

Boards, 24.5 cm.; Vol. I: [iv], [1]-[8], [1]-503 p.; Vol. II: [v], [1]-442, [i]-xcviii p.; atlas: [iv], 8 plates, 2 maps, 2 charts, dated 1822, atlas 30 cm.

At first known as the Yellowstone Expedition, for its intended destination, this group wintered near Council Bluffs, 1819-20. It then took a revised course along the Platte, down the Rockies, and back along the Arkansas. Near present Rocky Ford, Colorado, Long and others turned south to the Canadian river; the rest of his party continued down the Arkansas (see entry 30). The expedition produced the first scientific data on the flora and fauna of the general area of the SFT. For further explanation see "Major Long's Route from the Arkansas to the Canadian River, 1820," by John M. Tucker, in *New Mexico Historical Review*, Vol. XXXVIII, No. 3 (July 1963), pp. 185-219, with map and illus. James' account was reprinted, Cleveland: Arthur H. Clark Company, 1905, *Early Western Travels* series; and reprinted again, New York: AMS Co., 1970. Graff 2188; Howes J-41; Wagner-Camp 25.

328 [James, Harold L.]

Guidebook of Taos—Raton—Spanish Peaks Country, New Mexico and Colorado; New Mexico Geological Society, Seventeenth Field Conference, October 14, 15, and 16, 1966. [Socorro, 1966].

Cloth, illus. endpapers, [1]-128 p., plus 8 p. advts., maps, 28.5 cm.

Contains a good, brief general history of the SFT (pp. 107-18) by Harold L. James; reprinted as a separate pamphlet, Globe, Ariz.: Southwestern Monuments Assn., 1968. Contains good recent views of remains at Clifton House, Raton summit, Point of Rocks, and other locations. Another section contains a geological trip log through Raton Pass (pp. 31-33) and past the Spanish Peaks.

329 James, Thomas

Three Years Among the Indians and Mexicans. Waterloo, Ill.: Printed at the Office of the "War Eagle," 1846.

Wrappers, [ii], [1]-130 p., 22.4 cm.

James took a caravan over the SFT and arrived in Santa Fe on December 1, 1821—about two weeks after Becknell. James' account thus describes one of the earliest trips. Reprinted, St. Louis: Missouri Historical Society, 1916, with an introduction by Walter B. Douglas. The 1916 edition was reprinted in facsimile, Chicago: Rio Grande Press, 1962. Another useful edition was done at Philadelphia: J. B. Lippincott Co., 1962, with an introduction by A. P. Nasatir. See Graff for a fascinating account of finding the rare first edition. Graff 2193; Howes J-49; Wagner-Camp 121.

330 [Johnston, Joseph Eccleston]

Letter from the Secretary of War, Transmitting the Report of Colonel Johnston's Survey of the Southern Boundary Line of Kansas. U.S. 35th Cong., 1st sess., H.R. Exec. Doc. 103 [Serial 958]. Washington, April 16, 1858.

3 p., fldg. map, 22.5 cm.

Johnston touched the western part of the SFT along the Cimarron Cutoff on this survey. The map shows much of the Trail. Wagner-Camp 301a.

331 ⸻

"Surveying the Southern Boundary Line of Kansas: from the Private Journal of Col. Joseph E. Johnston," edited by Nyle H. Miller. *Kansas Historical Quarterly*, Vol. I, No. 2 (Summer 1932), pp. 104-39.

Portions of this journal describe the SFT.

332 Jones, Alexander E.

"Albert Pike as a Tenderfoot." *New Mexico Historical Review*, Vol. XXXI, No. 2 (April 1956), pp. 140-47.

A general review of Pike's first trip over the SFT in 1831, taken from standard sources and adding little that is new.

333 Jones, Hester

"The Spiegelbergs and Early Trade in New Mexico." *El Palacio*, Vol.

XXXVIII, Nos. 15-16-17 in one (April 10-17-24, 1935), pp. 81-89, ports.

Solomon Jacob Spiegelberg went to Santa Fe over the SFT at the time of Doniphan's expedition. Information on practices of early merchants, much of it from contemporary newspapers. The Spiegelberg brothers once bought a glittering wagon from a stranded circus, loaded it with merchandise, and took it down the trail to Chihuahua.

334 Jones, Horace

Up from the Sod: the Life Story of a Kansas Prairie County. Lyons, Kansas: Coronado Publishers, Inc., [c 1969].

Cloth, map endpapers, [1]-207 p., 22.2 cm.

Firsthand accounts by old-timers; otherwise a general history of Rice county, Kansas, through which the SFT runs. Frank Stahl describes a wagon train of Irwin & Jackson, large freighters in the 1850s; also an account of destruction of the H. C. Barrett train in 1864 (pp. 33-57). Some of the material is from Jones' earlier work, *The Story of Early Rice County,* same publisher, 1959.

335 [Jones, Nathaniel V.]

"Extracts from the Life Sketch of Nathaniel V. Jones," by Rebecca M. Jones. *Utah Historical Quarterly,* Vol. 4, No. 1 (Jan. 1931), pp. 3-23.

Jones was a sergeant in the Mormon Battalion on its march across the SFT and to California. Article contains only a small amount of SFT material; there is a long extract from his journal, but it begins with the departure from Santa Fe en route to California.

336 [Kansas. Laws. Statutes.]

An Act Declaring the Santa Fe Road a State Road.

In: Special Laws of Kansas, 1868. 88 pp. KHS.

337 ————

An Act Making Appropriation to Pay the Cost of Marking the Santa

Fe Trail in the State of Kansas and Providing a Penalty for the Defacement of Such Marks. N.P. [1905].

> 3 unnumbered pages. 23 cm.
> Kansas House bill 485, 1905. KHS.

338 [Kansas, Map]

"Explanation of Map." *Kansas Historical Collections*, Vol. IX (1905-1906), pp. 565-78, folding map.

A simplified map drawn by the Kansas State Historical Society to show routes important before 1854. Text gives capsule data on each trail and major point of interest; map shows routes of Long, Frémont, Butterfield, Holladay, SFT, Pony Express, and others. Useful in visualizing relationships of trails to each other.

339 [Kansas, Sites]

"Kansas Historical Markers." *Kansas Historical Quarterly*, Vol. X, No. 4 (Nov. 1941), pp. 339-68.

Full text of historical markers placed at Chouteau's Island, Council Grove, Fort Riley, Fort Harker, Fort Zarah, and other points.

340 ———

"A Survey of Historic Sites and Structures in Kansas." *Kansas Historical Quarterly*, Vol. XXIII, No. 2 (Summer 1957), pp. 113-80, illus. photos.

Capsule data on such SFT points as Lone Elm, Burlingame, Council Grove, Diamond Springs, Ft. Zarah, Pawnee Rock, Ft. Larned, Ft. Atkinson, The Caches, Ft. Dodge, Cimarron Crossing, Wagon Bed Springs, and Point of Rocks.

341 Karnes, Thomas L.

"Gilpin's Volunteers on the Santa Fe Trail." *Kansas Historical Quarterly*, Vol. XXX, No. 1 (Spring 1964), pp. 1-14.

While U.S. troops were fighting in Mexico, Indians were raiding along the SFT. To restore order, Missouri organized in 1847 the "Separate Battalion of Missouri Volunteers," also known as the "Indian Battalion" and as the "Oregon Battalion." Commander was William Gilpin, former executive officer to Doniphan. This article tells of a hectic twelvemonth spent by this raw outfit along the SFT in 1847-48. An incident of a female recruit is one of the most uproarious in SFT history.

342 ———

William Gilpin, Western Nationalist. Austin: University of Texas Press, [1970].

> Cloth, [x], [1]-383 p., 3 lvs., plus 4 leaves plates (maps, ports., views), biblio., index, 23.5 cm.

A scholarly biography of Gilpin (1815-1894) who was with Doniphan during the Mexican War and was also a military commander along the SFT in 1847-48. Part of the section dealing with 1848 was taken from Karnes' article in the *Kansas Historical Quarterly* (see preceding entry).

343   [Kearny, Stephen Watts]

Report of a Summer Campaign in the Rocky Mountains, &c., in 1845. U.S. 29th Cong., 1st sess., Sen. Doc. 1 [Serial 470]. Washington, Dec. 2, 1845.

> Pp. 210-220.

Also issued as House Doc. 2, Vol. I, (Serial 480), same session, with map. Kearny commanded the 1st Dragoons; they left Fort Leavenworth on May 18, 1845, went up the Platte river as far as Fort Laramie, then down through Colorado to Bent's Fort, along the SFT and back to Fort Leavenworth by August 24. For references to reprints of this report in *Niles' Register* and other contemporary journals see Wagner-Camp 117.

344   Keleher, William Aloysius

Turmoil in New Mexico, 1846-1868. Santa Fe: The Rydal Press, [c 1952].

Cloth, map endpapers, xiii, [1]-534 p., frontis., ports., plates, notes, index, 21.8 cm.

One section deals with the Kearny and Doniphan trips over the SFT. The text is general, but the extensive notes (pp. 108-38) add new biographical material on many participants.

345 Kelley, E. E.

"Some Southwest Kansas Pioneers." *Kansas Historical Quarterly*, Vol. VI, No. 1 (Feb. 1937), pp. 87-93.

Information on the Cimarron Cutoff near Garden City; history of the town of Ingalls, Kansas.

346 Kellogg, David

"Across the Plains in 1858: Diary of Daniel [David] Kellogg." *The Trail*, Vol. V, No. 7 (Dec. 1912), pp. 5-10.

Personal account by a traveler with a train of fourteen wagons going over the SFT from Kansas City to Bent's Fort, then on into Colorado.

347 Kendall, George Wilkins, 1809-1867

Narrative of the Texan Santa Fe Expedition, Comprising a Description of a Tour through Texas, and Across the Great Southwestern Prairies, the Camanche and Caygua Hunting-grounds, with an Account of the Suffering from Want of Food, Losses from Hostile Indians, and Final Capture of the Texans, and Their March, as Prisoners, to the City of Mexico. 2 vols. New York: Harper & Bros., 1844.

Cloth, 5 plates, fldg. map, 20 cm.; Vol. I: xii, [13]-405 p.; Vol. II: xii, [13]-406 p.

Generally considered the most complete work on this expedition, the men of which were imprisoned briefly at San Miguel del Vado on the SFT in 1842. There have been many editions, including a facsimile reprint of the first edition at Austin, Texas: The Steck Company, 1935, and at Ann Arbor, Mich.: University Microfilms, 1966. Graff 2304; Howes K-75; Wagner-Camp 110.

348 [Kingsbury, Gaines Pease]

Journal of the March of a Detachment of Dragoons under the Command of Colonel Dodge, during the Summer of 1835. U.S. 24th Cong., 1st sess., Sen. Doc. 209 [Serial 281]. Washington: Gales & Seaton, 1836.

38 p., 2 maps, 22.5 cm.

Also issued by the House, same session, Vol. 4, H.R. Doc. 181 (Serial 289), 39 pp., 2 fldg. maps. Also reprinted with maps in *American State Papers, Military Affairs*, Vol. VI, document 654, pp. 134-46, with maps. The Dragoons went along the Platte and returned via Bent's Fort and the SFT along the Arkansas. Details of Indian peace councils. See also entries under Lemuel Ford. Kingsbury kept the official journal for Dodge on this expedition. Graff 2335; Howes K-161; Wagner-Camp 63.

349 [Kirwan, John S.]

"Patrolling the Santa Fe Trail: Reminiscences of John S. Kirwan," edited by Merrill J. Mattes. *Kansas Historical Quarterly*, Vol. XXI, No. 8 (Winter 1955), pp. 659-87.

Kirwan was a private in Co. K, 4th U.S. Cavalry, based at Fort Riley and serving along the SFT on patrol duty, 1859-61. Although he saw no major action, Kirwan (1840-1908) wrote in a colorful and detailed style. Reprinted with same folios in blue wrappers, as a separate, 1955.

350 Lamar, Howard Roberts

The Far Southwest, 1846-1912: A Territorial History. Yale Western Americana Series, 12. New Haven: Yale University Press, 1966.

Cloth and paper over boards, [xiv], 1-560 p., 6 leaves plates, fldg. map, biblio., index, 24 cm.

A study of the political evolution of New Mexico, Colorado, Utah, and Arizona. Useful for its analysis of the SFT as a factor contributing to the development of these territories. Reprinted in facsimile paperback, New York: W. W. Norton & Co., 1970.

351 [Lane, William Carr]

Historical Sketch of Governor William Carr Lane, Together with Diary of His Journey from St. Louis, Mo., to Santa Fe, N. M., July 31st to September 9th, 1852. With annotations by Ralph E. Twitchell. Historical Society of New Mexico Papers, 20. Santa Fe: Historical Society of New Mexico, 1917.

> Pamphlet, lettered wrappers, saddle stitched, [1]-62 p., frontis. port., 23.4 cm.

The diary gives a good account of a Trail journey. Lane (1789-1863) was the first mayor of St. Louis, 1823; he was appointed by Pres. Fillmore as governor of New Mexico Territory in 1852 and resigned when Pierce was elected president in 1853. By a misprint the cover states it is "No. 4" in the Papers; it is really No. 20.

352 ———

"Letters of William Carr Lane, 1852-1854," edited by Ralph P. Bieber. *New Mexico Historical Review*, Vol. III, No. 2 (April 1928), pp. 179-203, illus., port.

Lane's letters to his family include an account of his journey over the SFT (pp. 187-88) and some comments on mail service over the Trail.

353 ———

"William Carr Lane, Diary," edited by Wm. G. B. Carson. *New Mexico Historical Review*, Vol. XXXIX, No. 3 (July 1964), pp. 181-234; No. 4 (Oct. 1964), pp. 274-332.

Much of the diary relates to affairs in New Mexico, but there is an account of his return trip over the SFT (pp. 303-23), in October 1853.

354 [Larimer, William H. H.]

Reminiscences of General William Larimer and of His Son William H. H. Larimer, Two of the Founders of Denver City, Compiled from Letters and from Notes Written by the Late William H. H. Larimer of Kansas City, Missouri. Edited by Herman S. Davis. Lancaster, Pa.: New Era Printing Company, 1918.

Leather and boards, [1]-256 p., ports., facsims., fldg. genealogical chart, index, 24.7 cm.

Wm. H. H. Larimer (1840-1910) went over the SFT in 1858 (pp. 45-75) to Bent's Fort. He knew Alexander Majors and other prominent figures. Some data on mail lines. The work was printed for private distribution. Graff 2400; Howes L-102.

355 La Tourette, Genevieve

"Fort Union Memories." *New Mexico Historical Review,* Vol. XXVI, No. 4 (Oct. 1951), pp. 277-86, illus.

Memoirs of social life at the fort, which in 1877 was still served by wagon freighters from the end of the railroad in Colorado. The author's father was fort chaplain, 1877-90. Reprinted as a separate pamphlet, Las Vegas, N.M.: Fort Union, Inc., Box 93; n.d.

356 Laumbach, Verna

"Las Vegas Before 1850." *New Mexico Historical Review,* Vol. VIII, No. 4 (Oct. 1933), pp. 241-64.

Some information on the effects of SFT trade in this New Mexico town before 1850, drawn chiefly from Gregg and similar sources.

357 Laut, Agnes Christian, 1871-

Pilgrims of the Santa Fe. New York: Frederick A. Stokes Company, 1931.

Cloth, dec. endpapers, x, [1]-363 p., 44 illus., index, 21 cm.
Popularly written; a general secondary account of the Trail.

358 Lavender, David

Bent's Fort. Garden City, N.Y.: Doubleday & Company, Inc., 1954.

Cloth, map endpapers, [1]-450 p., notes, biblio., index, 21.5 cm.

The most comprehensive history of this SFT fort, with extensive and useful notes. Perhaps the best selling recent book on any aspect of the Trail, useful for pleasure reading as well as study. Reprinted, Gloucester, Mass.: Peter Smith, 1968. Lavender's work is cited by most recent writers on the SFT.

359 ———

Trail to Santa Fe. Boston: Houghton Mifflin Company, 1958.

A juvenile.

360 Layne, J. Gregg

Western Wayfaring: Routes of Exploration and Trade in the American Southwest. Introduction by Phil Townsend Hanna; maps by Lowell Butler. Los Angeles: Automobile Club of Southern California, 1954.

> Half cloth and green paper over boards, v, 1-63 p., 2 leaves, 30 maps in text, index, 28.4 cm. "One hundred copies . . . specially printed and bound for the Zamorano Club of Los Angeles."

Layne wrote a series of articles for *Westways* magazine on twenty-nine famous expeditions and trails, here gathered in book form. Those relating to the SFT are trails of Pike, Pattie, Ewing Young, Mormon Battalion, Army of the West, and the SFT itself.

361 Lecompte, Janet

"Gantt's Fort and Bent's Picket Post." *The Colorado Magazine,* State Historical Society of Colorado, Vol. XLI, No. 2 (Spring 1964), pp. 111-25, illus.

Descriptions of two trading posts that briefly preceded Bent's Fort: a post built by John Gantt, sometimes called Fort Cass; and a post built by William Bent, shown on at least one map as Fort William. Both were on the Arkansas river a short distance above its junction with Huerfano creek. A well documented account, including a letter from Gantt to Mexican officials, translated into Spanish by Alexander Le Grand.

362 [Lee, John D.]

"'Diary of the Mormon Battalion Mission: John D. Lee," edited by Juanita Brooks. *New Mexico Historical Review*, Vol. XLII, No. 3 (July 1967), pp. 165-99; and No. 4 (Oct. 1967), pp. 281-332.

John D. Lee was assigned to ride with the Battalion to Santa Fe and return from there with the soldiers' pay. This article reprints his round trip diary of 1846. See Howes L-208.

363 Lee, John Thomas

"The Authorship of Gregg's *Commerce of the Prairies*." *Mississippi Valley Historical Review*, Vol. XVI, No. 4 (March 1930), pp. 451-66.

L. Bradford Prince had stated that Gregg's book was written by John Bigelow from materials furnished by Gregg. Lee made a thorough study of Bigelow's own records and concludes that while Bigelow aided Gregg, as perhaps did one other person, the work remains essentially that of Gregg.

364 ————

Josiah Gregg and Dr. George Engelmann. Worcester, Mass.: American Antiquarian Society, 1931.

> Pamphlet, blue wrappers, saddle stitched, [1]-52 p., 24.7 cm.

Reprinted from the *Proceedings* of the Society for October, 1931. Dr. Engelmann was a physician and botanist who came to Saint Louis in 1833. Gregg was interested in botany and collected specimens for Engelmann along the SFT. This pamphlet contains much of their correspondence, with added biographical data on Gregg.

365 [Leitensdorfer, Eugene]

Eugene Leitensdorfer. Mr. Joseph J. Davis, for the Committee of Claims, Submitted the following Report. U.S. 45th Cong., 2nd sess., H.R. Report 189 [Serial 1822]. Washington, Feb. 8, 1878.

> 1 p., 22.5 cm.

Leitensdorfer states he is now in poverty, but that he was a wealthy merchant in Santa Fe during the Mexican War and induced the Pueblo Indians to remain peaceful during Kearny's advance. He asks $100,000 for such services; the Committee declines.

366 [Lewis, Meriwether]

Original Journals of the Lewis and Clark Expedition, 1804-1806. Edited by Reuben Gold Thwaites. 8 vols. New York: Dodd, Mead & Co., 1904-05.

In Vol. IV, pp. 382-90, it mentions that on their return trip in 1806, the explorers met Captain John McClallan "on a speculative expedition to the confines of New Spain to trade up the Platte with Panis & Otooes, then to Santa Fee (*sic*)." Graff 2485; Howes L-320; Wagner-Camp 13.

367 Lindsey, David, ed.

"The Journal of an 1859 Pikes Peak Gold Seeker." *Kansas Historical Quarterly,* Vol. XXII, No. 4 (Winter 1956), pp. 321-41.

The journal of twenty-year-old William W. Salisbury on his trip from Cleveland, Ohio, to Colorado in 1859, over the SFT. Excellent footnotes.

368 Little, James A., 1831-

What I Saw on the Old Santa Fe Trail: A Condensed Story of Frontier Life Half a Century Ago. Plainfield, Indiana: The Friends Press, [1904].

Printed wrappers, side stitched, [ii], [1]-127 p., frontis. port., 19 cm.

Little was an Indiana man who went to Kansas in 1854, went over the SFT with a wagon train of Russell, Majors & Waddell, and spent his later years in Kansas. A relatively scarce book, usually priced above the value of its contribution. Graff 2512; Howes L-384. KHS, UNM.

369 Long, Margaret

The Santa Fe Trail: Following the Old Historic Pioneer Trails of the

Modern Highways. Denver: The W. H. Kistler Stationery Company, [c 1954].

> Cloth, map endpapers, viii, [1]-281 p., plus 29 p. plates, 2 fldg. maps, index, 24.3 cm.

An extensive guide for anyone who wishes to retrace, as far as is possible, the SFT along modern roads. Careful mileage readings are given from Westport to Santa Fe, with separate logs for side trips on variant Trail routes. Gives texts of many markers, list of stage stations in N.M. (p. 275), and logs noted by early travelers.

370 ———

"The Santa Fe Trail on the Cimarron in Colorado." *The Colorado Magazine*, The State Historical Society of Colorado, Vol. XIV, No. 3 (May 1937), pp. 115-18, map.

Gives precise details as to where the Cimarron branch of the SFT cuts off to cross extreme southeastern Colorado. Map shows locations of markers placed by the D.A.R., ca. 1908.

371 [Look]

The Santa Fe Trail: A Chapter in the Opening of the West. New York: Random House, [1946].

> Cloth, [1]-[271] p., 267 illus., 24.5 cm.

A general history of the SFT (pp. 25-89), early railroad days (pp. 90-184), and the modern period, compiled by the editors of *Look* magazine. A reasonably good collection of illustrations, although not all relate to the Trail.

372 Loomis, Noel M., and Abraham P. Nasatir

Pedro Vial and the Roads to Santa Fe. American Exploration and Travel Series, 49. Norman: University of Oklahoma Press, [1967].

> Cloth, xxix, [1]-[570] p., 8 leaves plates, maps, biblio., index, 24 cm.

The only complete work on Pedro Vial, first trailblazer of the Southwest, who was assigned by the Spaniards to find a route from Santa Fe to St. Louis. He did this on a round trip in the summers of

1792-93. Instructions to Vial and his diary are included (pp. 369-79, 397-405). The work also includes a broad review of French ventures toward New Mexico and Spanish expeditions toward the east and northeast.

373 ———

The Texan-Santa Fe Pioneers. American Exploration and Travel Series, 25. Norman: University of Oklahoma Press, 1958.

> Cloth, xviii, [1]-[331] p. facsim., ports., scenes, maps (1 fldg.), biblio., index, 23.5 cm.

A recent, comprehensive study of the Texan-Santa Fe expedition. "This writer suggests that the entire structure of fear and hatred of New Mexicans against Texans was manufactured by Armijo and his sycophants" (p. 161). A useful biographical roster (pp. 193-255) is included.

374 Lowe, Percival Green, 1828-

"Address of ———." *Kansas Historical Collections,* Vol. V (1896), pp. 93-99.

A paper read before the annual meeting of the Kansas State Historical Society in 1894. Lowe was with "B" troop, 1st Dragoons, and this paper tells of the summer campaign of his troop along the SFT in 1852 to control the Indians.

375 ———

Five Years a Dragoon, '49 to '54, and Other Adventures on the Great Plains. Kansas City: The Franklin Hudson Publishing Co., 1906.

> Cloth, [ii], [1]-[418] p., frontis. port., scenes, index, 19.9 cm.

Lowe joined B Troop, 1st Dragoons, and saw service along the SFT in 1852-54; he went over the Trail in 1862 with a train of 6-mule wagons (excellent description, pp. 364-69). Later he was a government freight contractor over the Trail in 1868-69, and his last project was chaining (measuring) the Trail from Fort Leavenworth to Fort Union in 1876. Reprinted, Norman: University of Oklahoma Press, 1965. Graff 2550; Howes L-526.

376 ———

"Recollections of Fort Riley." *Kansas Historical Collections*, Vol. VII (1901-1902), pp. 101-13.

Fort Riley was not on the SFT but its history was linked strongly with that of the Trail. Biographical data on Lowe and memoirs of the fort, 1852-54. He was later an overland freighter and in 1862 herded 840 mules and horses over the Trail.

377 Loyola, Sister Mary

"The American Occupation of New Mexico, 1821-1852." *New Mexico Historical Review*, Vol. IX, No. 1 (Jan. 1939), pp. 34-75; No. 2 (April 1939), pp. 143-99; No. 3 (July 1939), pp. 230-86.

A documented study of the Anglo-American advance into New Mexico. The first three chapters are most useful, describing in general the early traders and trappers. There is also material on the Texan-Santa Fe Expedition. Written chiefly from published sources. Also issued as a separate, in wrappers, with an added preface and index, as Historical Society of New Mexico *Publications in History*, No. VIII, September 1939, viii, 166 p.

378 Lubers, H. L.

"William Bent's Family and Indians of the Plains." *The Colorado Magazine*, State Historical Society of Colorado, Vol. XIII, No. 1 (Jan. 1936), pp. 19-22.

Details on William Bent and others of the family, written by a Bent descendant.

379 Lummis, Charles Fletcher

"The Santa Fe Trail." *The Land of Sunshine*, Vol. 8, No. 4 (Mar. 1898), pp. 185-86.

Lummis reviews Inman's just-published *Santa Fe Trail* and says the author's historical introduction is worthless, while praising Inman for the material based on personal experience and acquaintance.

380 Lyman, George D.

John Marsh, Pioneer: the Life Story of a Trail-blazer on Six Frontiers.
New York: Charles Scribner's Sons, 1930.

Cloth, 394 p., illus. Also an edition of 150 ltd., signed, boxed.

Marsh was on the upper Mississippi and on the Missouri; he
fought in the Indian wars and settled in California in his later years.
A short section describes his experiences as an unsuccessful storekeeper
at Independence, 1833-35, serving SFT traders. He also made a trip
over the Trail. Reprinted, same publisher, 1947. Howes L-578.

381 McClendon, R. Earl

"Daniel Webster and Mexican Relations: the Santa Fe Prisoners."
Southwestern Historical Quarterly, Vol. XXXVI, No. 4 (April 1933),
pp. 288-311.

A documented review of the diplomatic efforts of the U.S. government to secure freedom for Texans and others taken prisoner during the Texan-Santa Fe expedition in 1841-42. At that time Daniel
Webster was Secretary of State in the Harrison-Tyler administration.

382 McClung, Quantrille D., compiler

*Carson—Bent—Boggs Genealogy: Line of William Carson, Ancestor
of "Kit" Carson, Famous Scout and Pioneer of the Rocky Mountain
Area, with the Western Branches of the Bent and Boggs Families with
Whom "Kit" was Associated, and the Line of Samuel Carson, Sup-
posed to be a Brother of William Carson.* [Denver]: Denver Public
Library, 1962.

Wrappers, plastic comb binding, [x], ii, 1-214 p., index, 28 cm.

A professionally compiled genealogy of these famous clans,
often with brief comments on their activities along the SFT. A de-
finitive work.

383 McClure, James R.

"Taking the Census and Other Incidents in 1855." *Kansas Historical
Collections*, Vol. VIII (1903-1904), pp. 227-50.

Personal experiences along the SFT from Council Grove to "110" Creek in 1855. Most of the article refers to Fort Riley.

384 McCoy, John

Pioneering on the Plains; Journey to Mexico in 1848; the Overland Trip to California. Kaukauna, Wisc.: [printed for the author], [c 1924].

> Pamphlet, side stapled, cover title, [iv], 115 unnumbered p., 26 cm.

Letters of four brothers: Alexander, William, John, and Samuel F. McCoy, relating to experiences at Independence, along the SFT (pp. 21-28), and en route to California. Good material on Independence in 1838. KSH.

385 McDermott, John Francis, ed.

"Isaac McCoy's Second Exploring Trip in 1828." *Kansas Historical Quarterly,* Vol. XIII, No. 6 (May 1945), pp. 400-62, ports.

Notes by McCoy, who made two trips from Missouri into the Indian country in 1828. Neither was over the SFT, but on the second trip he crossed the Trail and described wagon trains seen. He also observed that in 1828 only eastbound caravans were attacked by Indians.

386 ———

"The Remarkable Life and Adventures of John Eugene Leitensdorfer." *Bulletin of the Missouri Historical Society,* Vol. XV, No. 2 (Jan. 1959), pp. 105-17.

John E. Leitensdorfer's son, Eugene, became a Santa Fe trader and merchant. John himself probably never traveled the Trail, but his fantastic career offers a treasure trove for anyone researching the life of his son. John was an Austrian cavalry cadet, a botanist in Egypt, a Capuchin friar, an engineer in Turkey, a surgeon on a British sloop of war, and a Missouri physician. His son took John's memoirs over the Trail to Santa Fe, where they remain an unfound treasure.

387 [McFerran, J. C.]

Message of the President of the United States, and Accompanying Documents, to the Two Houses of Congress, at the Commencement of the First Session of the Thirty-Ninth Congress. Report of the Secretary of War, Vol. I. U.S. 39th Cong., 1st sess., H.R. Exec. Doc. 1 [Serial 1249]. Washington, 1865.

Major J. C. McFerran reports (pp. 744-50) on a trip over the SFT, with descriptions of Fort Lyon, Fort Dodge, and Fort Larned. His diary is included. This presidential message occupies several volumes, Serials 1244-54, but see only the volume cited above.

388 McHendrie, A. W.

"Trinidad and Its Environs." *The Colorado Magazine,* State Historical Society of Colorado, Vol. VI, No. 5 (Sept. 1929), pp. 159-70, illus.

A local history with emphasis on the SFT period.

389 McKay, Robert H.

Little Pills: An Army Story; Being Some Experiences of a United States Army Medical Officer on the Frontier Nearly a Half Century Ago. Pittsburg, Kans.: Pittsburg *Headlight,* 1918.

Khaki cloth, [1]-127 p., 3 leaves plates, 22.5 cm.

Personal memoirs of an Army doctor in Kansas, New Mexico, Oklahoma, and Colorado, 1869-76. He describes a stage trip from the end of the railroad at Sheridan, Kans., 400 miles to Santa Fe; also a description of the return over the SFT in 1869 to Fort Dodge. Good description of fellow officers as types. Graff 2618; Howes M-122.

390 McKinnan, Bess

"The Toll Road Over Raton Pass." *New Mexico Historical Review,* Vol. II, No. 1 (Jan. 1927), pp. 83-89.

An early general account of this pass, the road built by Richens L. Wootton, and the accounts of his tolls.

391   [McKnight, Robert]

Message of the President of the United States Transmitting . . . Information Relative to the Arrest and Imprisonment of Certain American Citizens at Santa Fe, by Authority of the Government of Spain. U.S. 15th Cong., 1st sess., Sen. Doc. 197 [Serial 11]. Washington: printed by E. DeKrafft, April 15, 1818.

> 23 p., p. 2 blank, 22.5 cm.
> Probably the earliest Congressional document relating wholly to the Santa Fe trade. A most important document, including letters from the U.S. and Spanish governments, depositions, and other accounts relative to the arrest of Robert McKnight, James Baird, and J. Farro in 1812; Auguste Choutcau and Jules de Mun in 1817. McKnight was not freed until 1821. See Graff, 2633-2638, for location of manuscript material by McKnight. Wagner-Camp 15.

392   Magoffin, Susan Shelby, 1827-1855

Down the Santa Fe Trail and into Mexico: The Diary of Susan Shelby Magoffin, 1846-1847. Edited by Stella M. Drumm. New Haven: Yale University Press, 1926.

> Cloth, xxv, [1]-294 p., frontis., port., fldg. map, appendix, biblio., index, 24.4 cm.
> Journal of young Mrs. Samuel Magoffin, who accompanied her trader husband over the SFT during the Mexican War. Graff (2656) justly calls it "one of the great Santa Fe Trail diaries." Reissued in paperback, New Haven: Yale University Press, 1962. Howes M-211.

393   [Mail Route]

New Mexico—Increased Facilities for Communication with the States. U.S. 33rd Cong., 1st sess., H.R. Misc. Doc. 53 [Serial 741]. Washington, April 4, 1854.

> 1 p., 22.5 cm.
> The Legislative Council of New Mexico asks for establishment of a postal route from Independence to Santa Fe.

394 Majors, Alexander, 1814-

Seventy Years on the Frontier: Alexander Majors' Memoirs of a Lifetime on the Border. Edited by Prentiss Ingraham; preface by "Buffalo Bill" (W. F. Cody). Chicago and New York: Rand, McNally & Company, 1893.

> Cloth, colored endpapers, [1]-325 p., 3 p. advts., frontis. port., ports., scenes, 19.8 cm.

Majors freighted on his own from 1848 to 1855 and then joined the famous partnership of Russell, Majors & Waddell. In his early years, Majors traveled the SFT (pp. 102-06, 128-41), but the later partnership was noted more for its role in the Utah "war," the Overland Mail, and the Pony Express. Good information on wagon freighting. Reprinted, Columbus: Long's College Book Co., 1950; and again more recently, Minneapolis: Ross & Haines. Graff 2664; Howes M-232.

395 Malin, James C.

Grasslands Historical Studies: Natural Resources Utilization in a Background of Science and Technology. Vol. I: Geology and Geography. Lawrence, Kansas: published by author, 1541 University Dr., 1950.

> Perfect (edge glued) binding, printed wrappers, xii, 1-[378] p., frontis., appendixes, duplicator processed from typewritten original, 21.7 cm.

A study of how geography and geology influenced Southwestern expansion. Has good SFT statistics for 1855-60, taken from *Western Journal of Commerce.* Reprinted as *Grassland of North America* . . ., Magnolia, Mass.: Peter Smith, Publisher, Inc., 1967.

396 Maloney, Alice Bay

"John Gantt, 'Borderer'." *California Historical Society Quarterly*, Vol. XVI, No. 1, Part 1 (March 1937), pp. 48-60.

Gantt was a Mountain Man connected incidentally with the SFT. He and his partner Blackwell had a trading post on the upper Arkansas in 1831. Written chiefly from such sources as Hugh Evans, Lemuel Ford, and Hiram Chittenden (q.v.).

397 Manning, William Ray

"Diplomacy Concerning the Santa Fe Road." *Mississippi Valley Historical Review*, Vol. I, No. 4 (March 1915), pp. 516-31.

A review of diplomatic correspondence, chiefly between the years 1823-29, pointing out that all frictions between the U.S. and Mexican governments regarding the SFT did not end with Mexican independence in 1821. Taken chiefly from manuscripts in the archives. Persons interested in Mexican-U.S. diplomatic relations, concerned only indirectly with the SFT, will find guidance in a recent work: *A Bibliography of United States-Latin American Relations Since 1910*, by David E. Trask, Michael C. Meyer, and Roger R. Trask (Lincoln: University of Nebraska Press, 1968).

398 ————

Early Diplomatic Relations Between the United States and Mexico. Baltimore: The Johns Hopkins Press, 1916.

Cloth, xi, 1-406 p., biblio., index, 20 cm.

One of the best discussions of diplomatic relations concerning the opening and first survey of the SFT, 1823-26, taken chiefly from correspondence in archives. See pp. 166-89. Delivered as an Albert Shaw lecture in diplomatic history, 1913. Reprinted, Westport, Conn.: Greenwood Press, Inc., 1968; also available from other reprint firms.

399 Marcy, Randolph Barnes, 1812-1887

The Prairie Traveler. A Hand-book for Overland Expeditions, with Maps, Illustrations, and Itineraries of the Principal Routes between the Mississippi and the Pacific. New York: Harper & Brothers, 1859.

Cloth, [xiv], [15]-340 p., illus. dwgs., fldg. map, 17 cm.

A how-to-do-it book widely used by emigrants over all Western trails. It describes equipment to carry, methods of organizing a wagon train, techniques of avoiding dangers and attacks, and twenty-eight itineraries including the SFT. Reprinted, New York: 1861; London: 1860, 1863; N.Y., 1950, ltd. 250 boxed; and Williamstown, Mass.: Corner House, 1968. Graff 2676; Howes M-279; Wagner-Camp 335.

400 Margry, Pierre, ed., 1818-1894

Découvertes et Etablissements des Francais dans l'Ouest et dans le Sud de l'Amerique Septentrionale, 1614-1754. 6 vols. Paris: Maissonneuve et Cie., 1879-1888.

> Wrappers, 619, 618, 656, 654, 698, and 750 p., fldg. maps, facsims., 25 cm.

A massive storehouse of original documents of French explorers in North America, 1614-1754. Vol. VI, Pt. 2, contains information on the Mallet brothers (pp. 465-92) and the Sieur de Bourgmont (pp. 398-452). For an English translation of the Mallet material, see our entry 211. De Bourgmont's early trip led to French interest in possible trade with Santa Fe. His document has been translated by Beatrice Paddock and published by the Wichita, Kansas, Public Library, 1936. The Maissonneuve edition is found most often, but there was a Paris edition by Jouaust, 1876-1886, same pagination. Graff 2680; Howes M-283. UNM.

401 [Marmaduke, Meredith Miles]

M. M. Marmaduke and Others. U.S. 35th Cong., 1st sess., H.R. Report 293 [Serial 965]. Washington, April 17, 1858.

> 2 p., 22.5 cm.

A favorable committee report on Marmaduke's claim for payment. He made a trip over the SFT in 1828 and on the return journey lost 600 head of livestock when attacked by the Pawnee Indians along the Trail.

402 ————

"Santa Fe Trail: M. M. Marmaduke Journal," edited by Francis A. Sampson. *Missouri Historical Review,* Vol. 6, No. 1 (Oct. 1911), pp. 1-10.

One of the best descriptions of the notable 1824 caravan over the SFT. The wagons left Franklin, Mo., May 18, 1824, and reached Santa Fe on July 31. Marmaduke stayed ten months before returning east. Issued also as a separate pamphlet in wrappers, by the *Review;*

see Graff 2683. Text reprinted in A. B. Hulbert's *Southwest on the Turquoise Trail* (q.v.). For another account see entry under Storrs, Augustus.

403 Marshall, James Leslie, 1891-

Santa Fe: The Railroad That Built an Empire. New York: Random House, [c 1945].

> Buckram, map endpapers, xvi, [1]-465 p., 16 leaves plates, appendixes, index, 21.8 cm.

One of the most readable books about the building of this great railroad and what happened as its inched west to replace the Trail. More exciting than the work by L. L. Waters (q.v.) but not as scholarly. Beyond these two books, literature on the railroad declines into repetition as far as the Trail is concerned.

404 Mathews, John Joseph

The Osages: Children of the Middle Waters. Civilization of the American Indian Series, 60. Norman: University of Oklahoma Press, [1961].

> Cloth, xx, [1]-826 p., colophon leaf, 4 maps in text, biblio., index, 23.6 cm.

A detailed study of the first major tribe encountered by SFT travelers, drawn from many sources (not keyed to text). The Osage treaty of 1825 paved the way for the opening of the Trail.

405 Mattison, Ray H.

Historical Aspects of the Santa Fe Trail. N.p., n.d. [ca. 1962].

> 16 leaves, duplicator processed from typewritten original, in paper covers, frontis. photo, 27.7 cm.

A general summary of Trail history, given as an address by Mattison at the annual meeting of the Santa Fe Trail Highway Association at Council Grove on December 9, 1962.

406 Maury, Dabney Herndon, 1822-1900

Recollections of a Virginian in the Mexican, Indian and Civil Wars. New York: Charles Scribner's Sons, 1894.

Cloth, xi, [1]-279 p., frontis. port., 20.2 cm.

Maury was sent to Fort Union with the Mounted Rifles as their adjutant, prior to the Civil War. He describes their march over the SFT. Also a London edition, 1894, and two later U.S. printings, 1894. Graff 2724; Howes M-440.

407 Mead, James R.

"The Saline River Country in 1859." *Kansas Historical Collections*, Vol. IX (1905-1906), pp. 8-19.

Personal experiences along the eastern portion of the SFT in 1859.

408 ————

"Trails in Southern Kansas." *Kansas Historical Collections*, Vol. V (1896), pp. 88-93.

A paper read at the Kansas State Historical Society's annual meeting, January 17, 1893. Mead was in Kansas in 1859 and saw the SFT. Good descriptions of roadway, wagons, and merchandise.

409 Meline, James Florissant, 1811-1873

Two Thousand Miles on Horseback; Santa Fe and Back; a Summer Tour through Kansas, Nebraska, Colorado, and New Mexico, in the Year 1866. New York: Hurd and Houghton, 1867.

Cloth, x, [1]-317 p., fldg. map, 18.3 cm.

Meline left Fort Leavenworth in June 1866, went up the Platte and down the South Platte to Denver; then south to Trinidad, Santa Fe, and Albuquerque. He returned east via the SFT and went to St. Louis in September. The return trip (pp. 261-99) was over the Cimarron Cutoff. Other editions were published in 1868 and 1873. Reprinted, Albuquerque: Calvin Horn, Publisher, 1966. Graff 2743; Howes M-488.

410 Meriwether, David

My Life in the Mountains and on the Plains: The Newly Discovered

Autobiography by David Meriwether. Edited by Robert A. Griffen. The American Exploration and Travel Series, 49. Norman: University of Oklahoma Press, [c 1965].

> Cloth, xxi, [1]-[302] p., 6 leaves plates, biblio., index, 23.4 cm.

Meriwether first went to New Mexico in 1820 by a route that occasionally touched points along the SFT. He was arrested, released, and made his way back east. He served as governor of New Mexico, 1853-57, and this autobiography describes his trip west over the Trail and two round trips to the East, 1853-56. Useful descriptions of stages used.

411   Miller, Harry G., Jr., and LeRoy R. Hafen

Bent's Fort on the Arkansas. Drawings by Harry G. Miller, Jr. Denver: State Historical Society of Colorado, [c 1954].

> Pamphlet, green wrappers, saddle stitched, 28 unnumbered leaves printed on one side only, including 24 p. of drawings with hand-lettered text, 20.8 cm.

A general history in popular form, brief but accurate.

412   Miller, William H.

The History of Kansas City, Together with a Sketch of the Commercial Resources of the Country with which It is Surrounded. Kansas City: Birdsall & Miller, 1881.

> Cloth, vi, [5]-264 p., fldg. map of Kansas City, 24.8 cm.

Most of the Santa Fe material is taken from Gregg, but pp. 43-45 contain reminiscences of Col. E. C. McCarty, who made trips over the SFT from 1828 to 1857. Graff 2800; Howes M-619. KHS.

413   [Mills, T. B.]

Report on the Internal Commerce of the United States for the Fiscal Year 1889. Part II of Commerce and Navigation: The Commercial, Industrial, Transportation, and Other Interests of Arkansas, Colorado, Dakota, Indian Territory, Kansas, Missouri, Montana, Nebraska, New Mexico, Texas, and Wyoming. U.S. 51st Cong., 1st sess., H.R. Exec. Doc. 6, Part 2[Serial 2738]. Washington, 1889.

xxxiii, 897 p., 22.5 cm.

T. B. Mills wrote the section on New Mexico (pp. 559-635), which contains a general history of the SFT (pp. 561-66). There is also some mention of the Trail in Kansas (p. 187) and in the Texas Panhandle (pp. 644-45). Seth Hays & Co., Council Grove, Kansas, provided statistics of traffic over the Trail, and some of the material is not readily available from other sources. As a New Mexico document on economic history, this is of major interest.

414 [Missouri Legislature]

Memorial of the Legislature of Missouri Praying that Adequate Protection be Extended by the Government to the Trade between that State and Mexico. . . . U.S. 20th Cong., 2nd sess., Sen. Doc. 52 [Serial 181]. Washington: Jan. 26, 1829.

> 3 p., 22.5 cm.

This memorial asks for establishment of a military post where the SFT crosses the Arkansas river. It also asks that British fur traders be excluded from U.S. territory but specifies chiefly the upper Missouri river region.

415 [Missouri Republican]

Publications of the Nebraska State Historical Society. Vol. XX. Edited by Albert Watkins. Lincoln: Published by the Society, 1922.

> Cloth, [xvi], 1-400 p., frontis. port., ports., facsims., scenes, index, 24.2 cm.

This work bears no title other than volume number. It includes hundreds of excerpts from the *Missouri Republican* newspaper, 1808-61, given chronologically, relating to fur trade and other ventures along the Missouri and Arkansas rivers. There are also items from the *Missouri Intelligencer*, 1819-26. A minority of the items, but still a useful number, refer to the SFT, including material on Charles Bent, dragoons, forts, Becknell, mails, Pawnee, etc.

416 Möllhausen, Heinrich Balduin

"Over the Santa Fe Trail through Kansas in 1858." Translated by John

A. Burzle, edited and annotated by Robert Taft. *Kansas Historical Quarterly*, Vol. XVI (Nov. 1948), pp. 337-80.

First English translation from Möllhausen's German work, *Reisen in die Felsengebirge Nord-Amerikas bis zum Hoch-Plateau von Neu-Mexiko . . .* (Leipzig, 1861). Möllhausen was with the Ives' expedition on the Colorado river in 1857-58 and returned east over the SFT from Santa Fe to Fort Leavenworth in 1858. Dr. John S. Newberry was also along, as was F. W. von Egloffstein, Ives' topographer. Möllhausen saw the SFT with an artist's eye for details, and he recorded campfire tales. The full work is scarce even in German (see Graff 2850; Howes M-712; Wagner-Camp 362). His earlier work, *Diary of a Journey from the Mississippi to the Coasts of the Pacific . . .*, with the Whipple expedition, does not deal with the SFT. This article from the *Quarterly* was also published by the Kansas Historical Society as a separate reprint in 1948, in wrappers.

417 Moody, Ralph

The Old Trails West. New York: Thomas Y. Crowell Company, 1963.

Cloth, map endpapers, 306 p., maps, biblio., index.

Covers the Santa Fe and Oregon Trails, plus such other trails as the Gila, El Camino Real, Old Spanish, etc. A general review.

418 ————

Stagecoach West. New York: Thomas Y. Crowell Company, [c 1967].

Cloth, map endpapers, x, 1-341 p., biblio., index, maps, ports., scenes, facsims., 23.9 cm.

A general work on the major stage lines of the West, with useful information on design and operation of stagecoaches. One chapter on the SFT (pp. 59-67).

419 Moore, Milton

"An Incident on the Upper Arkansas in 1864." *Kansas Historical Collections*, Vol. X (1907-1908), pp. 414-17.

Indian attacks on wagon trains of Stuart, Slemmons & Co.; also a letter from George Bent.

420 Moorhead, Max L.

New Mexico's Royal Road: Trade and Travel on the Chihuahua Trail.
Norman: University of Oklahoma Press, [c 1958].

> Cloth, xi, [1]-234 p., colophon leaf, 4 maps, 8 views from early art, biblio., index, 22 cm.

An extremely important study, based on original sources. The Chihuahua Trail was an extension of the Santa Fe Trail southward from Santa Fe. It existed prior to the SFT. Much commerce from Missouri went the full distance, and the work therefore contains much SFT information.

421 [Mooso, Josiah, 1803-]

The Life and Travels of Josiah Mooso: A Life on the Frontier among Indians and Spaniards, Not Seeing the Face of a White Woman for Fifteen Years. Winfield, Kansas: Telegram Print, 1888.

> Cloth, [xii], [13]-400 p., frontis. port., 19.9 cm.

Mooso spent his boyhood in Canada and became a fur trader on the upper Missouri river. In the 1840s he made a trip over the SFT (pp. 192-205). A rambling discourse, sparse in details; sometimes indexed under Alice G. Limerick as author or editor. Graff 2885; Howes M-784. KSH.

422 Morehouse, George Pierson

"Diamond Springs, the Diamond of the Plain." *Kansas Historical Collections,* Vol. XIV (1915-1918), pp. 794-804.

This spring, in present Morris county, Kansas, was noted by George C. Sibley in 1825. Waldo, Hall & Co. built a stone stage station there after 1849. On one ocasion 1,500 oxen stampeded and were killed falling into a gulch. Dick Yeager, a Quantrill guerrilla officer, raided along the SFT to Diamond Springs in 1863.

423 ———

"A Famous Old Crossing on the Santa Fe Trail." *Kansas Historical Collections,* Vol. VIII (1903-1904), pp. 137-43, illus. photos.

Describes the crossing of the Neosho river at Council Grove, Kansas. The first wooden bridge was built in the 1860s and was replaced by an iron bridge, which was washed out by a flood in 1903. Summary data on leading figures who traveled the Trail. Also issued as a separate, in wrappers.

424 ————

"An Historic Trail through the American Southwest." *Journal of American History*, Vol. 3, No. 3 (1909), pp. 461-70, illus.

A general summary of the earliest trips along the SFT. Morehouse states that Becknell had only three wagons on his trip in 1822, and that wagons did not come into general use until the Storrs' caravan in 1824.

425 Morgan, Dale L.

Jedediah Smith and the Opening of the West. Indianapolis: The Bobbs-Merrill Company, Inc., [c 1953].

> Cloth, map endpapers, [1]-458 p., 6 leaves of plates incl. frontis., appendixes, notes, index, 22.2 cm.

Acknowledged as the most scholarly work on Smith, who met his death on the Cimarron section of the Trail in 1831. Smith was a monumental figure but was more significant in the Far West than along the SFT. Morgan's excellent notes give many sidelights on fur trade and exploration. Reported reprinted, Magnolia, Mass.: Peter Smith; also in facsimile paperback with all plates and map, Lincoln: University of Nebraska Press, 1964.

426 Mumey, Nolie, 1891-

"John Williams Gunnison: Centenary of His Survey and Tragic Death, 1853-1953." *The Colorado Magazine*, State Historical Society of Colorado, Vol. XXXI, No. 1 (Jan. 1954), pp. 19-32.

Gunnison made a survey of a possible railroad route through the central Rockies to the Pacific in 1853. He left in June and proceeded from Westport along the SFT to Bent's Fort (pp. 22-24).

427 ————

Old Forts and Trading Posts of the West: Bent's Old Fort and Bent's New Fort on the Arkansas River. Denver: Artcraft Press, 1956.

> Buckram, [xx], 1-239 p., ports., plans, scenes, facsims., and maps (4 fldg., incl. 1 at back), index, issued unopened, ltd. 500 numbered and signed, 26 cm.

Probably ranks second only to David Lavender's book as a study in depth of Bent's forts. Chiefly a collection of excerpts from scores of other sources, some previously unpublished, describing the forts.

428 Napton, William Barclay

Over the Santa Fe Trail in 1857. Kansas City, Mo.: Franklin Hudson Publishing Co., 1905.

> Printed wrappers, side stitched, [1]-99 p., 17.4 cm.

Personal memoir of a wagon train trip over the SFT, pp. 3-72. Last half of book describes a trip to the upper Missouri river in 1858. A perceptive personal narrative of a young man's experiences. SFT portion reprinted, Santa Fe: Stagecoach Press, 1964, ltd. 650; also a deluxe reprint ltd. 99 copies. Graff 2944; Howes N-9.

429 Nasatir, Abraham Phineas

Before Lewis and Clark: Documents Illustrating the History of the Missouri, 1785-1804. 2 vols. St. Louis: Historical Documents Foundation, 1952.

> Cloth, 23.5 cm. Vol. I: [xviii], 1-375 p., 5 fldg. maps; Vol. II: [xiii], 376-853 p., maps and facsims. in text, index.

An essential for any study of trading ventures up the Missouri and into New Mexico. A short historical essay on the Missouri river, 1673-1804, is followed by a massive collection of documents, 1790-1804, most of them here translated and published for the first time. Many of them are to or from such men as Antonio Rengel, Pedro Cavallos, Jacques Clamorgan, Zenon Trudeau, Charles De Lassus, Manuel Lisa, Joseph Robidoux, and others who were concerned with Santa Fe trade. Graff 2945.

430 ————————

"Jacques Clamorgan: Colonial Promoter of the Northern Border of New Spain." *New Mexico Historical Review*, Vol. XVII, No. 2 (April 1942), pp. 101-12.

Clamorgan was a merchant in the upper Mississippi valley as early as 1783 or prior. In 1807 he secured an American license to trade with the Pawnee, and he used this as a device to go to Santa Fe with three companions, a slave, and "four cargoes of goods." Nasatir says Clamorgan was the first man to take a cargo of trade goods west to Santa Fe and sell it at a profit.

431 ————————

"Jacques D'Eglise on the Upper Missouri, 1791-1795." *Mississippi Valley Historical Review*, Vol. XIV, No. 1 (June 1927), pp. 47-71.

D'Eglise went up the Missouri river in 1790 to hunt and trade. In the Mandan country he met a Frenchman who had been in communication with New Mexico and had a Mexican saddle and bridle. For the next several years D'Eglise was a trader on the upper Missouri, at times associated with Jacques Clamorgan's company. With Lorenzo Duroche he ascended the Missouri, probably in 1804, hoping to find a short route to New Mexico, and it is inferred that D'Eglise reached the Mexican province.

432   Nichols, Roger L.

General Henry Atkinson; a Western Military Career. Norman: University of Oklahoma Press, [1965].

> Cloth, xiv, [1]-243 p., frontis. port., 11 plates, 9 maps in text, biblio., index, 23.5 cm.

Henry Atkinson (1782-1842) was one of the most important military figures along the SFT from 1819 to 1842. In 1825 he urged establishment of a fort on the Arkansas to guard the SFT, and in 1829 he sent a detachment under Major Bennet Riley to escort a wagon train. Useful in understanding the role of the military along the Trail in its early days.

433 [Niles Register]

One of the most important periodicals carrying news of the Western frontier. Volumes 1-76 were published from September 1811 to 1849, containing many SFT entries. Reprinted volumes are now available from University Microfilms, Ann Arbor, Michigan; also reprinted, New York: Arno Press, Inc., 1967, in 76 vols. Available on microfiche from Bell & Howell Co., Micro Photo Div., Cleveland.

434 O'Connor, Thomas F., ed.

"Narratives of a Missionary Journey to New Mexico in 1867." Mid-America, Vol. 19, New Series, Vol. 8, No. 1 (Jan. 1937), pp. 63-67.

Two narratives by members of the same caravan over the SFT, May-July, 1867. One is by Sister M. Kotska of the Sisters of Loretto, going to join Sister Blandina in Santa Fe. The other is by Mr. John Geatley who happened to be on the same trip. Archbishop Lamy also joined the wagon train at Fort Larned. Details of Indian troubles and death from cholera.

435 Oglesby, Richard Edward

Manuel Lisa and the Opening of the Missouri Fur Trade. Norman: University of Oklahoma Press, [1963].

Cloth, [xiv], [1]-246 p., 6 leaves plates, map, appendixes, biblio., index, 23.5 cm.

Perhaps the best-documented study to date on Lisa. In 1806 Lisa formed a partnership with Jacques Clamorgan to send a trading expedition toward Santa Fe, and Clamorgan left on that trip in 1807. In 1812 Lisa also sent Charles Sanguinet toward Santa Fe with trade goods, but all goods were lost in an Indian attack. The work also has material on the Santa Fe expedition of Robert McKnight and James Baird (pp. 123-24). Of special value is the bibliography with a detailed list of manuscript collections at the Missouri Historical Society in Saint Louis.

436 [Oklahoma]

"Preliminary Report of Survey of Inscriptions Along Santa Fe Trail in

Oklahoma." *The Chronicles of Oklahoma*, Vol. XXXVII, No. 3 (Autumn 1960), pp. 310-22, illus.

Report of a committee of the Oklahoma Historical Society. The SFT ran through Cimarron county in the far northwestern corner of the Oklahoma Panhandle. The committee examined three major campsites, and the article lists scores of names and inscriptions found cut in rocks.

437 Oliva, Leo E.

"Fortifications on the Plains: Fort Dodge, Kansas, 1864-1882." In *The 1960 Brand Book of the Denver Posse of the Westerners*. Boulder, Colo.: Johnson Publishing Co., 1960. Pp. 136-79.

A short, authoritative account of this fort on the SFT.

438 ———

Soldiers on the Santa Fe Trail. Norman: University of Oklahoma Press, [c 1967].

Cloth, xi, [1]-226 p., colophon leaf, ports., scenes, maps (1 fldg.), biblio., index, 23.4 cm.

The most recent comprehensive study of military protection along the SFT, from 1829 to 1880, drawn from primary sources such as military reports and correspondence.

439 Omer, George E., Jr.

"An Army Hospital: From Dragoons to Rough Riders—Fort Riley, 1853-1903." *Kansas Historical Quarterly*, Vol. XXIII, No. 3 (Winter 1957), pp. 337-67, illus.

Details of army hospital life at Fort Riley, established to serve as protection for Western travelers.

440 Omwake, John

The Conestoga Six-horse Bell Teams of Eastern Pennsylvania. Cincinnati: Printed for the Author, 1930.

Cloth, 136 p., illus., 28.5 cm.

The best authoritative work on the Conestoga wagon, which originated in Pennsylvania. Apparently some Conestogas were used in the early SFT trade, but the genuine Conestoga was not the most common wagon when freighting reached its peak. General features of the Conestoga were adapted by such famed Trail wagon makers as Espenscheid and Murphy. Howes O-85.

441 Otero, Miguel Antonio, 1859-

My Life on the Frontier, 1864-1882: Incidents and Characters of the Period when Kansas, Colorado, and New Mexico were Passing Through the Last of their Wild and Romantic Years. New York: Press of the Pioneers, 1935.

> Cloth, [x], 1-293 p., index, 23.4 cm. Also issued in an edition with added plates, ltd. 750, numbered, and signed.

The author's father was a New Mexican who took his family east to Westport in 1862 to open a wholesale grocers and outfitting business. The firm moved successively to Leavenworth, Fort Harker, Ellsworth, Hays City, Sheridan, Kit Carson, and Granada as the railhead moved west. Otero describes conditions and events in the end-of-track towns as the SFT grew shorter. He wrote two more volumes covering subsequent years. Both were issued by the University of New Mexico Press; the 1882-1897 volume was numbered II; the third had no volume number. Graff 3136; Howes O-141.

442 [Pacific Railroad Explorations and Surveys]

Reports of Explorations and Surveys, to Ascertain the Most Practicable and Economical Route for a Railroad from the Mississippi River to the Pacific Ocean . . . 1853-4, Volume II. U.S. 33rd Cong., 3d sess., H.R. Ex. Doc. 91 [Serial 792]. Washington: A. O. P. Nicholson, Printer, 1855.

> Cloth, [1]-128; [1]-132; [1]-45; [v], [1]-185; [1]-50; [1]-28; and [1]-22 p.; plates, maps, 29.8 cm.

Beginning in 1853, several expeditions were sent out by the government to survey possible routes for a railroad to the Pacific coast. One of these surveys began along the general route of the SFT: the survey made by Captain J. W. Gunnison. He was killed by Indians, and the final report was written by Lieut. E. G. Beckwith. The reports were issued in a set of volumes, octavo size, and shortly afterward in the larger (quarto size) set, of which Volume II is described here as being most generally available. For full bibliographic details, see Wagner-Camp 261-67, with comment on various editions. Gunnison left Fort Leavenworth in June 1853 and went via Council Grove, Pawnee Rock, and to Bent's Fort (pp. 11-28, first section of Vol. II), which he reached on July 29. Other pages detail certain barometric and geographical data. In section two (pp. 125-31) there is a list of botanical specimens collected. Howes P-3.

443 [Pancoast, Charles Edward, 1818-]

A Quaker Forty-niner: the Adventures of Charles Edward Pancoast on the American Frontier. Edited by Anna Paschall Hannum; foreword by John Bach McMaster. Philadelphia: University of Pennsylvania Press, 1930.

> Cloth, map endpapers, xv, 1-402 p., frontis., port., illus., index, 23.3 cm.

Pancoast (b. 1818) had been a Mississippi river pilot and went to California during the gold rush. He left Fort Leavenworth in April 1849 with a wagon train guided by James Kirker, via the SFT to Santa Fe (pp. 178-220). The rest of the memoirs, written forty years later, deal with his California experiences. A useful firsthand account. Graff 3180.

444 Pantle, Alberta

"History of the French-speaking Settlement in the Cottonwood Valley." *Kansas Historical Quarterly,* Vol. XIX, No. 1 (Feb. 1951), pp. 12-24, and No. 2 (May 1951), pp. 174-206; ports.

Part of this settlement was in Marion county, Kansas, on the SFT. Mentions ranches and supply points on the Trail. Biography of Francis Soyez (p. 177), a wagon freighter.

445 Parish, William J.

The Charles Ilfeld Company: A Study of the Rise and Decline of

Mercantile Capitalism in New Mexico. Harvard Studies in Business History, XX. Cambridge: Harvard University Press, 1961.

Cloth, adv. leaf, [xxii], [1]-431 p., illus., maps, tables, appendixes, notes, biblio., 24 cm.

Chiefly a study of a New Mexico firm over many years, but the first chapters review the rise of mercantilism in New Mexico which began with the arrival of the merchant traders over the SFT, including Solomon Spiegelberg, Sigmund Seligman, Gustave Elsberg, Jacob Amberg, and others.

446 ———

"The German Jew and the Commercial Revolution in Territorial New Mexico." *New Mexico Historical Review,* Vol. XXXV, No. 1 (Jan. 1960), pp. 1-29; and No. 2 (April 1960), pp. 129-50.

Most of the early Jewish merchants went to New Mexico over the SFT. Good information on Albert Speyer, Eugene Leitsendorfer, Jacob Amberg, Charles Ilfeld, Solomon and Nathan Bibo, and others. Several were traders on the Trail before they settled in New Mexico.

447 Parker, John W.

"The 'Windwagon' of Westport." *Missouri Historical Review,* Vol. XXV, No. 4 (July 1931), pp. 528-29.

In 1853 the Westport & Santa Fe Overland Navigation Company was formed at Westport. A twenty-five foot long wagon was built and equipped with a sail. On its maiden "voyage" it was wrecked and the company thereupon disbanded. Reprinted from the Kansas City *Journal-Post* of Jan. 4, 1931.

448 Parker, William Thornton

Personal Experiences among our North American Indians from 1867 to 1885. Northampton, Mass.: [Published by Author], 1913.

Cloth, [1]-232 p., 5 plates, frontis. port., issued uncut, 24.5 cm.

Parker served with military units in Kansas, Texas, Colorado, and New Mexico; he also wrote a small book about Fort Cummings.

In 1867 he rode with 300 recruits from Fort Leavenworth to Fort Union (pp. 11-44) over the SFT. A 46-page supplement to *Personal Experiences . . .* was published in 1918 but has not been examined. Graff 3197; Howes P-94. KHS, N.

449 Parkhill, Forbes

The Blazed Trail of Antoine Leroux. Westernlore Great West and Indian Series, XXX. Los Angeles: Westernlore Press, 1965.

> Cloth, colored endpapers, [1]-235 p., colophon leaf, biblio., index, 20.8 cm.

Antoine Leroux (1801-1861) was a noted trapper and guided many expeditions, but apparently seldom ventured east of Bent's Fort. His services were often used by military and civilian groups west of that point.

450 Parkman, Francis, Jr., 1823-1893

The California and Oregon Trail: Being Sketches of Prairie and Rocky Mountain Life. New York: G. P. Putnam, 1849.

> Cloth, [1]-448 p., 19 cm.

Although generally considered to be only an Oregon Trail item, the last part of this work describes a journey by Parkman down the Arkansas river and along the SFT in 1846, during which he met U.S. military units marching west. Recent editions, available from many sources in both cloth and paperback, are usually titled *The Oregon Trail.* Graff 3201; Howes P-97; Wagner-Camp 170.

451 Parsons, William Bostwick

The Gold Mines of Western Kansas; Being a Complete Description of the Newly Discovered Gold Mines, Different Routes, Camping Places, Tools & Outfit; and Containing Everything Important for the Emigrant and Miner to Know. Lawrence, Kansas: Printed for the Author, 1858.

> Green paper wrappers, [1]-45 p., plus 3 p. advts., 18.9 cm.

Colorado then was known as Western Kansas, and this was the first guide book issued during the Pike's Peak gold rush. The second

(1859) edition is better, and its text is reprinted in full in LeRoy R. Hafen's *Pike's Peak Gold Rush Guidebooks of 1859* (q.v.). Parsons describes the SFT or southern route (pp. 172-78 in Hafen). Graff 3205; Howes P-110; Wagner-Camp 305b.

452 Pattie, James Ohio

The Personal Narrative of James O. Pattie of Kentucky, Being an Expedition from St. Louis, through the Vast Regions Between that Place and the Pacific Ocean. . . . Edited by Timothy Flint. Cincinnati: Printed and Published by John H. Wood, 1831.

> Cloth, [xii], 13-300 p., 5 leaves plates, 19.8 cm. (In first printing, p. 251 is numbered 151.)

Pattie's book, a classic on the Southwest, is more than an incidental SFT item. He joined Sylvester Pratte's trading expedition on the Platte, headed southwest across Kansas, and reached the upper Arkansas. From there they went to Santa Fe, apparently along a rough approximation of the later SFT. They reached Santa Fe November 5, 1824. When the book was published, editor Flint included an appended account of a trip over the SFT in 1825 by a Dr. Willard: *Inland Trade with New Mexico*. This is a useful and important source in itself. For details on the several editions of the Pattie work, see Wagner-Camp 45 and Howes P-123. Reprints include Cleveland: A. H. Clark, 1905; Chicago: R. R. Donnelley, 1930; and Philadelphia: J. B. Lippincott, 1962. For a version written to interest the general reader, see *The Swallowing Wilderness; The Life of a Frontiersman: James Ohio Pattie*, by Stanton A. Coblentz (New York: Thomas Yoseloff, 1961). Graff 3216. N.

453 Paxson, Frederic Logan, 1877-

The Last American Frontier. New York: The Macmillan Company, 1910.

> Cloth, [xii], 1-402 p., 4 p. advts., 5 leaves plates incl. frontis., sources, index, 19.6 cm.

A general exposition on the Far Western frontier. The chapter on the SFT (pp. 53-69) tells how the Trail brought such new problems as long-distance government, plus an end to the sharply defined Indian frontier as wagon freight lines thrust westward through Indian lands. Reprinted, New York: Cooper Square Publishers, Inc., 1970.

454   Payton, William

The Last Man over the Trail. N.p., n.d. [c 1939].

> Pamphlet, overhang dec. wrappers, [iv], 1-60 p., frontis. port., illus., 21.5 cm.

The *Kansas Historical Quarterly* says this was published by the Kinsley, Kansas, *Graphic.* Payton (b. 1870) had no personal knowledge of the pre-railroad SFT, but his father, Kit Payton, was a cousin of Kit Carson and acquired general information about the Trail. Disconnected general memoirs. Some data on William Drannan (pp. 43-60), whom the author admired.

455   Pearson, Nels

The Old Santa Fe Trail and Other Poems of the Plains. Kansas City, [1920].

A book of poems, not a scholarly study.

456   Peattie, Donald Culross

"The Santa Fe Trail." *Yale Review,* Vol. XXXV, No. 2 (Winter 1946), pp. 242-50.

Writing: excellent; content: general. Peattie states that only "eleven white men lost their scalps on the Santa Fe Trail between 1821 and 1843," which is doubtful unless several were killed but not scalped.

457   Peck, Robert Morris

"Recollections of Early Times in Kansas Territory." *Kansas Historical Collections,* Vol. VIII (1903-1904), pp. 484-507.

Peck was in the 1st Cavalry in Kansas, 1857. Details of a march along the SFT to Bent's Fort and beyond in a campaign against the Cheyenne. Officers on this march included such later notables as Sumner, Johnston, Sturgis, Stuart, Hancock, and Sedgwick. See also entry 271.

458   Pelzer, Louis, 1879-

Henry Dodge. Iowa Biographical Series. Iowa City: The State Historical Society of Iowa, 1911.

Cloth, [xv], 1-266 p., frontis. port., notes, index, 21.5 cm.

Dodge was the first colonel of the 1st Dragoons. Pages 113-27 describe their famous march to the Rocky Mountains in 1835. Part of their return trip was along the SFT.

459   ————

Marches of the Dragoons in the Mississippi Valley, 1833-1850. Iowa City: State Historical Society of Iowa, 1917.

Cloth, x, 282 p., index.

One of the best sources on general history of the Dragoons, cited by all authoritative writers on the subject. Chapter VI describes the expedition of the Dragoons to the Rocky Mountains in 1835. Howes P-188.

460   Perkins, Margaret, compiler

Echoes of Pawnee Rock. Wichita: Woman's Kansas Day Club, 1908.

Moire glassine jacket over printed wrappers, tied with ribbon on side, [1]-[60] p., 19 cm.

A collection of old-timers' memoirs. Two of the best are an account of a buffalo hunt near Pawnee Rock in 1874 by H. A. Bower, and life in a stage station dugout by Adolph Roenigk. Pawnee Rock, which stood tall before quarrying operations reduced its size, was an important landmark on the Trail. KHS.

461   Perrine, Fred S.

"Military Escorts on the Santa Fe Trail." *New Mexico Historical Review,* Vol. II, No. 2 (April 1927), pp. 175-93; No. 3 (July 1927), pp. 269-304; Vol. III, No. 3 (July 1928), pp. 265-300.

The first installment is chiefly the report of Major Bennet Riley, dated Nov. 22, 1829, describing his escort of a caravan along the SFT, reprinted verbatim in the garbled form in which it appeared in *American State Papers, Military Affairs*, Vol. IX, pp. 277-80. The second installment contains the full report of Captain Clifton Wharton, July 21, 1834, with numerous supporting orders and letters. The third installment revises the first, as Perrine inserts errata and omitted material and reprints Riley's full journal taken from the original manuscript. The first two installments were also issued as reprints, in wrappers, as *Historical Review* reprint no. 6 in two parts. The third installment was never issued as a separate.

462 Peterson, Charles E.

"Manuel Lisa's Warehouse." *Bulletin of the Missouri Historical Society*, Vol. IV, No. 2 (Jan. 1948), pp. 59-91, illus.

A historical sketch of the warehouse and details of its reconstruction in 1941. Appended are useful notes and documents, including an inventory of Lisa's estate at the time of his death. The warehouse was built in St. Louis in 1818.

463 Peyton, John Lewis

The Adventures of My Grandfather: With Extracts from His Letters, and Other Family Documents, . . . with Notes and Biographical Sketches of Himself and His Son, John Howe Peyton, Esq. London: John Wilson, MDCCCLXVII.

Cloth, x, [1]-249 p., 4 p. advts., port., 21.5 cm.

A curious volume containing letters indicating that the grandfather, John Rowzee Peyton (1752-1799), had been imprisoned at Santa Fe and made his way overland to St. Louis in the spring of 1774. At St. Louis he wrote three letters, the first dated May 10, 1774, telling how he had been shipwrecked off the mouth of the Rio Grande, captured by the Spaniards and taken to Santa Fe, where he managed to escape. The book was reprinted, Ann Arbor: University Microfilms, 1965. The three letters were reprinted in *New Mexico Historical Re-*

view, Vol. IV, No. 3 (July 1929), pp. 239-72. They were again reprinted as 3 Letters from St. Louis, Denver: Libros Escogidos, 1958, ltd. 350 incl. 50 with a colored frontis., and again as A Virginian in New Mexico, Santa Fe: Press of the Territorian, 1967. Graff 3265; Howes P-275.

464   Phillips, Paul Chrisler

The Fur Trade. 2 vols. Norman: University of Oklahoma Press, 1961.

> Cloth, ports., maps, illus., index, 24 cm. Vol. I: xxvi, 686 p.; Vol. II: viii, 696 p.; boxed.

One of the more recent works on the fur trade, with useful SFT material. Dr. Phillips died in 1956 when he was ready to start completion of the Southwestern section. That portion was completed by his associate, J. W. Smurr.

465   Pike, Albert, 1809-1891

"Narrative of a Journey in the Prairie." Publications of the Arkansas Historical Association, Vol. 4, Conway, Ark., 1917, pp. 66-139.

The first reprint of Pike's account of his trip on the SFT, which had originally appeared as a serial in the columns of his newspaper, The Arkansas Advocate, in 1835. See next entry.

466   ———

Prose Sketches and Poems, Written in the Western Country. Boston: Light and Horton, 1834.

> Cloth, label on spine, viii, 9-200 p., 19 cm.

Pike was twenty-two when he left Independence in September, 1831, and went over the SFT with a caravan led by Charles Bent. They went by the Cimarron route and took the road to Taos instead of Santa Fe. By 1832, Pike had returned and settled permanently in Arkansas. After his book was published he wrote articles for The Boston Pearl and Literary Gazette, with better descriptions of the Trail. His book was reprinted in Arkansas Historical Collections, Vol. II, but the most useful reprint was at Albuquerque: Calvin Horn, Publisher,

1967, with an introduction by David J. Weber and including some of the sketches from *Pearl*. Graff 3285; Howes P-365; Wagner-Camp 50.

467 Pike, Zebulon Montgomery, 1779-1813

An Account of Expeditions to the Sources of the Mississippi, and through the Western Parts of Louisiana, to the Sources of the Arkansas, Kans, La Platte, Pierre Juan, Rivers; Performed by Order of the Government of the United States During the Years 1805, 1806, and 1807; And a Tour through the Interior Parts of New Spain, when Conducted through These Provinces, by Order of the Captain-General, in the Year 1807. Philadelphia: C. & A. Conrad & Co., 1810.

> Boards, 277, 65, 53, and 87 p., 4 maps, 2 charts. Maps sometimes issued in a separate atlas volume. For complete bibliographic details of this first edition see Graff 3290, Howes P-373, or Wagner-Camp 9.

First report of a U.S. government expedition into the Southwest. Beginning students of the West may be confused by the various titles and editions of this work. Pike made two expeditions, the second almost immediately after the first. In August 1805 Pike secured supplies at St. Louis and went up the Mississippi to explore its sources. He went as far as Minnesota and was back in St. Louis in April 1806. A separate report was published later describing that trip. On July 15, 1806, he left on his second expedition, with instructions to go up the Arkansas river to its source, cross to the Red river, and descend it on his return. His route up the Arkansas followed, in good part, the later SFT. North of Taos his party was captured by the Mexicans. Pike was taken to Mexico and later released, returning across Texas to Louisiana. His combined report of the two expeditions was published in 1810. A London edition appeared in 1811, and this was reprinted at Denver in 1889. It was followed by a three volume edition edited by Elliott Coues (N.Y. 1895), including a slim volume of maps. Scholars have preferred the 1895 edition for its annotations, clarity, and appended documents. Milo M. Quaife edited an edition entitled *The Southwestern Expedition of Zebulon Pike* (Chicago 1925), and Stephen H. Hart did another, entitled *Zebulon Pike's Arkansaw Journal* (Denver 1932). Pike's second expedition is often called his Southwestern Expedition. All are SFT items. The latest edition of the com-

plete original work is that edited and with new notes by Donald
Jackson, American Exploration Series, 48 (Norman: University of
Oklahoma Press, 1966). The Coues edition was reprinted, Minneapolis: Ross & Haines, 1965, three volumes bound in two. There is no
doubt that Pike's reports were known to some of the earliest subsequent expeditions venturing toward Santa Fe. N.

468 Pino, Pedro Bautista

*Noticias Históricas y Estadisticas de la Antigua Provincia del Nuevo-
México, Presentadas por su Diputado en Cortés, D. Pedro Bautista
Pino, en Cadiz el año de 1812, Adicionadas por el Lic. D. Antonio
Barreiro en 1839; y Ultimamente Anotadas por el Lic. Don José Agus-
tín de Escudero, para la Comision Militar de la Republica Mexicana.*
Mexico: Imprenta de Lara, 1849.

> Printed wrappers, iv, [1]-98 p., 4 p., index, map, 21.5 cm.
> See comments under Carroll, H. Bailey, *Three New Mexico
Chronicles.* Graff 3297; Howes P-383.

469 Place, Marion T.
First Book of the Santa Fe Trail. Watts, Ill., 1966.

> A juvenile.

470 Porter, Clyde, and Mae Reed Porter
Matt Field on the Santa Fe Trail. Collected by Clyde and Mae Reed
Porter; edited by John E. Sunder. American Exploration and Travel
Series, 29. Norman: University of Oklahoma Press, [1960].

> Cloth, xxix, [1]-322 p., color frontis., ports., scenes, map of SFT, index,
> 23.5 cm.
> In 1839 Matt Field (1812-1844) went over the SFT with a
caravan. Later he was assistant editor of the New Orleans *Picayune,*
where this collection of narrative verses and eighty-five articles first
appeared. They describe places and incidents on the Trail.

471 Powell, H. M. T.
The Santa Fe Trail to California, 1849-1852: The Journal and Draw-

ings of H. M. T. Powell. Edited by Douglas S. Watson. San Francisco: The Book Club of California, [1931].

> Cloth, [xv], [1]-272 p., illus., map, ltd. 300, 34 cm.

A handsome, scarce, and important work. Powell's party left Greenville, Ill., in April 1849 and went over the SFT (pp. 10-74) to Santa Fe, reaching there on July 16. They continued to California, where Powell made all of the sketches included in the book. He returned east via Panama. Graff 3334; Howes P-525.

472 Preuss, Charles, 1803-1854

Exploring with Frémont: the Private Diaries of Charles Preuss, Cartographer for John C. Frémont on his First, Second, and Fourth Expeditions to the Far West. Translated and edited by Erwin G. and Elisabeth K. Gudde. American Exploration and Travel Series, 26. Norman: University of Oklahoma Press, [c 1958].

> Cloth, [xxx], [1]-162 p., 8 leaves of plates, map, index, 23.5 cm.

Most useful, as far as the SFT is concerned, for its introduction giving data about Preuss. Frémont's second expedition left Westport on May 30, 1843; his fourth trip started from there on October 21, 1848. Both journeys were over the SFT and beyond, but Preuss' diaries have only one page of SFT material for the 1843 trip and nothing about the Trail in the 1848 entries.

473 Pride, W. F.

The History of Fort Riley. N.p., 1926.

> Cloth, [vi], 9-339 p., ports., scenes, 2 fldg. maps (one at back), 23.4 cm.

Fort Riley was named for Major Bennet Riley, who commanded a dragoon escort on the SFT. The fort was established to provide military protection on the Kansas frontier and along the SFT. A useful source for any study of military activities along the Trail.

474 Prince, LeBaron Bradford, 1840-1922

Old Fort Marcy, Santa Fe, New Mexico: Historical Sketch and Panoramic View of Santa Fe and Its Vicinity. Santa Fe: New Mexican Printing Co., 1912.

Pamphlet, green wrappers, saddle stitched, [1]-16 p., scenes, plan, 23.5 cm.

Brief history of the first U.S. fort southwest of the Arkansas, built in 1846 at the end of the SFT.

475   Quinn, Vernon, 1881-

War-paint and Powder-horn. New York: Frederick A. Stokes Company, 1929.

Cloth, dec. endpapers, xiv, [1]-298 p., plates (1 colored), map, 20 cm.

A popularized general history of the SFT. Based on historical research; a good introduction to the lore of the Trail but not useful to the scholar.

476   Raber, Charles

"Personal Recollections of Life on the Plains from 1860 to 1868." *Kansas Historical Collections,* Vol. XVI (1923-1925), pp. 316-41.

Raber made many trips over the SFT. One of the better personal memoirs, with names, dates, places, and details of freighting.

477   Rainey, George

No Man's Land: The Historic Story of a Landed Orphan. Enid, Okla.: George Rainey, 1937.

Cloth, 245 p., frontis., illus., 22 cm.

The SFT nicks the far northwest corner of the Oklahoma Panhandle along the Cimarron Cutoff. Rainey discusses this region briefly in a chapter on the Trail. An edition was also issued at Guthrie in 1937.

478   Rainey, Thomas Claiborne

Along the Old Trail: Pioneer Sketches of Arrow Rock and Vicinity. Vol. I. Marshall, Mo.: Marshall Chapter, Daughters of the American Revolution, 1914.

Overhang paper wrappers, side stitched, [1]-94 p., 1 leaf, ports., 19.2 cm. Also an edition of 50 signed copies.

Arrow Rock was a landing on the Missouri river and a prominent starting point for SFT travelers. Rainey was born in Tennessee and went to Missouri in 1852, arriving at Arrow Rock in 1865. Most of the historical text dealing with the town and the SFT was taken from Louis Houck's history of Missouri (q.v.), but there are some old-timers' memoirs appearing here for the first time. Only one volume was ever published. Howes R-19. KHS.

479 [Read, H. W.]

H. W. Read. Mr. Merrimon Submitted the Following Report. U.S. 43rd Cong., 1st sess., Sen. Report 173 [Serial 1586]. Washington, March 17, 1874.

> 1 p., 22.5 cm.

In 1863 Read resigned as a Treasury clerk and went over the SFT to Santa Fe, en route to become a postmaster at Tucson. He was asked to superintend a shipment of $200,000 in currency over the Trail, a task that "was attended with some danger." He asks for compensation; the Claims Committee approves $1,000 for services.

480 Richardson, William H.

Journal of William H. Richardson, a Private Soldier in Col. Doniphan's Command. Baltimore: Printed by Jos. Robinson, 1847.

> [1]-84 p., 19 cm.; also reported issued in wrappers.

A journal of personal experiences with Doniphan's men on their march over the SFT during the Mexican War. Reprinted in the *Missouri Historical Review*, Vol. XXII, No. 2 (Jan. 1928), pp. 193-236; No. 3 (April 1928), pp. 331-60; and No. 4 (July 1928), pp. 511-42; also issued by that *Review* as a separate. There were other editions in 1848 and 1849 with 96 pp. Graff 3496; Howes R-262; Wagner-Camp 137.

481 Richey, W. E.

"The Real Quivira." *Kansas Historical Collections*, Vol. VI (1897-1900), pp. 477-85.

Data on the expedition of Coronado into present Kansas in 1541, with a supporting comment by F. W. Hodge advancing the possibility that the Spanish explorer's men may have traveled a route that became the SFT where it crosses the Arkansas river.

482   Richie, Eleanor L.

"Background of the International Boundary Line of 1819 along the Arkansas River in Colorado." *The Colorado Magazine*, State Historical Society of Colorado, Vol. X, No. 4 (July 1933), pp. 145-56.

A documented general review of explorations by both Spanish and French along the Arkansas, written from published sources. From 1819 to 1848 the Arkansas was a boundary between the nations; for that reason Bent's Fort was built on the northern bank.

483   Riddle, Kenyon

Records and Maps of the Old Santa Fe Trail. Raton, N.M.: *Raton Daily Range*, 1948.

> Pamphlet, heavy brown paper wrappers, saddle stitched, halftone frontis. pasted inside front cover, [1]-36 p., five maps in back pocket, 23 cm.

Riddle grew up in Kansas and made a long and serious effort to retrace personally the SFT as it existed in the 1940s. His hand-lettered maps trace the route in great detail, with modern roads also indicated. In later editions the work grew to a full-sized clothbound book of 104 pp. and seven maps, plus a cardboard mileage scale, available from John K. Riddle, 1311 Willow Road, West Palm Beach, Florida. The maps are more reliable than the sources used for the text.

484   Rideing, William H.

A-Saddle in the Wild West: a Glimpse of Travel among the Mountains, Lava Beds, Sand Deserts, Adobe Towns, Indian Reservations, and Ancient Pueblos of Southern Colorado, New Mexico, and Arizona. New York: D. Appleton and Company, 1879.

> Cloth, [1]-165 p., plus 8 p. advts. (varies), 16 cm.

Rideing was an Eastern newspaper correspondent who spent the years 1875-76 in the Southwest with the Wheeler Survey. Contains one of the best graphic descriptions of a stage ride from Santa Fe to the end of the railroad at Las Animas, Colo. (pp. 156-65). Graff 3503.

485   Ridge, Martin, and Ray Allen Billington

America's Frontier Story: A Documentary History of Westward Expansion. New York: Holt, Rinehart and Winston, [c 1969].

> Paper, xxi, [1]-657 p., illus., 23.5 cm.

A recent college-level reader with selections from important contemporary writers connected with events along the Trail. Contains material by or about James Wilkinson, Gregg, Pattie, Ruxton, Pike, Frémont, Alexander Majors, and others.

486   Riley, Bennet

Message from the President in Reply to a Resolution of the Senate Regarding Protection of Trade between Missouri and Mexico. Major Riley's Report. U.S. 21st Cong., 1st sess., Sen. Doc. 46 [Serial 192]. Washington, Feb. 8, 1830.

> 9 p., 22.5 cm.

Riley's own report of his military escort service along the SFT in 1829, published in a badly edited, garbled form. See also entries 461 and 675. Wagner-Camp 41.

487   [Roads]

Military Road from Fort Leavenworth to Fort Riley. U.S. 34th Cong., 3rd sess., H.R. Report 172 [Serial 912]. Washington, Jan. 31, 1857.

> 3 p., 22.5 cm.

A road was requested from Westport to Fort Union; the Committee on Military Affairs says such a road may be desirable for trade but not for military purposes. Report is adverse except for a road from Fort Leavenworth to Fort Riley.

488   ———

Military Road from Fort Union to Santa Fe. 35th Cong., 1st sess., H.R. Report 372 [Serial 966]. Washington, May 11, 1858.

4 p., 22.5 cm.

A favorable report from the Committee on Military Affairs on construction of a road, with cost estimates and accurate mileages between points on the route. For another report on this project, see U.S. 36th Cong., 1st sess., H.R. Report 509 (Serial 1069), 3 pp., with almost identical contents.

489   Roberts, B. H.

The Mormon Battalion: Its History and Achievements. Salt Lake City: The Deseret News, 1919.

Cloth, v, [1]-96 p., fldg. map in front, ports., facsims., 20 cm.

History of the march of the Mormon Battalion over the SFT during the Mexican War, 1846. A few copies have been noted in wrappers.

490   [Robidoux, Antoine]

Antone Robidoux. U.S. 34th Cong., 1st sess., H.R. Report 226 [Serial 870]. Washington, July 19, 1856.

1 p., 22.5 cm.

The Claims Committee is favorable to a memorial from Robidoux, who asks for recompense of travel funds. He had been an interpreter with Kearny in 1846 over the SFT and on to California, where he was wounded and had to return to New Orleans by ship at his own expense. The printed document misspelled his name. The matter was brought before the committee again in later years; see U.S. 35th Cong., 2nd sess., H.R. Report 60 (Serial 1018); and again, U.S. 36th Cong., 1st sess., H.R. Report 496 (Serial 1069), 1860.

491   Robidoux, Orral Messmore

Memorial to the Robidoux Brothers: A History of the Robidouxs in America; Manuscript, Titles, Quotations, and Illustrations. Kansas City, Mo.: Smith-Grieves Company, 1924.

Cloth, [1]-311 p., map, 24.1 cm.

184

Mrs. Robidoux gathered this useful miscellany of disconnected short documents dealing with her family's history, especially the Mountain Men, Antoine and Louis Robidoux. Contains some data on the SFT, chiefly for the years 1832-46 (pp. 156-82). See entry 618. Graff 3522; Howes R-360. KHS, N.

492 Robinson, Jacob S.

Sketches of the Great West: A Journal of the Santa-Fe Expedition, Under Col. Doniphan, Which Left St. Louis in June, 1846. . . . Portsmouth, N.H.: Portsmouth Journal Press, 1848.

Boards, [1]-71 p., 14 cm.

Robinson was with the 1st Missouri Mounted Volunteers who went over the SFT in 1846 during the Mexican War. He was at Bent's Fort on July 21 and describes his personal experiences. Reprinted, Princeton: Princeton University Press, 1932, as *A Journal of the Santa Fe Expedition Under Colonel Doniphan.* Graff 3530; Howes R-368; Wagner-Camp 154. N.

493 Robinson, W. Stitt, ed.

"The Kiowa and Comanche Campaigns of 1860 as Recorded in the Personal Diary of Lt. J. E. B. Stuart." *Kansas Historical Quarterly,* Vol. XXIII, No. 4 (Winter 1957), pp. 382-400.

Stuart was with the 1st Cavalry under Major John Sedgwick in a summer campaign from Fort Riley to the Arkansas river and thence along the SFT to a point beyond Bent's New Fort. See entry 271.

494 Rowland, Buford

"Report of the Commissioners on the Road from Missouri to New Mexico, October, 1827." *New Mexico Historical Review,* Vol. XIV, No. 3 (July 1939), pp. 213-29, 2 maps.

Report of the commissioners who were sent by the U.S. to survey the SFT, 1825-27.

495 [Roy, Jean Baptiste]

"'Jean Baptiste Roy, St. Louis Fur Trader." *Bulletin of the Missouri Historical Society,* Vol. III, No. 3 (April 1947), pp. 85-93.

A biographical sketch of Roy, who was interpreter on Hugh Glenn's expedition to Santa Fe in 1821-22.

496   [Ruddock, Samuel Adams]

Northwest Coast of America. Mr. Bayliss, for the Select Committee to Which the Subject had been Referred, made the Following Report. U.S. 19th Cong., 1st sess., H.R. Report 213 [Serial 142]. Washington, May 15, 1826.

> 32 p., 22.5 cm.

Only the first page relates to the Santa Fe trade; the rest concerns the Far Northwest. Samuel Adams Ruddock (p. 1) left Council Bluffs on May 12, 1821. He went along the Platte river and then south to Santa Fe, where he arrived on June 8, 1821. This was some months prior to Becknell. However, Ruddock failed to see the possibilities for commerce and continued northwest to the Columbia.

497   Russell, Marian Sloan, 1845-1936

"Memoirs of Marian Russell," edited by Mrs. Hal Russell. *The Colorado Magazine,* State Historical Society of Colorado, Vol. XX, No. 3 (May 1943), pp. 81-95; No. 4 (July 1943), pp. 140-54; No. 5 (Sept. 1943), pp. 181-96; No. 6 (Nov. 1943), pp. 226-38; Vol. XXI, No. 1 (Jan. 1944), pp. 29-37; No. 2 (Mar. 1944), pp. 62-74; No. 3 (May 1944), pp. 101-11.

Also issued in book form, Evanston, Ill.: Branding Iron Press, 1954, with some variance in contents. Marian Russell made five trips over the Trail, 1852-62. She and her husband ran a trading post on the Trail at Tecolote, N.M., 1866-71. Together with the memoirs of Susan Magoffin (q.v.), this is one of the two best detailed accounts by a woman traveler over the SFT.

498   [Russell, William H.]

Report: The Committee of Claims, to Whom was Referred the Memorial of Russell & Jones. . . . U.S. 32nd Cong., 1st sess., Sen. Report 304 [Serial 631]. Washington, July 21, 1852.

2 p., 22.5 cm.

A claim for compensation for extra expenses incurred when a large wagon train was caught in a severe snowstorm at San Jose, near Las Vegas, N.M., in November 1850. It was hauling 684,834 lbs. of government supplies. James Brown died as a result of exposure when he went to Santa Fe for help. For another report on this same claim, see U.S. 33rd Cong., 1st sess., H.R. Report 59 [Serial 742], Washington, 1854.

499   Ruxton, George Augustus Frederick

Adventures in Mexico and the Rocky Mountains. London: John Murray, 1847.

> Cloth, adv. leaf, viii, [1]-332 p., 16 p. advts., 17.7 cm. Also in two parts, in wrappers.

Ruxton had gone first to Mexico, then north to Santa Fe and eastward on the SFT. The latter portion contains some material on Bent's Fort and the Trail. He is recognized as one of the great classic writers on the Mountain Men in the 1840s. The Newberry Library has a collection of Ruxton documents (Graff 3613-23). Part of this work was reissued in 1916 as *Wild Life in the Rocky Mountains,* and sections were also included in Clyde and Mae Porter's *Ruxton of the Rockies* (Norman: University of Oklahoma Press, 1950). Graff 3620; Howes R-553; Wagner-Camp 139.

500   Ryus, William Henry, 1839-

The Second William Penn: A True Account of Incidents that Happened along the Old Santa Fe Trail in the Sixties. Kansas City, Mo.: Frank T. Riley Publishing Co., [c 1913].

> Cloth, dec. endpapers, [1]-176 p., frontis. port., ports., 19.7 cm. Cover title: *The Second William Penn, Treating with Indians on the Santa Fe Trail, 1860-66.* Also issued in printed wrappers, side stitched.

The unusual title came from a statement that Ryus "got along with Indians as well as William Penn did." Firsthand account of staging on the SFT. Ryus was also a sutler for a time at Fort Union. He knew Carson, Wootton, and Maxwell. Reprinted, Fort Davis, Tex.: Frontier Book Co., 1968. Graff 3628.

501 Sabin, Edwin LeGrand, 1870-

Kit Carson Days, 1809-1868: Adventures in the Path of Empire. Chicago: A. C. McClurg & Co., 1914.

> Cloth, xv, 1-669 p., frontis., plates, index, 20.7 cm.

Sabin's biography of Carson, which remains the pioneer scholwork upon which all later works have been based. Reprinted, same publisher, 1919. Scholars usually prefer the revised two-volume edition (New York, Press of the Pioneers, 1935; ltd. 1,000 copies plus 200 signed). For comments on Carson's role along the SFT see entries in this bibliography under Harvey Carter and Marion Estergreen. Graff 3630; Howes S-1.

502 Sage, Rufus B.

Scenes in the Rocky Mountains, and in Oregon, California, New Mexico, Texas, and the Grand Prairies; or Notes by the Way, during an Excursion of Three Years, with a Description of the Countries Passed Through, including Their Geography, Geology, Resources, Present Condition, and the Different Nations Inhabiting Them; by a New Englander. Philadelphia: Carey & Hart, 1846.

> Wrappers, xii, 13-303 p., 18.3 cm. First copies issued in wrappers, with later copies of first edition in boards, with folding map. First issue has folios 77-78 on inner margins.

LeRoy R. Hafen says this is "exceptionally accurate and . . . full of valuable information." Howes, S-16, says this is "an intelligent narrative of extensive travels from the Platte to the Arkansas, including the best contemporary account of . . . Snively's expedition." Sage left Independence in September 1841 and went northwest to Fort Platte, returning to Independence in 1842. He was back in the Rockies in 1842-1843, and in 1843 he joined Col. Charles Warfield's unit of Texans who were later connected with the Snively expedition. In 1844, Sage returned to Van Buren, Arkansas, arriving in July, over a route that included much of the SFT. The book went through several editions, the most useful to scholars being the 1956 two-volume set by the Arthur H. Clark Co., Glendale (Vols. IV and V, The Far West and the Rockies Historical Series), which includes the full text, annotated by LeRoy R. Hafen, together with many of Sage's letters, two folding maps, and index. For information on other editions, see Graff 3633, Howes S-16, and Wagner-Camp 123. N.

503 [St. Vrain, Ceran]

Sureties of St. Vrain. Report: The Committee of Claims, to Whom was Referred Senate Bill No. 7. U.S. 29th Cong., 1st sess., H.R. Report 298 [Serial 489]. Washington: Ritchie & Heiss, Feb. 18, 1846.

    1 p., 22.5 cm.

A brief report urging that the bill be amended; proposed amendments were not printed in this document.

504 St. Vrain, Paul Augustus

Genealogy of the Family of De Lassus St. Vrain. Kirksville, Mo.: privately published, 1943.

    Pamphlet, 36 unnumbered p.

A scarce genealogy with details on Ceran St. Vrain, the noted SFT trader. Library of Congress.

505 Sampson, Francis A.

"Glimpses of Old Missouri by Explorers and Travelers." *Missouri Historical Review*, Vol. 1, No. 4 (July 1907), pp. 247-66.

    Brief data on the Spanish expedition from Santa Fe toward Missouri in 1719, taken from Dumont de Montigny's *Memoires historiques sur la Louisiane* . . . , Paris, 1753.

506 [Sanderson, J. L.]

Biographical Sketch of Col. J. L. Sanderson, of St. Louis, Mo. Kansas City, Mo.: Ramsey, Millett & Hudson, 1880.

    Limp calf, 8 p., frontis., 20 cm.

A brief biography of Sanderson, a founder and later owner of the noted Barlow and Sanderson's stage line over the SFT. Graff 3668. N.

507 Sanford, Albert B.

"Life at Camp Weld and Fort Lyon in 1861-62: An Extract from the Diary of Mrs. Byron N. Sanford." *The Colorado Magazine*, Historical Society of Colorado, Vol. VII, No. 4 (July 1930), pp. 132-39, illus.

Camp Weld was within present Denver, but Fort Wise (later Fort Lyon) was on the Arkansas. Pp. 135-37 contain descriptions of life at the fort, with SFT stagecoaches passing.

508 [Santa Fe and the Far West]

"Santa Fe and the Far West." *Niles National Register*, Vol. LXI, Dec. 4, 1841, p. 209.

Articles in *Niles National Register* are not generally listed in this bibliography, but this one has been the subject of much interest and was reprinted several times: in *Nouvelles Annales des Voyages et des Sciences Geographiques*, Vol. XCIII, pp. 308-13; in *New Mexico Historical Review*, Vol. V, No. 3 (July 1930), pp. 299-304; and in book form, Los Angeles: Glen Dawson, 1949, under the same title and with an introduction by Dale L. Morgan, ltd. 200 copies. It describes a trip over the SFT and on to California by a party that left in May 1841. Henry R. Wagner believed Dr. John Lyman was the author; Morgan believes it was written by John McClure. Wagner 86.

509 [Santa Fe Trail Highway Association]

Take a Santa Fe Trail Trip. N.p., 1961.

Wrappers, 48 p., fldg. map, illus. dwgs., 24 cm.

A modern travel guide to the SFT, which follows U.S. Highway 56 from Missouri to New Mexico, following U.S. 85 for the last section. Includes the text of many roadside historical markers and brief histories of towns along the way. Reissued several times in recent years; currently available from Walter D. Young, Box 1115, Hugoton, Kansas.

510 Seabrook, S. L.

"Expedition of Col. E. V. Sumner Against the Cheyenne Indians,

1857." *Kansas Historical Collections*, Vol. XVI (1923-1925), pp. 306-15.

As told to Seabrook by Major Sebastian Gunther (1831-1909), who served on the campaign. Part of the march was via the SFT and Bent's Fort.

511   Sears, W. H.

"Cowboy Life at Bent's Fort and on the Arkansas." *The Colorado Magazine*, State Historical Society of Colorado, Vol. XXXI, No. 3 (July 1954), pp. 193-201.

Sears was a cowboy in the vicinity of Fort Wise and Bent's New Fort in 1876, and he describes the ruins.

512   Segale, Rosa Maria (Sister Blandina), 1850-

At the End of the Santa Fe Trail. [Columbus, Ohio: Columbian Press, c 1932].

Cloth, [viii], [1]-347 p., frontis. port., ports., scenes, 20.5 cm.

Sister Blandina went by train to the end of track at Kit Carson, Colorado, in December 1872 and from there by stage over the SFT to Trinidad. In 1876 this Sister of Charity went, still by stage over the SFT, to Santa Fe. Minor but colorful items about the Trail. Reprinted, Milwaukee: Bruce Publishing Co., 1948.

513   Settle, Raymond W.

"The Role of Russell, Majors & Waddell in Western Overland Transportation." In: *The American West: An Appraisal.* Santa Fe: Museum of New Mexico Press, [1963].

A paper read at a Western History Association conference, dealing with reasons for the firm's failure: bad luck, overconfidence, poor judgment, and reckless management.

514   Settle, Raymond W., and Mary Lund Settle

"The Early Careers of William Bradford Waddell and William Hepburn Russell: Frontier Capitalists." *Kansas Historical Quarterly*, Vol. 26, No. 4 (Winter 1960), pp. 355-82, illus.

Biographical data on these two men who began their careers as wagon freighters on the SFT. Also reprinted as a separate pamphlet.

515 ———

"Napoleon of the West." *Annals of Wyoming*, Vol. 32, No. 1 (April 1960), pp. 5-47, illus.

An excellent brief biography of William Hepburn Russell (1812-1872), who started as a clerk in the J. & R. Aull store at the eastern end of the SFT in 1830 and rose to become a partner in Russell, Majors & Waddell. Russell was a wagon freighter by 1847; he was a partner of James Brown (q.v.) in 1850 and of Alexander Majors in 1854.

516 ———

"Origin of the Pony Express." *Bulletin of the Missouri Historical Society*, Vol. XVI, No. 3 (April 1960), pp. 199-212.

The Pony Express never operated along the SFT, and the extensive literature on the Express need not be listed in this bibliography except for two essential points mentioned in this article: the first regular couriers west of the Missouri were those along the SFT during the Mexican War; and the firm of Russell, Majors & Waddell, who launched the Pony Express, began as a firm of freighters on the Trail.

517 ———

War Drums and Wagon Wheels: The Story of Russell, Majors and Waddell. Lincoln: University of Nebraska Press, [c 1966].

Cloth, x, [1]-268, appendixes, chronology, bibliography, index, 23.6 cm.

The main emphasis is on freighting during the Utah campaign of 1857-58, but there is much on the rise of SFT freighting, with facts, figures, names, wagon design, teamsters' methods, and biographical sketches.

518   Sharp, Mamie Stine

"Home-coming Centennial Celebration at Council Grove, June 27 to July 2, 1921." *Kansas Historical Collections*, Vol. XVI (1923-1925), pp. 528-69, illus. photos.

A compilation of papers read at the celebration, many containing useful SFT material: John Maloy on Matteo Boccalina, the "hermit priest;" and R. M. Armstrong's memoirs of sixty years at Council Grove, 1865-1925, with data on stage lines.

519   Sheridan, Philip H.

Outline Descriptions of the Posts in the Military Department of the Missouri, Commanded by Lieutenant General P. H. Sheridan; Accompanied by Tabular Lists of Indian Superintendencies, Agencies and Reservations, and a Summary of Certain Indian Treaties. Chicago: Headquarters Military Division of the Missouri, 1876.

264 p., maps, 22.5 cm.

Contemporary descriptions of SFT Forts Dodge, Harker, Larned, Leavenworth, Lyon (II), Marcy (Santa Fe), and Union. The maps not only show fort plans but often show the vicinity, with locations of trails. A much smaller edition was issued at Chicago in 1870, under George Hartsuff (Howes H-271) and again in 1872 under Sheridan. The 1876 edition, generally the most useful, has been reprinted, Bellevue, Nebr.: The Old Army Press, 1969. Howes S-394.

520   ———

Record of Engagements with Hostile Indians Within the Military Division of the Missouri, from 1868 to 1882. Washington: Government Printing Office, 1882.

Wrappers, [1]-112 p., index, 22.5 cm.

Contains descriptions of about four hundred engagements, arranged by years and briefly described. Graff 3753 says there was an edition published at Chicago in 1882 which may have been the first issue. Reprinted, facsimile, Bellevue, Nebr.: The Old Army Press, 1969, in both cloth and paperback. Many of the incidents occurred along the SFT. Howes S-395.

521   Shields, Clara M. F.

"The Lyon Creek Settlement." *Kansas Historical Collections*, Vol. XIV (1915-1918), pp. 143-70, illus.

Chiefly on German settlements along Lyon creek but contains material about the Lost Springs station on the SFT in Marion county, first operated in 1859.

522   Smith, Duane Allen

"The Army and Western Transportation." In: *1959 Brand Book of The Denver Posse of The Westerners*, Vol. XV, [c 1960], pp. 279-308.

A brief, scholarly review of the role of Army units along the SFT, from the Rangers in 1832 to the Dragoons in 1834 and later.

523   Smith, Ezra Delos

"Jedediah S. Smith and the Settlement of Kansas." *Kansas Historical Collections*, Vol. XII (1911-1912), pp. 252-60.

Biographical data on Smith, by his great-grandson. In 1818 Smith went over what became the SFT with a packtrain that was to meet a Mexican merchant near present Fort Dodge. When the merchant failed to appear, the trader went back. Smith and two others waited for the Mexican and went with him to Santa Fe over what became the Cimarron Cutoff. Smith was later killed near the Cimarron river on a trip west over the SFT.

524   Smith, Henry

The Santa Fe Trail: The Trip over It in 1863, Made by a Youth of Sixteen. N.p.: Kellogg-Baxter Printing Co., [1907].

Pamphlet, colored wrappers, 20 p., 17.6 cm.

A firsthand account, written by Smith and read by his daughter, Mrs. M. T. Burwell, Jr., before "The Athena" Ladies Club of Goodland, Kansas, March 6, 1907. Smith was sixteen in 1862 when he went along to tend the extra oxen on a train of thirty wagons hauling supplies from Fort Leavenworth to Fort Union. They went via Raton Pass to avoid possible capture by the Confederates. KSH.

525   Smith, John Calvin

The Illustrated Hand-book, a New Guide for Travelers through the United States of America: Containing a Description of the States, Cities, Towns, Villages, Watering Places, Colleges, etc., etc., with the Railroad, Stage, and Steamboat Routes. . . . New York: Sherman & Smith, MDCCCL.

Cloth, [1]-[234] p., frontis.

Lists mileage (p. 221) between stops by stage over the SFT from St. Louis to Santa Fe via Mora, N.M., as Fort Union was not yet built. A description of Santa Fe (p. 168) adds that "it is the nominal capital of the province of Santa Fe, or New Mexico, although, according to the claims of the late Republic of Texas, it is within the bounds of that state." Smith issued several similar guide books. Howes S-614. KSH.

526   Smith, Leonard K.

Forty Days to Santa Fe. Boston, 1938.

Fiction.

527   Smyth, Bernard Bryan

The Heart of the New Kansas: A Pamphlet Historical and Descriptive of Southwestern Kansas. Great Bend, Kansas: B. B. Smyth, Book and Job Printer, 1880.

Pamphlet, wrappers, side stapled, viii, 9-168 p., 17.8 cm.

Contains some firsthand memoirs: "Indian Fight at the Arkansas" by James M. Fugate, 1853; pioneer experiences of Homer H. Kidder, who went over the SFT at least a hundred and fifty times as a mail carrier for Barlow & Sanderson; plan of Fort Zarah.

528   [Snively, Jacob]

Message from the President of the United States to the Two Houses of Congress, at the Commencement of the Second Session of the Twenty-eighth Congress. U.S. 28th Cong., 2nd sess., Sen. Doc. 1 [Serial 449]. Washington: Gales & Seaton, printers, Dec. 3, 1844.

702 p., 22.5 cm.

Contains Snively's own report of the seizure of his expedition by U.S. forces, together with complaints from the government of Texas to the U.S. concerning the episode (pp. 96-112). One of the most important documents on the subject. Wagner-Camp 103.

529 Spalding, Charles C.

Annals of the City of Kansas: Embracing Full Details of the Trade and Commerce of the Great Western Plains, together with Statistics of the Agricultural, Mineral and Commercial Resources of the Country West, South and South-west, Embracing Missouri, Kansas, the Indian Country, and New Mexico. Kansas City: Van Horn & Abeel's Printing House, 1858.

Cloth, [1]-111 p., 7 plates incl. frontis., 22.6 cm.

Frequently cited as a source of statistics on the Santa Fe Trade. "It is estimated that there are at least 300 merchants and freighters now engaged. . . ." Also issued, 1858, in wrappers; very rare. Reprinted, excellent facsimile, Kansas City, Mo.: Frank Glenn Publishing Co., 1950. Graff 3917; Howes S-805; Wagner-Camp 309.

530 Spear, Stephen Jackson

"Reminiscences of the Early Settlement of Dragoon Creek, Wabaunsee County." *Kansas Historical Collections,* Vol. XIII (1913-1914), pp. 345-63.

Memoirs about a small town near Wilmington, Kansas, which is at the junction of the SFT and the branch trail from Fort Leavenworth. Mentions 500 wagons a day at height of the Pike's Peak gold rush; material on mail stages; covers years 1857-67.

531 Sperry, Armstrong

Wagons Westward: The Old Trail to Santa Fe. Chicago: John C. Winston Co., [1936].

Fiction.

532 [Stage Lines]

"Carrying the Mail to Santa Fe 100 Years Ago." *Kansas Historical Quarterly*, Vol. XVIII, No. 1 (Feb. 1950), p. 97.

Reprints an item from *The Western Journal*, St. Louis, September 1850, with material on stages of Waldo, Hall & Co., and the heavy armament drivers carried.

533 Stanley, F. (pseud. of Anthony Crocchiola)

Fort Union, New Mexico. N.p., n.d. [c 1953].

Cloth, xiii, 1-305 p., 9 leaves plates, biblio., 22.2 cm.

The first book-length work on the history of Fort Union.

534 ——

Raton Chronicle. [Denver: World Press Publishing Co., c 1948].

Printed paper wrappers, sewn, [xii], [1]-146 p., illus. ports., scenes, biblio., 21.5 cm.

A local history of Raton, with brief data on the Clifton House, stage lines, and Willow Springs ranch. See also entry 128. Howes C-893.

535 Stanley, [Mrs.] W. E.

"Marking the Santa Fe Trail." *Santa Fe Employees Magazine*, Vol. 1, No. 3 (Feb. 1907), pp. 63-65, illus.

A general article describing the program then being carried out to mark the SFT. Written by a state regent of the D.A.R.

536 [Steele, John]

"Extracts from the Journal of John Steele." *Utah Historical Quarterly*, Vol. 6, No. 1 (Jan. 1933), pp. 3-28.

Steele was with the Mormon Battalion and was one of those who marched to Santa Fe and then turned back to rejoin the Mormon exodus. Part of his narrative tells briefly of the trip to Santa Fe and back as far as Bent's Fort (pp. 7-14).

537 Stephens, F. F.

"'Missouri and the Santa Fe Trade." *Missouri Historical Review*, Vol. X, No. 4 (July 1916), pp. 233-62; and Vol. XI, Nos. 3-4 in one (April-July 1917), pp. 289-312.

The editor of the *Review* noted that "no articles of greater value and accuracy have been printed in the *Review* than these." Dr. Stephens pays most attention to the economic and legal aspects of the SFT. The fact that Missouri was recognized as a hard money state and a mule state was due to the influx of specie and livestock over the Trail. A serious attempt to analyze the mechanics of the trade and the early role of the government in encouraging commerce. Widely used by later writers.

538 ⸺

"Nathaniel Patten, Pioneer Editor." *Missouri Historical Review*, Vol. IX, No. 3 (April 1915), pp. 139-55.

Useful because Patten was editor and co-owner of *The Missouri Intelligencer and Boon's Lick Advertiser*, which began publication at Franklin, Missouri, in April 1819. This newspaper at the eastern end of the SFT was often first to print important Trail news.

539 Stoddard, Amos

Sketches, Historical and Descriptive, of Louisiana. Philadelphia: Mathew Carey, 1812.

> Boards, viii, [1]-172, 175-488 p., 1 leaf, 23.5 cm.

The printer skipped two folios (173-74) but omitted no text. See pp. 46, 147, 453-57 for mention of early Spanish ventures east and northeast from New Mexico, trade along the Missouri and Red rivers, and other mentions of trade possibilities between New Mexico and the regions of Louisiana and Missouri. Reported reprinted, New York: AMS Press. Graff 3994; Howes S-1021. KHS, N.

540 Storrs, Augustus

Answers of Augustus Storrs, of Missouri, to Certain Queries upon the

Origin, Present State, and Future Prospect, of Trade and Intercourse between Missouri and the Internal Provinces of Mexico, Propounded by the Hon. Mr. Benton. U.S. 18th Cong., 2nd sess., Sen. Doc. 7 [Serial 108]. Washington: Printed by Gales & Seaton, Jan. 3, 1825.

> 14 p., 1 leaf, 22.5 cm.

One of the earliest Congressional documents dealing wholly with the SFT. Storrs was one of the leaders of a wagon train over the Trail in 1824. He wrote detailed answers to twenty-two questions asked by Senator Thomas Hart Benton, and Benton had the material issued as a congressional document. This led to a survey of the Trail. Reprinted in *Niles Register,* January 15, 1825; reprinted as *Santa Fe Trail: First Reports, 1825,* Houston: Stagecoach Press, 1960; also in *American Scene,* Vol. VI, No. 4 (1965), and in A. B. Hulbert's *Southwest on the Turquoise Trail.* Storrs later became a U.S. consul and is worthy of an extensive paper. Graff 3998; Wagner-Camp 29.

541   Strate, David K.

Sentinel to the Cimarron: The Frontier Experience of Fort Dodge, Kansas. Dodge City: Cultural Heritage and Arts Center, [1970].

> Cloth, [1]-[148] p., 8 leaves plates, biblio., index, 21 cm. Also in wrappers.

A recent work, professionally written from broad research and with all sources cited. Strate deals with the military campaigns against the Indians, garrison life at the fort, and Indian attacks on wagon trains along the SFT.

542   Stratton, Royal B.

Life among the Indians: Being an Interesting Narrative of the Captivity of the Oatman Girls, among the Apache and Mohave Indians; Containing also an Interesting Account of the Massacre of the Oatman Family, by the Apache Indians, in 1851. . . . San Francisco: Whitton, Towne & Co., 1857.

> Cloth, iv, [5]-183 p., port., illus. woodcuts. Second edition in same year had title beginning *Captivity of the Oatman Girls.* . . .

This narrative is best known for its description of the massacre in Arizona, but it also contains SFT material in its first pages. The

Oatmans joined a wagon train that left Independence in August 1850. Reprinted, San Francisco: Grabhorn Press, 1935; Upper Saddle River, N.J.: Gregg Press, Inc., 1970. Graff 4006; Howes S-1068; Wagner-Camp 294. N.

543   Stullken, Gerhard

My Experiences on the Plains. Wichita: The Grit Printery, 1913.

> Pamphlet, tan wrappers, [1]-36 p., frontis. port., 20.3 cm.

Stullken (1840-1916) served with the 9th Wisconsin Battery, Light Artillery, 1861-65. His unit went from Ft. Leavenworth up the Platte and to Denver, then down to Fort Union. Later he saw service along the Mountain Branch of the SFT to Bent's Fort and east to Council Grove. A facsimile reprint has been issued recently by Harold Humburg, Ness City, Kansas. Graff 4023; Howes S-1108. KSH, N.

544   Sunder, John E.

Bill Sublette, Mountain Man. Norman: University of Oklahoma Press, [c 1959].

> Cloth, xv, [1]-279 p., ports., scenes, maps, biblio., index, 23.5 cm.

Biography of William Lewis Sublette, with a description (pp. 93-100) of a trip over the SFT with a caravan in 1831. They left Independence in April and were back in October. Jedediah Smith was killed on this trip. Based on original documents.

545   ———

"British Army Officers on the Santa Fe Trail." *The Colorado Magazine,* State Historical Society of Colorado, Vol. XXIII, No. 2 (Jan. 1967), pp. 147-58.

An interesting account of a jaunt along the SFT from Westport to its crossing of the Arkansas. Seven British army officers, on leave from service in Canada, left Westport for a hunting trip along the Trail in September 1840 and returned in late October. Information was taken from the journal of Lt. William Fairholme, a member of the party.

546 ———

"Solomon Perry Sublette: Mountain Man of the Forties." *New Mexico Historical Review*, Vol. XXXVI, No. 1 (Jan. 1961), pp. 49-61.

Sublette's first venture was a clothing store in Independence, in 1836. He later became a trapper and in 1848 entered the Santa Fe trade briefly.

547 [Survey]

Boundary—United States and Mexico. Message from the President . . . Concerning the Boundary between the United States and the Republic of Mexico. U.S. 25th Cong., 1st sess., H.R. Doc. 42 [Serial 311]. Washington, Oct. 3, 1837.

94 p., 22.5 cm.

Includes correspondence between the U.S. and Mexico (pp. 7-8, 21-22) concerning the opening and surveying of the SFT and Mexico's reluctance on the matter.

548 Taft, Robert

"The Diamond of the Plain." *Transactions of the Kansas Academy of Science*, Sept., 1950.

Diamond Spring is located about four miles west and one mile north of the present town of Diamond Springs, Kansas, on what is locally known as the old Whiting ranch. During SFT days the spring was an important stopping point. The article has also been issued as a separate of four unnumbered pages. KHS.

549 [Talbot, Thomas]

Report: The Committee on Indian Affairs, To Whom was Referred the Petition of Thomas Talbot and Others. U.S. 29th Cong., 2nd sess., Sen. Doc. 75 [Serial 494]. Washington: Ritchie & Heiss, Jan. 18, 1847.

2 p., 22.5 cm.

Returning in 1827 from Santa Fe after trading, the Talbot party was attacked by Pawnee Indians and lost a hundred head of stock.

They petitioned unsuccessfully in 1828, 1832, and 1833. They petitioned again later in 1847, see U.S. 30th Cong., 1st sess., Sen. Report 11 (Series 512) and, same session, H.R. Report 299 (Serial 525) with identical text.

550 Taylor, Benjamin Franklin, ed.

Short Ravelings from a Long Yarn, or Camp March Sketches of the Santa Fe Trail; from the Notes of Richard L. Wilson. Chicago: Geer & Wilson, *Daily Journal* Office, 1847.

> Wrappers, 64 p., 22.5 cm.
> A good account of a trip over the SFT, apparently in 1841, by a large party whose captain was named Houck. First published in serial form in the *Daily Journal* and type forms held to print this pamphlet with double-column pages. Reprinted, Santa Ana, Calif.: Fine Arts Press, 1936, with a scholarly introduction by Henry R. Wagner. Graff 4709; Howes T-45; Wagner-Camp 142.

551 Taylor, Creswell

" 'Charles Bent Has Built a Fort'." *Bulletin of the Missouri Historical Society,* Vol. XI, No. 1 (Oct. 1954), pp. 82-84.

> Taylor replies to an article by LeRoy R. Hafen, "When Was Bent's Fort Built?" (q.v.), with text of a letter by Ceran St. Vrain stating the fort was built in 1834. The letter, written in 1847, is in the National Archives.

552 Taylor, Morris F.

"Confederate Guerrillas in Southern Colorado." *The Colorado Magazine,* State Historical Society of Colorado, Vol. XLVI, No. 4 (Fall 1969), pp. 304-23.

> While they were not equal in importance to Quantrill's men in Kansas, free-ranging bands of Confederates plundered along the SFT's Mountain Branch in Colorado. Headed by such men as Joel McKee, James Reynolds, and George "Madison," these groups attacked wagon trains. A carefully documented study.

553 ———

First Mail West: Stagecoach Lines on the Santa Fe Trail. Albuquerque: University of New Mexico Press, [c 1971].

Cloth, x, 1-253 p., plus 4 leaves plates and map, biblio., index, 24.5 cm.

A thorough scholarly work on the development of mail routes and stagecoach lines over the SFT, 1850-79. Based on original research in documents, postal records, and contemporary accounts, it gives the best account to date of such firms as Waldo, Hall & Co.; Hockaday & Hall; Hall & Porter; Barlow & Sanderson; and similar lines.

554 ———

"Fort Wise." *The Colorado Magazine*, State Historical Society of Colorado, Vol. XLVI, No. 2 (Spring 1969), pp. 93-119, illus., ports.

A history of the building and early operations of Fort Wise, built in 1860 on the SFT Mountain Branch adjacent to Bent's New Fort east of present Las Animas, Colo. In 1862 the name of the post was changed to Fort Lyon.

555 ———

A Sketch of Early Days on the Purgatory. Trinidad, Colo.: Risley Printing Co., [c 1959].

Pamphlet, tan wrappers, saddle stitched, [1]-48 p., 23.3 cm.

A local history of the area around Trinidad, Colorado. The Mountain Branch of the SFT left the Arkansas river near Bent's Old Fort and roughly paralleled the Purgatoire river into what is now Trinidad. The Spaniards had named it El Rio de Las Animas Perdidas en Purgatorio (the river of souls lost in purgatory). Later it was known as the Purgatoire, the Picketwire, and the Purgatory. After the railroad bypassed the Cimarron Cutoff in 1872, the Mountain Branch of the SFT remained the only branch in use until the railroad went through Raton Pass.

556 ———

Trinidad, Colorado Territory. [Trinidad: Trinidad State Junior College, c 1966].

Cloth, map endpapers, xiii, 1-214 p., illus., biblio., index, 23.5 cm.

A well researched and professional local history of the town of Trinidad, located at the north end of Raton Pass on the Mountain Branch of the SFT.

557 Taylor, Ross M.

We Were There on the Santa Fe Trail. New York: Grosset & Dunlap, Inc., 1960.

A juvenile, non-fiction.

558 Taylor, Zachary M.

California and New Mexico. Message from the President of the United States, Transmitting Information in Answer to a Resolution of the House of the 31st of December, 1849, on the Subject of California and New Mexico. U.S. 31st Cong., 1st sess., H.R. Exec. Doc. 17 [Serial 573]. Washington, Jan. 24, 1850.

976 p., fldg. maps, 22.5 cm.

A basic work on New Mexico and California. Material on the SFT is limited but useful: a report on the killing of Dr. White; report of J. S. Calhoun on Indians along the Trail; and information on Bent, St. Vrain, and Co.

559 Templeton, Sardis

The Lame Captain: The Life and Adventures of Pegleg Smith. Great West and Indian Series, XXVIII. Los Angeles: Westernlore Press, 1965.

Cloth, [1]-239 p., illus., index, 21 cm.

A biography of Thomas Long "Pegleg" Smith, written for the general reader. Smith is best known for his connection with a famous lost mine in California, but he was with a pack train as part of the SFT caravan in 1824 (pp. 37-40).

560 [Texan-Santa Fe Expedition]

American Citizens Arrested by Mexicans. Resolution of the Legisla-

ture of Kentucky in Relation to Certain American Citizens Captured by a Military Force of Mexicans. U.S. 27th Cong., 2nd sess., H.R. Doc. 42 [Serial 402]. Washington: 1842.

2 p., 22.5 cm.

Urges "the most energetic action" by the U.S. in response to Mexican arrest of members of the Texan-Santa Fe expedition.

561 ————

American Citizens Captured Near Santa Fe. Message from the President . . . in Relation to American Citizens Captured Near Santa Fe, &c. U.S. 27th Cong., 2nd sess., H.R. Doc. 49 [Serial 402]. Washington, Jan. 20, 1842.

7 p., 22.5 cm.

An important collection of documents and correspondence relative to this expedition.

562 ————

John T. Howard. Resolution of the Legislature of the State of Maryland, relating to John T. Howard, a Prisoner in Mexico. U.S. 27th Cong., 2nd sess., H.R. Doc. 154 [Serial 403]. Washington, Mar. 24, 1842.

1 p., 22.5 cm.

The Maryland assembly asks the U.S. to seek freedom for Howard, a Maryland citizen who was with the Texan-Santa Fe Expedition.

563 ————

Message from the President of the United States, Communicating . . . Copies of Correspondence with the Government of Mexico. U.S. 27th Cong., 2nd sess., Sen. Doc. 325 [Serial 398]. Washington, June 15, 1842.

104 p., 22.5 cm.

One of the most important Congressional documents concerning the Texan-Santa Fe expedition, containing letters from prisoners, correspondence between the two governments, statements, and depositions. Some of the prisoners were taken along the SFT from San Miguel to Santa Fe.

564 ──────

Relations with Mexico. Message of the President . . . Transmitting Copies of Papers upon the Subject of the Relations between the United States and the Mexican Republic. U.S. 27th Cong., 2nd sess., H.R. Doc. 266 [Serial 405]. Washington, July 14, 1842.

> 42 p., 22.5 cm.

Contains good material on the Texan-Santa Fe expedition and also on general relations between the U.S. and Mexico during the period of the Texas Republic.

565 [Texas: Snively Expedition]

Documents Showing the Description and Value of the Arms Taken from a Party of Texans within the Territory of the United States, by Capt. Cooke, 1st Reg't. Dragoons, June 30, 1843, and Deposited at Fort Leavenworth, Mo. U.S. 29th Cong., 1st sess., Sen. Doc. 43 [Serial 472]. Washington: Ritchie & Heiss, Jan. 8, 1846.

> 3 p., 22.5 cm.

A letter from Major Clifton Wharton, with the report of a board of survey and an itemized list of weapons with the value of each.

566 Thoburn, Joseph Bradfield, 1866-

"The Dragoon Campaigns to the Rocky Mountains." *Chronicles of Oklahoma*, Vol. VIII, No. 1 (March 1930), pp. 35-41.

Thoburn did some excellent work as a historical detective to prove that James Hildreth never wrote the book entitled *The Dragoon Campaigns to the Rocky Mountains*, although Hildreth may have taken the manuscript to a publisher. Hildreth had been discharged for disability before the campaign began as described in the book. Thoburn presents a case for William L. G. Miller as author. Miller was a former British officer, and Thoburn believes that he served in both the British army and the Dragoons under other names.

567 Thomas, Alfred Barnaby

After Coronado: Spanish Exploration Northeast of New Mexico, 1696-1727; Documents from the Archives of Spain, Mexico, and New Mexico. Civilization of the American Indian Series, 9. Norman: University of Oklahoma Press, [1935].

> Cloth, [xiv], 1-[308] p., 1 map in text, 1 fldg. map, notes, biblio., index, 23.6 cm.

A long historical introduction and a collection of valuable documents, most of them here translated and published for the first time. Devoted chiefly to Spanish explorations outward from New Mexico and French moves toward the province, leading eventually to commerce and the SFT. Reprinted, same publisher, 1969.

568 ———

"Documents on the Northern Frontier of New Mexico, 1818-1819." *West Texas Historical Yearbook,* 1928.

Documents relating to Jules de Mun, A. P. Chouteau, James Long, and others venturing toward the northeastern boundary of New Mexico. Reprinted in *New Mexico Historical Review,* Vol. IV, No. 2 (April 1929), pp. 146-77; and reprinted therefrom as a separate, Santa Fe: Historical Society of New Mexico, *Review* Reprint No. 14. Some related information can also be found in "The Journals of Jules de Mun," edited by Thomas Maitland Marshall, *Missouri Historical Society Collections,* Vol. 3, 1928.

569 ———

"The First Santa Fe Expedition." *Chronicles of Oklahoma,* Vol. IX, No. 2 (June 1931), pp. 195-208.

A study of the trip made by Pedro Vial from Santa Fe to St. Louis in 1792 and his return journey in 1793, with translations of Spanish documents and Vial's diary of the return trip.

570 ———

The Plains Indians and New Mexico, 1751-1778: A Collection of

Documents Illustrative of the History of the Eastern Frontier of New Mexico. Coronado Cuarto Centennial Publications, 1540-1940, XI. Albuquerque: University of New Mexico Press, 1940.

> Cloth, [xvi], 1-232 p., biblio., index, 27.2 cm.

Translations of valuable documents found in Spain and Mexico, with others from archives in the U.S. Several of these deal with the French traders Jean Chapuis and Louis Feulli in 1752, including a full list of their trade goods. Thomas' introduction reviews French intrusions toward Santa Fe, using data from Bolton but adding some new material. An important source work.

571 ———

"The Yellowstone River, James Long, and Spanish Reaction to American Intrusion into Spanish Dominions, 1818-1819." *New Mexico Historical Review,* Vol. IV, No. 2 (April 1929), pp. 164-177.

The title defines the general content, but there is also mention of Spanish inscriptions on rocks along the Cimarron in the Oklahoma Panhandle (p. 168). Reprinted from the *West Texas Historical Year Book,* 1928.

572 Thompson, Albert W.

"Kit Carson's Camp Nichols in No Man's Land." *The Colorado Magazine,* State Historical Society of Colorado, Vol. XI, No. 4 (July 1934), pp. 179-86, plan.

No Man's Land was a term applied to the Oklahoma Panhandle; the SFT crossed the far western tip of the region. Carson's command of troops from Fort Union built Camp Nichols in June 1865 and abandoned it in September. It was located four or five miles east of the New Mexico line and about one mile north of the SFT. Included is an interview with Mrs. Marion Russell, who describes her stay at Camp Nichols in 1865.

573 ———

"Notes." *Old Santa Fe,* Vol. III, No. 11 (July 1916),) pp. 276-79, 282-85, map.

Thompson was a local historian engaged in writing a history of Clayton county, New Mexico. He identified local landmarks and variant routes in Oklahoma and northeastern New Mexico along the SFT.

574 ———

"Ruins of Forts on the Santa Fe Trail." *El Palacio*, Vol. XII, No. 7 (April 1, 1922), pp. 93-94.

Describes a visit to the site of Bent's New (or lower) Fort on the Arkansas river in 1922, not far from Lamar, Colorado.

575 ———

"Thomas O. Boggs, Early Scout and Plainsman." *The Colorado Magazine*, State Historical Society of Colorado, Vol. VII, No. 4 (July 1930), pp. 152-60, port.

A brief biography of Boggs, an employee of the Bents and friend of Kit Carson. Included is text of a dictation by Boggs to Thompson in 1889, describing a trip Boggs made over the SFT in 1846 with dispatches from Santa Fe to Fort Leavenworth (pp. 156-57).

576 Thompson, Enid T.

"Fort Stevens." *The Colorado Magazine*, State Historical Society of Colorado, Vol. XLIII, No. 4 (Fall 1966), pp. 303-07, illus.

Fort Stevens was to have been built on a plateau at the foot of the Spanish Peaks, south of the Arkansas river. Construction was started in the summer of 1866 but halted less than three months later. Documents relative to the fort are reprinted in this article.

577 Thomson, Matt

Early History of Wabaunsee County, Kansas, with Stories of Pioneer Days and Glimpses of Our Western Border. Alma, Kansas: Matt Thomson, 1901.

Cloth, [1]-368 p., index, viii p., maps, ports., scenes, 22.1 cm.

In part a firsthand account. Thomson's father was a station agent on the mail stage line over SFT at Elm Creek, 1859-62 (pp. 205-20). Matt later rode the Trail himself. Describes Indian attack on mail coach in 1859 (pp. 104-05). Howes T-214. KSH.

578   Tisdale, Henry

"Travel by Stage in the Early Days." *Kansas Historical Collections,* Vol. VII (1901-1902), pp. 459-64.

Firsthand material by a stage line executive with data on several Kansas lines and especially on the Hall & Porter operations in 1860.

579   Todd, Edgeley W.

"Bent's Fort in 1846." *The Colorado Magazine,* State Historical Society of Colorado, Vol. XXXIV, No. 3 (July 1957), pp. 206-10.

Newspaper descriptions of the fort in 1846, chiefly from the Saint Louis *Reveille.*

580   Toponce, Alexander

Reminiscences of Alexander Toponce, Pioneer, 1839-1923. [Salt Lake City: Century Printing Co., c 1923.]

Cloth, [1]-248 p., frontis. port., ports., scenes, 17.9 cm.

Toponce freighted in Montana, Wyoming, Idaho, and Nevada in the 1860s and later. Contains a firsthand account (pp. 28-32) of mail stage lines on the SFT in the late 1850s. The work was published by Mrs. Katie Toponce. Reprinted, Norman: University of Oklahoma Press, 1971. Graff 4165; Howes T-300. KHS.

581   [Treaties]

"Indian Treaties and Councils Affecting Kansas." *Kansas Historical Collections,* Vol. XVI (1923-1925), pp. 746-72.

Summary information on treaties, with dates, locations of meetings, and terms. Those concerning the SFT were with the Sioux in 1825 (p. 750); the Cheyenne, Crow, and Osage in 1825 (p. 751); and a treaty to protect the survey party of Sibley and Brown. There were other similar treaties with Pawnee and Omaha tribes.

582 ———
Message from the President . . . in Relation to the Western Boundary of the United States. U.S. 18th Cong., 2nd sess., Sen. Doc. 52 [Serial 115]. Washington: Gales and Seaton, Printers, Jan. 17, 1825.

4 p., 22.5 cm.

Reports that Mexican government is generally favorable to continuing the boundary as defined in the treaty between U.S. and Spain in 1819, by which the Arkansas river was part of the boundary.

583 ———
Treaties with Mexico: Treaty of Amity, Commerce, and Navigation. . . . U.S. 22nd Cong., 1st sess., H.R. Doc. 225 [Serial 220]. Washington, May 1, 1832.

27 p., 22.5 cm.

A message from President Jackson with text of the treaty signed in 1831, giving nationals of each country the same rights to trade as given to others in the country visited. Essentially it protected U.S. traders in Mexico. No specific mention of the SFT trade, except as it mentions the Arkansas river as a boundary.

584 Trego, Frank H.
Boulevarded Old Trails in the Great Southwest. New York: Greenberg, Publisher, [1929].

Cloth, xviii, 1-262 p., illus., map, 21 cm.

Trego took a motor trip in the late 1920s, and one section of his tour was along the SFT from Trinidad, Colorado, to Santa Fe. His account of this region (pp. 20-25) is so general as to be inconsequential.

585 Tucker, John M.
"Major Long's Route from the Arkansas to the Canadian River, 1820."

New Mexico Historical Review, Vol. XXXVIII, No. 3 (July 1963), pp. 185-219, illus., fldg. map.

In 1820 Major Stephen H. Long led a government expedition into the Rocky Mountains. It added much to knowledge of the region soon to be traversed by the SFT, although Long's trip touched only part of the Arkansas on his return. For a full journal, see entries 30 and 137. This article describes a careful attempt to retrace Long's route from the Arkansas to the Canadian.

586   Twitchell, Ralph Emerson

Dr. Josiah Gregg, Historian of the Santa Fe Trail. Historical Society of New Mexico, Papers, No. 26. Santa Fe, 1924.

> Pamphlet, saddle stitched, frontis., [1]-45 p., 22.8 cm.

A biography of Gregg.

587   ————

The History of the Military Occupation of the Territory of New Mexico from 1846 to 1851 by the Government of the United States, Together with Biographical Sketches of Men Prominent in the Conduct of the Government During That Period. Denver: The Smith-Brooks Printing Company, Publishers, 1909.

> Cloth, [xvi], [17]-394 p., frontis., ports., facsims., scenes, 22.7 cm.

Describes the formation and march of the Army of the West in 1846 over the SFT, but is more useful for biographical sketches of David Waldo, James Magoffin, Richard H. Weightman, and others. Reprinted in facsimile, Chicago: Rio Grande Press, 1963.

588   ————

The Leading Facts of New Mexican History. 5 vols. Cedar Rapids: The Torch Press, 1911-1917.

> Cloth, indexed, 25 cm.; Vol. I: [xxi], 1-506 p., 87 leaves plates, 2 fldg. maps; Vol. II: [xxiii], [1]-631 p., 100 leaves plates, 1 fldg. table, 4 fldg. maps; Vol. III: xii, [1]-571 p., 70 leaves plates; Vol. IV: viii, [1]-567 p., 56 leaves plates; Vol. V: [x], [1]-505 p., 58 leaves plates.

With all his faults, Twitchell remains one of the great basic sources of New Mexican history. Vols. I (1911) and II (1912) were

issued in an edition limited to 1500 copies, plus a few using letters,
e.g., "F" instead of numerals to number copies. In 1917 three more
volumes were issued, III and IV with county histories and local
biographies, V with data on twentieth century events. Vol. II is especially useful for SFT history, with a chapter (pp. 91-146) devoted to
the Trail. This volume covers the period 1822-1912 and includes material on the Texan-Santa Fe Expedition, the Mexican War, and the
Civil War. Vol. III has SFT data in the chapter on Mora county (pp.
389-426), including the Indian attacks on Dr. White, on Ambrosio
Armijo's train, and on Allison's caravan. There is also an eastbound
table of mileages from a Spanish document. Vol. IV has SFT information on pp. 18-37, 196-201, 209-10, and 515-33, with data on
John Dold, the wagon freighter; Jedediah Smith; the Snively affair,
etc. Vols. I and II reprinted, Albuquerque: Horn & Wallace, Publishers, 1963. Howes T-443.

589 ———

Old Santa Fe: The Story of New Mexico's Ancient Capital. Santa Fe:
New Mexican Publishing Co., [1925].

> Cloth, [1]-488 p., 39 leaves plates, index, ltd. 1000 numbered, 25.5 cm.
> Lamy plate usually missing at p. 362; art museum plate at p. 462 not in
> list of illustrations.

Has a useful section on the SFT (pp. 211-44), chiefly from
known sources but partly from obscure documents. Valuable for its
picture of conditions at the western end of the Trail. Reprinted, Chicago: Rio Grande Press, 1963.

590 ———

The Spanish Archives of New Mexico. 2 vols. Cedar Rapids: The
Torch Press, 1914.

> Cloth, indexed, 23.5 cm.; Vol. I: [xxiv], [1]-525 p., 21 leaves plates; Vol.
> II: [viii], [1]-683 p., 21 leaves plates.

These volumes are a calendar or chronological guide to thou-
sands of New Mexico Spanish documents prior to 1821. Entries give
only short clues to documents, not their contents. Those relating to
the SFT mention such names as Vial, La Lande, Purcell, Clamorgan,

McLanahan, and others in the period 1804-19. See documents 1714, 1834, 1859, 1888, 1992, 1953, 1980, 2001, 2090, 2171, 2183, 2187, 2249, 2291, 2311, 2320, 2325, 2340, 2363, 2427, 2646, 2672, 2714, and 2850. A more accurate calendar of the same documents has been prepared recently by the New Mexico State Records Center and Archives, Santa Fe. It corrects many of Twitchell's errors, and the documents themselves are now available on microfilm from this Center. Howes T-445.

591 ———

The Story of the Conquest of Santa Fe, New Mexico, and the Building of Old Fort Marcy, A.D. 1846. Papers, No. 24. [Santa Fe: Historical Society of New Mexico, 1923].

> Pamphlet, lettered wrappers, saddle stitched, [1]-63 p., ports., scenes, plan, 23.1 cm.

Fort Marcy was built hurriedly in 1846. The first half of this booklet describes the organization and march of U.S. troops over the SFT. The last half reprints many papers of James W. Magoffin, a SFT trader who conducted preliminary negotiations that aided the surrender of New Mexico. Reprinted, Truchas, N.M.: Tate Gallery, 1968, in cloth and paper.

592   Udell, John

Journal of John Udell, Kept During a Trip across the Plains, Containing an Account of the Massacre of a Portion of His Party by the Mohave Indians, in 1858. Suisun City: Solano County Herald, Print, 1859.

> Pamphlet, self-cover, sewed, [1]-45 p., 1 leaf, 21 cm.

Udell made several trips across the West: his fourth was via the SFT as far as Santa Fe, thence by Beale's road to California. The only known copy of this first edition is in the Coe Collection at Yale; they reprinted it facsimile, ltd. 200, in 1952 as No. 1 in their Western Historical Series. The second edition, Jefferson, Ohio: Ashtabula Sentinel Steam Press Print, 1868, was also reprinted, Los Angeles, N. A. Kovach, 1946. Graff 4231; Howes U-4; Wagner-Camp 346a.

593   Ulibarri, George S.

"The Chouteau-Demun Expedition to New Mexico, 1815-1817." *New Mexico Historical Review*, Vol. XXXVI, No. 4 (Oct. 1961), pp. 263-73.

In 1817 these two Frenchmen left Saint Louis on an expedition to trade with Indians at the head of the Arkansas river in what is now Colorado. They were arrested in 1817, taken to Santa Fe, and their goods confiscated. Their claims for compensation were not settled fully until 1851. Auguste P. Chouteau and Jules de Mun have been considered forerunners of the SFT trade.

594   Unrau, William E.

"Indian Agent vs. the Army: Some Background Notes on the Kiowa-Comanche Treaty of 1865." *Kansas Historical Quarterly*, Vol. XXX, No. 2 (Summer 1964), pp. 129-52.

Indian affairs along the SFT in 1865, based on research in original sources.

595   ———

"The Story of Fort Larned." *Kansas Historical Quarterly*, Vol. XXIII, No. 3 (Autumn 1957)), pp. 257-80, illus.

Fort Larned was built on the SFT in 1859 and abandoned in 1878. It was a center for military control of the Indians. The article has data on wagon trains. Also issued as a separate pamphlet. Unrau also wrote a 24-page *History of Fort Larned*, n.p., n.d. (1950s), containing essentially the same material.

596   Utley, Robert M.

"Fort Union and the Santa Fe Trail." *New Mexico Historical Review*, Vol. XXXVI, No. 1 (Jan. 1961), pp. 36-48.

A summary on military protection along the SFT in the 1850s and 1860s.

597 ―――――

Fort Union and the Santa Fe Trail: A Special Study of Santa Fe Trail Remains at and near Fort Union National Monument, New Mexico. National Survey of Historic Sites and Buildings. Santa Fe: U.S. Department of Interior, National Park Service, 1959.

> Wrappers, 2 p., v, 1-71 leaves text, 12 leaves plates, 6 leaves maps, duplicator processed on one side only, for limited internal distribution.

Title defines contents. Most of the text is identical with that of entry 596 above, but the book contains superb aerial views of Trail remains in the vicinity of Fort Union, plus detailed maps. Also includes data on Fort Barclay.

598 ―――――

Fort Union National Monument, New Mexico. National Park Service Historical Handbook Series No. 35. Washington, D.C., 1962.

> Pamphlet, saddle stitched, [iv], 1-68 p., maps, plans, ports., scenes, 23 cm.

The best short history of the fort, with information on the SFT.

599 [Vaill, ―――――]

"Journal of Mr. Vaill, during a Preaching Tour." *The Missionary Herald,* Vol. XXIX, No. 9 (Sept. 1833), pp. 366-71.

Vaill was on a tour through Kansas in May 1833 and was told Indians had killed some SFT traders eastbound in the winter of 1832-33. The traders are said to have buried $20,000 before they were killed. KSH.

600 Van Cleave, Errett

"Credit on the Santa Fe Trail: Business Pioneering in Pueblo Regions." *Credit and Financial Management,* Vol. 41, No. 10 (Oct. 1939), pp. 16-17.

Contains slight information on SFT traders' practices but is devoted chiefly to credit policies of the Charles Ilfeld Co. in the area around Las Vegas, N.M.

216

601   Vanderwalker, George F.

"Over the Santa Fe Trail in '64." *The Trail*, Vol. II, No. 1 (June 1909), pp. 16-18.

Personal memoirs of a trip over the Trail in 1864, by an ox-team driver.

602   Van Ravenswaay, Charles

"Arrow Rock, Missouri." *Bulletin of the Missouri Historical Society*, Vol. XV, No. 3 (April 1959), pp. 203-23, illus.

The director of the Missouri Historical Society gives a brief, documented history of the Missouri river town that for several years was an important eastern terminus of the SFT. Also reported issued as an offprint in pamphlet form.

603   Van Tramp, John C.

Prairie and Rocky Mountain Adventures; or, Life in the West; To Which will be Added a View of the States and Territorial Regions of our Western Empire: Embracing History, Statistics and Geography, and Descriptions of the Chief Cities of the West. Columbus: J. & H. Miller, 1858.

Cloth, vi, [7]-640 p., plus 61 plates, 21.5 cm.
A general work on the West, characterized by Henry R. Wagner as "a book made up with scissors." Material concerning the SFT is taken from Frémont, Gwinn H. Heap, Senator Benton, and similar sources. First printing lacks note on page 640. There were several later editions, often enlarged; that of 1868 has 795 pages including plates. Graff 4462; Howes V-43; Wagner-Camp 312.

604   Vernon, Joseph S.

Along the Old Trail: A History of the Old and a Story of the New Santa Fe Trail. Larned, Kansas: Tucker-Vernon, Publishers, [c 1910].

Lettered wrappers, side fastened with ribbon, [vi], [1]-110 p., 3 leaves, colored frontis., scenes, 22.8 cm.

217

A general history of the SFT, including reprint of a work by Robert M. Wright (q.v.). Useful for the photographs, such as comparative views of Pawnee Rock in 1865 and 1910. Copies vary; some have added sections on modern Kansas, bringing the total to 190 pp. in some issues. Known variants include ones about Las Animas, Colo., 1910; Barton county, Kans., 1910; Cimarron county, Kans., 1910; Larned, Kans., 1910; Western Kansas, 1910; and Dodge City, Kans., 1911. Howes V-77.

605   Vestal, Stanley (pseud. of Walter Stanley Campbell)

The Old Santa Fe Trail. Boston: Houghton Mifflin Company, [c. 1939].

> Cloth, front map endpaper, [xiv], [1]-304 p., 8 leaves plates, appendixes (tables), biblio., index, 21 cm.

A standard history for the general reader, with emphasis almost entirely on selected incidents that make exciting reading. Also issued in paperback, without index, New York: Bantam Books, 1957.

606   ———

Wagons Southwest: Story of Old Trail to Santa Fe. New York: American Pioneer Trails Association, 1775 Broadway, 1946.

> Pamphlet, saddle stitched, full color cover, 1 leaf, [iv], 1-50 p., illus. drawings, map, 17.7 cm.

Introduction by Howard R. Driggs. A brief resume of the Trail, condensed by Vestal (Campbell) from his *The Old Santa Fe Trail*.

607   Vilas, Jonas

"Old Franklin: A Frontier Town of the Twenties." *Mississippi Valley Historical Review*, Vol. IX, No. 4 (March 1923), pp. 269-82.

Old Franklin was on the northern bank of the Missouri river, opposite present Boonville. It began around 1816; by 1829 it was abandoned as families moved to New Franklin, two miles away, because of encroaching water. In 1822 it saw the early SFT trade. The article describes the people, stores, and scenes in the town.

608   Villard, Henry

The Past and Present of the Pike's Peak Gold Regions. St. Louis: Sutherland & McEvoy, Publishers, 1860.

> Cloth, [1]-112 p., 8 p. advts., 2 maps, frontis., 20.5 cm.; also in wrappers.

Excessively rare. Villard went to Colorado during the gold rush in 1859 as a Cincinnati newspaper correspondent. He then wrote this guide book, which includes seven pages of directions for those traveling the SFT or "Arkansas route" to Colorado. Reprinted, Princeton: Princeton University Press, 1932, in the Narratives of the Trans-Mississippi Frontier series. Graff 4486; Howes V-101; Wagner-Camp 366.

609   Voelker, Frederic E.

"Ezekiel Williams of Boon's Lick." *Bulletin of the Missouri Historical Society,* Vol. VIII, No. 1 (Oct. 1951), pp. 17-51.

The best documented study of Williams, a real person who figured strongly in Coyner's *The Lost Trappers* (q.v.). He traveled down the Arkansas in 1813; at his home William Becknell's group met in 1821 to plan the expedition that went to Santa Fe; and he was captain of a train of 53 wagons over the SFT in 1827.

610   Wagner, Henry Raup, and Charles L. Camp

The Plains and the Rockies: A Bibliography of Original Narratives of Travel and Adventure, 1800-1865. Third edition, revised by Charles L. Camp. Columbus: Long's College Book Company, 1953.

> Cloth, [viii], 1-601 p., 16 leaves facsimile plates, chronological list, index, 23.4 cm.

The largest and best edition, expanded beyond the editions of 1919, 1921, and 1937 (of which the first two were basically the same edition). It scrupulously describes 429 items listed by Wagner and 110 added by Camp. Considered essential in any bibliographical study of the West. All titles in it are being supplied on microfilm by the Lost Cause Press, 235 South Galt Ave., Louisville, Kentucky 40206.

611 [Wagon Freighting]

Memorial of the Legislature of Missouri Relative to a Grant of Land to the Teamsters Employed in the Mexican War. U.S. 31st Cong., 1st sess., H.R. Misc. Doc. 33 [Serial 581]. Washington, 1850.

2 p., 22.5 cm.

A memorial, dated March 12, 1849, requesting a bonus of land for those who drove freight wagons from Missouri to New Mexico during the war.

612 ————

Report of the Secretary of War, Communicating . . . Abstracts of the Proposals for Transporting Military Supplies from Fort Leavenworth Westward. . . . U.S. 38th Cong., 2nd sess., Sen. Exec. Doc. 31 [Serial 1209]. Washington, Mar. 3, 1865.

18 p., 22.5 cm.

Correspondence and documents on wagon freighting rates, bids, and contracts. Of SFT interest are letters from Henry S. Wright and Francisco Perea. Wright's late bid was lowest but was rejected; Perea hints at a combination in possible restraint of trade.

613 [Waldo, David]

David Waldo. U.S. 34th Cong., 1st sess., H.R. Report 284 [Serial 870]. Washington, July 25, 1856.

2 p., 22.5 cm.

Waldo, with William McCoy and Jabez Smith, had a train of 66 wagons hauling military supplies from Fort Leavenworth to Santa Fe and were caught in a severe snowstorm near Las Vegas in November 1850. Compensation is asked to cover the extra expenses incurred. Committee report is favorable, but payment apparently was not made. Brown, Russell & Co., another freighting firm, was caught in the same storm; see entry 498. Waldo applied again in 1859 and again was denied; see U.S. 35th Cong., 2nd sess., H.R. Report 56 (Serial 1018).

614 ————

Report of the Secretary of War, with Statements of Contracts . . .

During the Year 1850. U.S. 31st Cong., 2nd sess., Sen. Exec. Doc. 11 [Serial 589]. Washington, Jan. 8, 1851.

> 25 p., 22.5 cm.

Brief data on contracts to David Waldo and to Brown, Russell & Co. for freighting military supplies over the SFT.

615 Waldo, William

"Recollections of a Septuaginarian." *Glimpses of the Past*, Vol. 5, Nos. 4-6 in one (April-June 1938), pp. 62-94.

William (1812-1881) was a brother of David Waldo, noted Santa Fe trader. He made his first trip over the SFT in 1829 and was active for many years on the Trail. His memoirs were first published in 1880 by the Missouri Historical Society as *Biographical Sketches of Various Explorers, Fur-Traders, Trappers and Hunters.* They are here reprinted, edited by Stella M. Drumm, with additional material by Waldo not in the first publication. Waldo spent his later years in Texas.

616 Walker, Henry Pickering

The Wagonmasters: High Plains Freighting from the Earliest Days of the Santa Fe Trail to 1880. Norman: University of Oklahoma Press, [c 1966].

> Cloth, xii, [1]-[348] p., color frontis., 12 leaves of plates, 3 maps in text, biblio., index, 23.5 cm.

The most scholarly and extensive work to date on wagon freighting, with much on the SFT: economics, vehicles, teaming, companies, personalities, and techniques. An extensive bibliography, including much manuscript and other unpublished material.

617 Walker, Joel P.

A Pioneer of Pioneers: Narrative of Adventures thro' Alabama, Florida, New Mexico, Oregon, California &c. Early California Travels Series, XVII. Los Angeles: Glen Dawson, 1953.

> Paper over boards, [viii], 1-20 p., colophon leaf, 1 leaf, ltd. to 197 copies, printed by Wm. M. Cheney, 19.1 cm.

Firsthand memoirs, from a manuscript in the Bancroft Library. In May 1822 Walker went with a party of thirty men headed by Stephen Cooper, traveling along the Arkansas to Santa Fe (pp. 5-11). They returned to Missouri in the same year. Walker erroneously says "this was the first trip ever made from Missouri to Santa Fe"—but it was one of the earliest.

618   Wallace, William Swilling

Antoine Robidoux, 1794-1860: A Biography of a Western Adventurer. Early California Series, XIV. Los Angeles: Glen Dawson, 1953.

> Cloth, map endpapers, colored frontis., [xii], 1-[60] p., ltd. 450 copies, 18.6 cm.

A good biography of a significant early Mountain Man. He went over the Trail in 1852 and was with Kearny in 1846 as interpreter.

619   ———

"Was Heap's Journal Plagiarized?" In: *Brand Book of the Denver Westerners,* 1970, pp. 130-62.

A skilled archivist analyzes the article, "Ein Ritt nach Californien," published in *Das Buch der Welt* (Stuttgart, 1860). It was written by an author who signed his name only as Th. Gr. Wallace gives good evidence that it was probably plagiarized from the work of Gwinn Harris Heap (q.v.). It describes a trip over the SFT to Bent's Fort and beyond in 1853. The text contains much translation of the German work. See also Wagner-Camp 326b.

620   Walter, Paul A. F.

"New Mexico's Pioneer Bank and Bankers." *New Mexico Historical Review,* Vol. XXI, No. 3 (July 1946), pp. 209-25.

The first bank in New Mexico was chartered in 1870. Description of its first shipment of currency received in 1871: $135,000 sent in "three ambulances with an escort of 25 soldiers . . . ," over the SFT (pp. 219-20).

621   Ward, Dillis B.

Across the Plains in 1853. Seattle: Privately Printed, [1911].

Wrappers, string tied, [ii], [1]-55 p., 17.5 cm.

An account of one of the relatively few caravans that went to Oregon via the SFT. Ward went to Bent's Fort, north to Denver and the North Platte and on to Oregon. Graff 4530; Howes W-94.

622   Warner, Louis Henry, 1875-

Archbishop Lamy: An Epoch Maker. Santa Fe: New Mexico Publishing Corp., [c 1936].

Cloth, [1]-316 p., 22.5 cm.

A biography of the first archbishop in Santa Fe. Lamy made several trips over the SFT, his first in 1852 to bring the Sisters of Loretto to New Mexico. See entry 178. They left Independence on Aug. 1, 1852. He went east again in 1865 to bring the Sisters of Mercy. Included is his own brief account of a trip over the Trail in 1865, from a report he wrote in 1866.

623   Waters, Lawrence L.

Steel Trails to Santa Fe. Lawrence: University of Kansas Press, 1950.

Buckram, map endpapers, [xiv], [1]-500 p., maps, graphs, scenes, ports., sources, index, 23.5 cm.

A scholarly study of the building of the Atchison, Topeka and Santa Fe Railway. The first chapter (pp. 9-22) is a good, brief economic history of the SFT.

624   Waugh, Alfred S.

Travels in Search of the Elephant: the Wanderings of Alfred S. Waugh, Artist, in Louisiana, Missouri, and Santa Fe, in 1845-1846. Edited and annotated by John Francis McDermott. St. Louis: Missouri Historical Society, 1951.

Cloth, [xxii], [1]-153, biblio., index, 23.8 cm.

Only part of Waugh's journal survives, and of this a section describes his preparations at Independence for a trip over the SFT (pp. 90-114). Apparently he reached Santa Fe on June 24, 1846. A letter is appended, written July 14, telling of the situation in Santa Fe just before Kearny arrived (August 18) at the start of the Mexican War. The letter originally appeared in *Southern Literary Messenger*, Vol. XII (Dec. 1846), pp. 755-62.

625 Webb, James Josiah, 1818-1889

Adventures in the Santa Fe Trade, 1844-1847. Edited by Ralph P. Bieber. Southwest Historical Series, I. Glendale: Arthur H. Clark Company, 1931.

> Cloth, [1]-301 p., 5 leaves advts., 8 leaves of plates, fldg. map, 24.4 cm. Title on spine: *Journal of a Santa Fe Trader*.

Considered by many to be second only to the book by Josiah Gregg (q.v.) as a firsthand account by a major trader over the SFT. When Webb was twenty-six he borrowed six hundred dollars and entered the Santa Fe trade. By the time he was forty-three he had made enough on eighteen trips to retire. His account begins in the year that Gregg's account ends and the two works cover the full span of SFT trade up to U.S. occupation of New Mexico.

626 Webb, W. L.

"Independence, Missouri, a Century Old." *Missouri Historical Review*, Vol. XXII, No. 1 (Oct. 1927), pp. 30-50, illus.

A general review of the history of an important SFT terminus. Westport gained prominence over Independence because the Big Blue river near the latter town was often swollen in spring and delayed trains two weeks.

627 Webb, William Edward

Buffalo Land: An Authentic Account of the Discoveries, Adventures, and Mishaps of a Scientific and Sporting Party in the Wild West. . . . Cincinnati and Chicago: E. Hannaford & Company, 1872.

> Cloth, [xxiv], 25-503, illus. woodcuts, 21.5 cm.

A popularized account of a trip across the plains in the 1870s, written for a general audience. Some descriptions of SFT freighters at

Hays City (pp. 142-43) and of the Arkansas river valley (pp. 471-72). Reprinted 1873 and also at Philadelphia, 1874, apparently from the same stereotype plates.

628   Weber, David J., ed.

The Extranjeros: Selected Documents from the Mexican Side of the Santa Fe Trail. Santa Fe: Stagecoach Press, [1967].

> Cloth, [1]-43 p., colophon leaf, ltd. 600 copies, 21.6 cm.

Mexican records from ports of entry at the New Mexico end of the SFT, 1825-28, with names of 340 extranjeros (foreigners) who came through Taos and Santa Fe. Some of the dates confirm or revise previous conjectures of scholars as to earliest arrival of men such as Pattie.

629   ———

"Spanish Fur Trade from New Mexico, 1540-1821." *The Americas,* Vol. XXIV, No. 2 (Oct. 1967), pp. 122-36.

Weber is the recognized authority on the fur trade of northern New Mexico. Such trade was one of the early attractions that drew the Mountain Men and stimulated interest in trade with Santa Fe.

630   ———

The Taos Trappers: The Fur Trade in the Far Southwest, 1540-1846. Norman: University of Oklahoma Press, [c 1971].

> Cloth, 1-260 p., illus., maps, biblio., index, 24 cm.

The best work on the fur trade at the Santa Fe end of the Trail. Weber has worked from Spanish, Mexican, and American sources to present a detailed study of this area which was treated only as a segment in general works on the fur trade by Chittenden, Cleland, Phillips, and others.

631   Weichselbaum, Theodore

"Statement of Theodore Weichselbaum, of Ogden, Riley county, July 17, 1908." *Kansas Historical Collections,* Vol. XI (1909-1910), pp. 561-71.

Memoirs of a sutler at Kansas forts, 1856-69, with some mention of eastern portions of the SFT.

632   Wells, Eugene T.

"The Growth of Independence, Missouri, 1827-1850." *Bulletin of the Missouri Historical Society*, Vol. XVI, No. 1 (Oct. 1959), pp. 33-46.

In 1832 Independence dominated the Southwestern trade as an outfitting point. This capsule history, well researched, has useful data from contemporary newspapers commenting on the SFT trade. Much of the information is not readily available except in newspaper files.

633   Welty, Raymond L.

"Supplying the Frontier Military Posts." *Kansas Historical Quarterly*, Vol. VII, No. 2 (May 1938), pp. 154-69.

Wagon freighting, 1855-75, along the Santa Fe and other trails; taken chiefly from Congressional documents.

634   [Westport, Mo.]

Westport, 1812-1912: Commemorating the Centennial of the Santa Fe Trail. Kansas City, Mo.: Franklin Hudson Publishing Company, 1912.

Wrappers, 76 p., illus. photos.

A general review of the SFT and local events connected with the Trail. It has four chapters on the Battle of Westport. General Sterling Price, who had been to Santa Fe with Doniphan in 1846, was a Confederate commander in 1864. He swept north into Missouri on a massive raid. At Westport on October 22, 1864, 9,000 Confederate troops engaged General Alfred S. Pleasanton's Union force of about 20,000 men. After a desperate fight the Confederates retreated. It was the largest battle west of the Mississippi.

635   Wetmore, Alphonso, 1793-1848

Gazetteer of the State of Missouri, with a Map of the State, from the Office of the Surveyor-general, including the Latest Additions and Sur-

veys, to which is Added an Appendix, containing Frontier Sketches, and Illustrations of Indian Character. St. Louis: C. Keemle, 1837.

Cloth, xvi, [17]-382 p., frontis., 22.4 cm.

Includes a table of mileages between all stopping points from Independence to Santa Fe (pp. 269-70). Graff 4615; Howes W-296; Wagner-Camp 69. KSH.

636 ———

"Major Alphonso Wetmore's Diary of a Journey to Santa Fe, 1828." Missouri Historical Review, Vol. VIII, No. 4 (July 1914), pp. 177-97.

The diary covers a trip that began May 28, 1828, and reached San Miguel on August 2. Wetmore sent these extracts, together with a letter, to Secretary of War Lewis Cass in 1831. In the letter he gives data on trips by other caravans, 1821-1829. Introductory comments by F. F. Stephens.

637 ———

Message from the President of the United States Concerning the Fur Trade and the Inland Trade to Mexico. U.S. 22nd Cong., 1st sess., Sen. Doc. 90 [Serial 213]. Washington, Feb. 9, 1832.

85 p., 22.5 cm.

Contains Alphonso Wetmore's diary of a trip over the SFT, May 28-Aug. 2, 1828, with data on other caravans 1821-29. This diary was also reprinted in the Missouri Historical Review (see entry 636). Doc. 90 also contains Bennet Riley's report of Sept. 28, 1831, on men killed on the SFT expedition of 1823. It includes a list of others killed on the Trail or in its vicinity 1813-30. There is also a letter from Joshua Pilcher in which he states that he never engaged in the Santa Fe trade. Graff 4411; Wagner-Camp 46.

638 ———

Petition of Sundry Inhabitants of the State of Missouri, upon the Subject of a Communication between the Said State and the Internal Provinces of Mexico, with a Letter from Alphonzo Wetmore upon the

Same Subject. U.S. 18th Cong., 2nd sess., Sen. Doc. 79 [Serial 116]. Washington: Gales & Seaton, Feb. 14, 1825.

> 8 p., p. 2 blank, 22.2 cm.

Also issued, in same session, as H.R. Doc. 79 (Serial 116). Missouri asks that the route to Santa Fe be developed and protected. Wetmore comments on the traders' trips in 1821-24. Reprinted in *Santa Fe Trail: First Reports, 1825,* Houston: Stagecoach Press, 1960. Graff 2834; Wagner-Camp 30.

639 ———

Report . . . on Petition of Mary Smith Wetmore for a Pension. . . . U.S. 31st Cong., 2nd sess., Sen. Report 275 [Serial 593]. Washington, Feb. 10, 1851.

> 1 p., 22.5 cm.

The widow of Alphonso Wetmore asks that she be given a pension, as her husband had one until his death. Committee report is adverse.

640 Wheat, Carl I.

Mapping the Transmississippi West, 1540-1861. 5 vols. San Francisco: Institute of Historical Cartography, 1957-63.

> Cloth, reduced facsims. of maps (many fldg.), 38 cm. Vol. I: xiii, 1-264 p., 50 maps, index, 1957; Vol. II: xiii, 1-281 p., 58 maps, index, 1958; Vol. III: xiii, 1-349 p., 82 maps, index, 1959; Vol. IV: xiii, 1-260 p., 42 maps, index, 1960; Vol. V, Pt. I: [xix], 1-222 p., 50 maps, 1963; Vol. V, Pt. II: [iv], 223-487 p., 32 maps, index, 1963. Maps not in pagination.

The most comprehensive work on the subject, in five volumes bound as six. Wheat describes 1,302 maps of the West and reproduces 314 in reduced facsimile. Vol. II contains the maps concerning the SFT, including those of Pike and Frémont. Contents: Vol. I, The Spanish *Entrada* to the Louisiana Purchase, 1540-1804; Vol. II, From Lewis and Clark to Frémont, 1804-1845; Vol. III, From the Mexican War to the Boundary Surveys, 1846-1854; Vol. IV, From the Pacific Railroad Surveys to the Onset of the Civil War, 1855-1860; Vol. V, From the Civil War to the Geological Survey.

641 [Whilden, Charles E.)

"Letters from a Santa Fe Army Clerk, 1855-1856: Charles E. Whilden," edited by John Hammond Moore. *New Mexico Historical Review*, Vol. XL, No. 2 (April 1965), pp. 141-64.

In June 1855 Col. John B. Grayson left Fort Leavenworth with five hundred men en route over the SFT to New Mexico. Whilden was a clerk with the detachment, and on August 28 he wrote a letter home describing how their camp was destroyed by a prairie fire, plus other details of the trip.

642 Whitford, William Clarke

Colorado Volunteers in the Civil War: The New Mexico Campaign of 1862. Denver: The State Historical and Natural History Society, 1906.

Wrappers, [1]-159 p., illus., maps, 24.5 cm.

The first comprehensive history of the Civil War in New Mexico, with emphasis on the battle in Glorieta Pass on the SFT and views of such Trail points as Kozlowski's ranch, Pigeon's ranch, and Johnson's ranch. Reprinted, Boulder, Colo.: Pruett Press, Inc., 1963, with index added. Howes W-378.

643 Whitney, Carrie Westlake

Kansas City, Missouri: Its History and its People, 1808-1908. 3 vols. Chicago: The S. J. Clarke Publishing Co., 1908.

¾ leather and green cloth, all edges gilt, 3 vols.: [1]-688 p. and xiv p. index; [1]-684 p. and iv p. index; [1]-689 p. and iv p. index; illus., 26.4 cm.

Vol. I has a chapter on the SFT (pp. 149-78) and material on early Westport, with an 1855 plat of that town. Most of the information is general, but the illustrations are useful. The last two volumes are biographical.

644 Whittemore, Margaret, ed.

One-way Ticket to Kansas: the Autobiography of Frank M. Stahl. Edited by Margaret Whittemore. Lawrence: University of Kansas Press, 1959.

Cloth, [x], [1]-146 p., drawings, ports., scenes, index, 21.7 cm.

Stahl (b. 1841) went to Kansas in 1856 at the age of fifteen. In the spring of 1862 he drove six yoke of oxen with a wagon train over the SFT to Fort Union and later drove beef cattle from Fort Leavenworth to Fort Union over the Trail.

645 ――――

Sketchbook of Kansas Landmarks. Topeka: College Press, 1936.

Cloth, [1]-125 p., 1 leaf, illus. drawings, 26 cm.

Text is quite general, but the book is useful for the author's pebbleboard sketches of old structures along the Trail. Also issued in a second, revised edition in 1937 and again in 1965 as *Historic Kansas: A Centenary Sketchbook* (University Press of Kansas).

646 Willard, James F.

"A Raton Pass Mountain Road Toll Book." *The Colorado Magazine,* State Historical Society of Colorado, Vol. VII, No. 2 (March 1930), pp. 77-83.

An account book kept at the Wootton toll gate in Raton Pass, 1869-70, from a manuscript book at the University of Colorado. In seven months receipts were $6,548.

647 ――――

"Sidelights on the Pikes Peak Gold Rush, 1858-1859." *The Colorado Magazine,* State Historical Society of Colorado, Vol. XII, No. 1 (Jan. 1935), pp. 3-13.

The SFT route to the Colorado gold fields was longer than other routes but was used by many travelers because it was well known and had water.

648 [Williams, Ezekiel]

"Adventures in Colorado." *Missouri Historical Society Collections,* Vol. IV, No. 2 (1913), pp. 202-06.

Reprints a letter of Ezekiel Williams previously published in the

Missouri Gazette. Williams was the hero of David H. Coyner's *The Lost Trappers* (q.v.) and wrote of a party of trappers on the North Platte river in 1812. When the party disbanded, "four men decided to go to the Spanish settlements in New Mexico."

649 Williams, Joseph

Narrative of a Tour from the State of Indiana to the Oregon Territory, in the Years 1841-2. Cincinnati: For the Author, 1843.

Wrappers, 3-48 p.

Apparently only six copies remain of the original. In 1842 Williams returned via Bent's Fort and the SFT. A reprint edition limited to 250 copies was published at New York in 1921. Graff 4682; Howes W-471; Wagner-Camp 105.

650 [Willing, George M.]

"Diary of a Journey to the Pike's Peak Gold Mines in 1859," edited by Ralph P. Bieber. *Mississippi Valley Historical Review,* Vol. XIV, No. 3 (Dec. 1927), pp. 360-78.

Dr. Willing went via the SFT to Pueblo, Colorado, and on to the mines. His diary was first published in the *Daily Missouri Republican,* St. Louis, August 9, 1859. The SFT material (pp. 362-69) describes such details as Mexican ox-carts met on the Trail, as well as heavy traffic (1,351 wagons) heading west.

651 Wilson, Iris Higbie

William Wolfskill, 1798-1866: Frontier Trapper to California Ranchero. Western Frontiersmen Series, XII. Glendale, California: The Arthur H. Clark Company, 1965.

Cloth [1]-268 p., frontis. port., maps, ports., facsim., scenes, biblio., index, index, 24.5 cm.

Wolfskill went with Becknell on the first wagon train over the SFT in 1822; as did Ewing Young. Wolfskill and Young remained in New Mexico to trap down the Pecos river. In 1828 Wolfskill made a third trip west over the SFT as a trader with his own wagonload of goods. It was also his last trip, for in 1830 he opened the route north-west through Utah and southwest from there to California, where he settled.

652 Wilson, R. R., and Ethel M. Sears

History of Grant County, Kansas. [Wichita: Wichita Eagle Press, 1950].

> Cloth, [1]-278 p., frontis., ports., scenes.

Wagonbed Springs and four others SFT sites are located in this county. Their locations are given by township and range; otherwise there is little SFT data.

653 Winship, George Parker

"The Coronado Expedition, 1540-1542." In: *Fourteenth Annual Report of the Bureau of Ethnology to the Secretary of the Smithsonian Institution, 1892-93,* Part I, pp. 329-637, Washington: Government Printing Office, 1896.

> Contains the Spanish text and English translation of Pedro de Castañeda de Nacera concerning the Coronado expedition in 1541-42, together with other documents and a historical introduction. The material includes the earliest known references to Kansas in the area later traversed by the SFT. Howes W-571.

654 Winther, Oscar Osburn

The Transportation Frontier: Trans-Mississippi West, 1865-1890. Histories of the American Frontier Series. New York: Holt, Rinehart and Winston, [c 1964].

> Cloth, map endpapers, xiv, [1]-224 p., 16 leaves of plates, 3 maps in text, biblio., index, 23.2 cm.

A foremost expert on Western transportation presents a general study of wagon roads, railroads, and early highways. It deals broadly with wagon and coach traffic but has only limited material about the SFT.

655 Wislizenus, Frederick Adolphus, 1810-1889

Ein Ausflug nach den Felsen-Gebirgen im Jahre 1839. St. Louis: Wilh. Weber, 1840.

> Boards, [1]-[126] p., fldg. map, 27 cm.

Wislizenus (1810-1889) came to the U.S. in 1835 and settled near St. Louis. In 1839 he went with trappers up the Missouri and returned via Bent's Fort and the SFT. His book was first published in German at St. Louis and was reissued in English in 1912 by the Missouri Historical Society, St. Louis, as *A Journey to the Rocky Mountains in 1839*, with SFT material on pp. 140-47, ltd. 500 copies. English edition reprinted, Glorieta, N.M.: Rio Grande Press, Inc., 1969. Graff 4722; Howes W-596; Wagner-Camp 83.

656 ─────

Memoir of a Tour to Northern Mexico, Connected with Col. Doniphan's Expedition, in 1846 and 1847. 30th Cong., 1st sess., Sen. Misc. Doc. 26 [Serial 511]. Washington: Tippin & Streeper, Printers, 1848.

> 141 p., 3 fldg. maps, 22.5 cm.

Wislizenus started on a privately financed trip over the SFT in 1846, unaware that the war with Mexico had been declared. He joined the large caravan of Albert Speyer and went to Chihuahua. Appendixes list botanical specimens. There was also a German edition in 1850. The 1848 edition was reprinted, facsimile with biographical introduction, Albuquerque: Calvin Horn, Publisher,1969; also Glorieta, N.M.: Rio Grande Press, 1969. Graff 4723; Howes W-597; Wagner-Camp 159.

657 ─────

Resolutions . . . that there be Printed . . . [the] Memoirs of Dr. Wislizenus. . . . U.S. 30th Cong., 1st sess., Sen. Misc. Doc. 22 [Serial 511]. Washington: Tippin & Streeper, Printers, Jan. 3, 1848.

> 1 p., 22.5 cm.

Senator Benton proposes that Wislizenus' memoirs of his trip over the SFT and into Mexico be printed.

658 [Wolf, Lambert Bowman]

"Extracts from the Diary of Captain Lambert Bowman Wolf," edited by George Root. *Kansas Historical Quarterly*, Vol. I, No. 3 (Autumn 1932), pp. 195-210.

Wolf (1834-1918) was a cavalryman in Kansas for four years prior to the Civil War. The extracts relate experiences guarding emigrants and escorting mails along the SFT, 1856-61.

659 Wood, Dean Earl

The Old Santa Fe Trail from the Missouri River: Documentary Proof of the History and Route of the Old Santa Fe Trail. "Panoramic edition." Kansas City, Mo.: E. L. Mendenhall, Inc., Printers, [c 1955].

Buckram, [xiv], [1]-278 p., maps, scenes, index, 28.7 cm.

The most thorough study to date of the location of the eastern end of the SFT, with particular reference to modern Independence and Westport, Missouri. Wood graduated *magna cum laude* from Harvard in 1926, was president of the Kansas City Council of the American Pioneer Trails Association in 1953, and was assigned to locate, verify, and mark the SFT from Gardner, Kansas, east through Kansas City.

660 Wood, Henry

"Fort Union: End of the Santa Fe Trail." In: *The Westerners Brand Book*, Vol. III, Denver, 1949, pp. 205-56, illus.

A competent brief history of Fort Union, by a staff member of the National Park Service.

661 Woodward, Arthur

"Adventuring to Santa Fe." *New Mexico Historical Review*, Vol. XVII, No. 4 (Oct. 1942), pp. 288-93.

One of the relatively few examples of contemporary frontier humor connected with the SFT. A satirical journal of a trip over the Trail written in Biblical language and first published in the *Missouri Intelligencer*, August 5 and 19, 1825.

662 ⸻

"Sidelights on Bent's Old Fort." *The Colorado Magazine*, State Historical Society of Colorado, Vol. XXXIII, No. 4 (Oct. 1956), pp. 277-82, illus., port.

Data on the burning of the fort in 1849 and subsequent use of a remaining building by J. L. Sanderson's stage line.

663 [Workman, William]

"A Letter from Taos, 1826: William Workman," edited by David J. Weber. *New Mexico Historical Review*, Vol. XLI, No. 2 (April 1966), pp. 155-61.

William Workman went over the SFT in 1825, probably with the caravan captained by Augustus Storrs. He became a merchant and distiller in Taos, later moving to California. His letter, dated February 13, 1826, is one of the few that survive from the earliest days of trade over the Trail. It lists supplies needed and is addressed to his brother David—to whom Kit Carson was once apprenticed.

664 Wright, Muriel H., ed.

"The Journal of John Lowery Brown, of the Cherokee Nation, En Route to California in 1850." *Chronicles of Oklahoma*, Vol. XII, No. 2 (June 1934), pp. 177-213, illus.

Brown was a young Cherokee who went with others of his nation overland to California in 1850. Part of his journal (pp. 184-88) describes their journey along the SFT and the Arkansas to Bent's Fort.

665 Wright, Robert M.

"Personal Reminiscences of Frontier Life in Southwest Kansas." *Kansas Historical Collections*, Vol. VII (1901-1902), pp. 47-83.

To Denver in 1859; east over the SFT in 1862 with Russell, Majors & Waddell; early ranching west of Fort Dodge; post trader at Fort Dodge in 1867; wagon freighting along the SFT before 1870.

666 [Writers' Program]

Kansas: A Guide to the Sunflower State. American Guide Series. New York: The Viking Press, MCMXXXIX.

> Cloth, [xxii], 1-538 p., illus., chronology, biblio., index, fldg. map in back pocket, 21 cm.

This well-known series of state guides contains local history not readily available from any other source. Particularly useful in locating sites along the Trail. Scholars generally use the material with caution and seek additional verification before relying on the information.

667 ———

Missouri: A Guide to the "Show Me" State. American Guide Series. New York: Duell, Sloan and Pearce, [c 1941].

> Cloth, [xxx], [1]-652 p., illus., maps, chronology, biblio., index, 21 cm.
> See comments under entry 666.

668 ———

New Mexico: A Guide to the Colorful State. American Guide Series. New York: Hastings House, MCMXL.

> Cloth, map endpapers, xxxvii, [1]-458 p., illus., maps, chronology, biblio., index, 21 cm.
> See comments under entry 666.

669 Wyman, Walker D.

"Bullwhacking: a Prosaic Profession Peculiar to the Great Plains." *New Mexico Historical Review*, Vol. VII, No. 4 (Oct. 1932), pp. 297-310.

A good general review of the techniques of teamsters on wagon trains along the SFT.

670 ———

"Freighting: a Big Business on the Santa Fe Trail." *Kansas Historical Quarterly*, Vol. I, No. 1 (Spring 1931), pp. 17-27.

Brief general summary, useful for statistics taken from many contemporary newspaper accounts.

671 ———

"F. X. Aubry: Santa Fe Freighter, Pathfinder and Explorer." New Mexico Historical Review, Vol. VII, No. 1 (Jan. 1932), pp. 1-31, map.

Aubry was most noted for a fast horseback ride over the SFT in 1848. He was freighting goods over the Trail in 1847 or earlier and made his last trip in 1852.

672 ———

"Kansas City, Mo., a Famous Freighter Capital." Kansas Historical Quarterly, Vol. VI, No. 1 (Feb. 1937), pp. 3-13.

Data on freight traffic over the SFT, 1850-66, taken chiefly from contemporary commercial journals.

673 ———

"The Military Phase of Santa Fe Freighting, 1846-1865." Kansas Historical Quarterly, Vol. I, No. 5 (1932), pp. 415-28.

Useful material taken chiefly from Congressional documents, contemporary newspapers, and account books, relating to wagon freighting of military supplies on the SFT. Gives rates, tonnages, and contractors.

674 Young, Otis E

"Dragoons on the Santa Fe Trail in the Autumn of 1843." Chronicles of Oklahoma, Vol. XXXII, No. 1 (Spring 1954), pp. 42-51.

Written from a broad range of reliable sources, this article reviews the operations of the 1st Dragoons under Philip St. George Cooke along the SFT in late 1843. Their most important action was the disarming of a group of Texans under Jacob Snively earlier in the summer. Traders were alert during the autumn in fear of possible raids.

675 ———

The First Military Escort on the Santa Fe Trail, 1829: From the Journal and Reports of Major Bennet Riley and Lieutenant Philip St. George Cooke. American Trail Series, VII. Glendale: Arthur H. Clark Company, 1952.

> Cloth, [1]-222 p., 4 leaves of plates incl. front., fldg. map, appended documents, biblio., index, 24.5 cm.

The best scholarly study of the SFT in 1828-29, with emphasis on the military escort in 1829 under Major Riley. Young proves that all accounts of the 1829 escort march were written by P.S.G. Cooke (q.v.): the journal, the official report, and Cooke's account in his *Scenes and Adventures in the Army*, although Fred Perrine (q.v.) had previously maintained the journal and report were written by another.

676 ———

"Military Protection of the Santa Fe Trail and Trade." *Missouri Historical Review*, Vol. XLIX, No. 1 (Oct. 1954), pp. 19-32.

An excellent scholarly review of military protection along the Trail from 1829 to 1845.

677 ———

"The United States Mounted Ranger Battalion, 1832-1833." *Mississippi Valley Historical Review*, Vol. XLI, No. 3 (Jan. 1954), pp. 453-70.

This battalion existed for only one year and preceded the formation of the Dragoons. In the summer of 1833 this unit escorted a train of 103 wagons under Charles Bent along the SFT to the crossing of the Arkansas, where the train then entered Mexican territory (see pp. 462-64).

678 ———

The West of Philip St. George Cooke, 1809-1895. Western Frontiersmen Series, V. Glendale: Arthur H. Clark Company, 1955.

> Cloth, [1]-393 p., 9 leaves plates incl. frontis., fldg. map, biblio., index, 24.5 cm.

The best biography of Cooke and an especially useful work on
the military activities along the SFT. Cooke was with Bennet Riley's
escort unit along the Trail in 1829; he went with Henry Dodge's
dragoons to the Rockies in 1835 and returned along the Trail. In 1843
he was the leading U.S. officer concerned in the Snively affair, and in
1846 he was with the Army of the West and the Mormon Battalion
in their conquest of New Mexico. He commanded troops in New Mexico in 1853-54 and was at Fort Riley in 1855-57.

679 [Yount, George C.]

*George C. Yount and His Chronicles of the West; Comprising Ex-
tracts from His "Memoirs" and from the Orange Clark "Narrative."*
Edited by Charles L. Camp. Denver: Old West Publishing Company,
MCMLXVI.

> Cloth, xviii, 1-280 p., colored frontis., 3 leaves plates, fldg. map inside back,
> index, ltd. 1,250, 26.5 cm.

Yount was a trapper with Ewing Young, William Workman,
the Patties, Thomas L. Smith, and William Wolfskill. Part of the text
is from his own memoirs and part is from his story as dictated to Rev.
Orange Clark. He went over the SFT as a teamster in 1826; his last
years were spent in California. One chapter has good material on T. L.
"Pegleg" Smith, with some SFT material (pp. 226-27) that is brief but
useful.

680 Zerwekh, Sister Edward Mary, C.S.J.

"John Baptist Salpointe, 1825-1894." *New Mexico Historical Review*,
Vol. XXXVII, No. 1 (Jan. 1962), pp. 1-19; No. 2 (April 1962), pp.
132-54; No. 3 (July 1962), pp. 214-29; illus.

A biography of the second Archbishop of Santa Fe. Contains
an account of his trip west over the SFT in 1859 (pp. 7-9).

681 Zollinger, James Peter

Sutter: The Man and His Empire. New York: Oxford University Press,
1939.

Cloth, [xx], [1]-374 p., 7 leaves of plates incl. frontis., biblio., index, 22 cm.

A good biography of Johann Augustus Sutter (1803-1880), famous in California Gold Rush history. Sutter's first Western ventures (pp. 23-36) were two trips over the SFT as a trader in 1835-36, described here chiefly from manuscript sources and accounts in German language newspapers of the time. Reprinted, Gloucester, Mass.: Peter Smith.

ADDENDA

The following documents were noted during compilation of this bibliography. Although most of them are not excessively rare, for various reasons it was not possible to examine them personally. Rather than omit them, this list of suspects is presented as worth investigation. There is no assurance that they will contain useful SFT material, but the probability is that they do.

682 Baiseley, Albert H.

"Initiation of a Bullwhacker." *Motor Travel*.

A 1939 catalog of Edward Eberstadt & Sons states that this relates Baiseley's experiences along the SFT. It was reprinted, New York, 1923, in a twenty-four page pamphlet privately published by Robert Bruce, together with memoirs of two other old-timers who had traveled the Oregon and Cheyenne trails, under the title *Three Old Plainsmen*.

683 Bryan, Milton E.

The Flight of Time: Adventures on the Plains Sixty Years Ago. Troy, Kansas: Troy *Chief*, June 9, 1887.

Apparently reprinted as a separate. Cited by Otis E Young.

684 Burris, J. T.

"The Santa Fe Trail." In: *Proceedings of the Old Settlers' Association of Johnson County, Kansas*. 1907. KHS.

685 Carter, E. S.

The Life and Adventures of E. S. Carter, including a Trip across the Plains and Mountains in 1852, Indian Wars in the Early Days of Oregon in the Years 1854-5-6; Life and Experience in the Gold Fields of California, and Five Years' Travel in New Mexico. St. Joseph, Mo.: Combe Printing Company, 1896.

> 145 p.
>
> Graff 609 says that nearly every copy was destroyed by fire before distribution. From the title, it is possible that in some of his travels he went over the SFT. Howes C-186.

686 [Catholic]

"Overland from Cincinnati to Santa Fe in 1865." *American Catholic Historical Society of Philadelphia Record*, Vol. 44, 1933, pp. 375-78.

> Said to be a contemporary account.

687 Cedarholme, Caroline

A Narrative of the Dangerous Journey of Mrs. Caroline Cedarholme across the Deserts to Arizona. St. Paul, 1872.

> 32 p.
>
> Howes C-253 says there was also an edition with 45 p. at Indianapolis in 1872.

688 Crawford, Samuel Johnson

Kansas in the Sixties. Chicago: A. C. McClurg & Co., 1911.

> Cloth, xvii, 441 p., frontis., ports., 21.5 cm.
>
> Crawford was with the 2nd Kansas Cavalry in 1862-63 and the work is said to have some firsthand material on the SFT and also on the Battle of Westport.

689 Crump, R. P. [pseud., "Flacco"]

"The Snively Expedition." *Porter's Spirit of the Times*, Vol. IX, No. 8 (Oct. 16, 1860).

A Texan's account of this expedition. It was reprinted as a pamphlet of 18 pages, New York: Edward Eberstadt and Sons, Dec. 25, 1949. Wagner-Camp 103.

690 Dike, Sheldon H.

"Early Mail Contracts on the Santa Fe Trail." *American Philatelist*, Vol. 8 (April 1958).

691 Ebright, Homer K.

The History of Baker University, Baldwin, Kans., 1951.

Chapter IV said to contain SFT material.

692 Etrick, Carl F.

Dodge City Semi-Centennial Souvenir. Dodge City: The Etrick Company, 1922.

693 Flournoy, Elizabeth A.

Historic Spots on the Santa Fe Trail. N.p., Kellogg-Baxter Printing Co., n.d.

694 [Folsom, George F.]

Mexico in 1842: A Description of the Country, Its Natural and Political Features; With a Sketch of Its History, Brought Down to the Present Year; To Which is Added an Account of Texas and Yucatan; and of the Santa Fe Expedition. New York: C. J. Folsom, 1842.

Cloth, 256 p., map.
Pp. 128-35 said to describe his journey from St. Louis to Santa Fe. Graff 1372; Howes F-226; Wagner-Camp 91.

695 François des Montaignes [pseud.]

"The Plains, Being a Collection of Veracious Memoranda, Taken during the Expedition of Exploration in the Year 1845. . . ." *Western*

Journal & Civilian, Vol. 9, No. 1, to Vol. 10, No. 6, 1852-53, and Vol. 15, No. 4, March 1856.

Said to be a diary of a participant in Frémont's Third Expedition, which went along the SFT as far as Bent's Fort. It may have been written by Isaac Cooper. Wagner-Camp 217.

696   Gillmore, Parker

Travel, War, and Shipwreck. London: Hurst and Blackett, 1880.

> Cloth, 307 p., 4 p. advts.

Bibliographer J. C. Dykes says this contains "the adventures of an Englishman on the Santa Fe Trail." It is known that Gillmore wrote several books on travel.

697   Gladstone, Thomas H.

Kansas; or, Squatter Life and Border Warfare in the Far West. London: G. Routledge & Co., 1857.

Said to contain material on the SFT (pp. 160-61), reprinted from the *Times* of London. There was also an American and a German edition. Howes G-200.

698   Hartmann, George

Wooed by a Sphinx of Aztlan; The Romance of a Hero of Our Late Spanish-American War and Incidents of Interest from the Life of a Western Pioneer. Prescott, Ariz., 1907.

> Cloth, 125 p., frontis.

Includes material on a trip from Kansas to New Mexico in 1867. Parts of this work may be fictional.

699   Hurd, Charles W.

"Origin and Development of the Santa Fe Trail." *The Santa Fe Magazine*, Vol. XV, No. 1 (Sept. 1921), pp. 17-27.

700   Huston, J. P.

The Old Tavern at Arrow Rock. N.p., 1914.

Pamphlet, 12 p., frontis.
A local history of the early SFT days at Arrow Rock.

701 Jenkins, Paul B.

The Battle of Westport. Kansas City, Mo., 1906.

Cloth, 181 p. plus index, illus., maps.
An account of Price's Missouri raid.

702 [Kelly, Hiram]

Letters from Old Friends and Members of the Wyoming Stock Growers Association. Cheyenne: S. A. Bristol Company, 1923.

Said to contain a letter (pp. 14-21), from Kelly to H. E. Crain, dated March 22, 1915, and describing an Indian attack along the SFT in Sept. 1856.

703 [March of the First]

The March of the First, Being a History of the Organization, Marches, Battles and Service of the First Regiment, of Colorado Volunteers . . . , by a Private of the Regiment. Denver: Thomas Gibson & Co., 1863.

36 p., plus 4 p. advts.
The only known copy of this item was sold at the auction of Thomas W. Streeter's books in 1968. It contains a firsthand account of the march of this unit through Raton Pass and over the SFT to the Battle of Glorieta Pass in 1862. Howes M-272; Wagner-Camp 392b.

704 Methvin, John Jaspar

Andele; or, The Mexican-Kiowa Captive. A Story of Real Life among the Indians. Louisville: Pentecostal Herald Press, 1899.

Cloth, 184 p., illus.
Said to contain material on Bent's Fort, where Mexicans waited for news of relatives seized by Indians. The captive in this instance was Andres Martinez. Graff 2764; Howes M-562.

705 [Mexico]

La Diplomacia Mexicana. Vol. II, pp. 13-14, 17-21.

In this book Torrens, the Mexican charge d'affaires in Washington, D.C., reports to his government that an expedition is about to leave Kentucky for Santa Fe for the purpose of opening a mine and starting trade; he urges that this traffic be regulated or prohibited.

706 [Military Transportation]

Report on the Transportation of United States Troops and Military Stores over the Atchison, Topeka and Santa Fe Railroad during 1875-1876. Washington: Quartermaster-General's Office, 1876.

Ben Perley Poore lists this item in his *Descriptive Catalogue of Government Publications,* p. 1029. Any troops or supplies destined for New Mexico and the Southwest would have continued another 200 miles or more along the SFT at that time. Poore says the report has 199 pp., indicating a broad scope of data.

707 Minor, Elinor, and Grace Minor

"William McCoy." *Journal of the Jackson County Historical Society,* Missouri, No. 7 (Spring 1968), p. 6ff.

708 Napton, William Barclay

The Past and Present of Saline County, Missouri. Chicago: B. F. Bowen & Co., 1910.

709 Rath, Ida E.

Early Ford County. North Newton, Kans., 1964.

According to Bolton, Coronado crossed the Arkansas in what is now Ford county.

710 Sargent, Charles S.

"Josiah Gregg." *Garden and Forest,* Vol. VII, No. 2 (Jan. 10, 1894), p. 12.

711   Schmidt, Heine

Ashes of My Campfire. Vol. I. Dodge City: Journal, Publishers, 1952.

    Contains a chapter headed "Twenty-four Miles on the Santa Fe Trail."

712   [Shepard, Elihu H.]

The Autobiography of Elihu H. Shepard. St. Louis, 1869.

    275 p., 2 ports.
    Said to contain Shepard's personal memoirs of service during the Mexican War, including a trip over the SFT. Howes S-386.

713   Stahl, Frank M.

"The Old Santa Fe Trail." *The Plebeian,* Vol. I, No. 1 (Feb. 1894), pp. 15-20.

714   Sterling, Edith

"Following the Santa Fe Trail through Kansas." *Daughters of the American Revolution Magazine,* Vol. XCVII (Nov. 1963), pp. 901-03.

715   Vee, Jay [pseud. of John Thomas Vanderlip]

Wild Oats. Topeka: Crane & Company, 1914.

    Contains a chapter on the SFT.

716   [Waldo, David]

"Dr. David Waldo." *Journal of the Jackson County Historical Society, Missouri,* No. 11 (Spring 1968), p. 6ff.

717   Ward, Christopher

A Yankee Rover: Being the Story of the Adventures of Jonathan Drew During His Travels in the South and Far West by Road, River and Trail in the Years 1824-29. New York, 1932.

    Cloth, 232 p.
    Said to include a description of a trip over the SFT.

718   Webb, W. L.

The Centennial History of Independence, Mo. N.p., 1927.

Cloth, 294 p.

Material on the SFT, Civil War battles at the eastern end of the Trail, and local history.

INDEX TO
CONGRESSIONAL DOCUMENTS

Entry numbers refer to items, not to pages.

27th Cong., 2nd sess., H.R. Doc. 402. Entry 560
28th Cong., 1st sess., Sen. Doc. 390. Entry 197
28th Cong., 1st sess., H.R. Doc. 30. Entry 222
28th Cong., 1st sess., H.R. Report 77. Entry 173
28th Cong., 2nd sess., Sen. Doc. 1. Entry 528
28th Cong., 2nd sess., Sen. Doc. 174. Entry 229
28th Cong., 2nd sess., H.R. Doc. 166. Entry 229
28th Cong., 2nd sess., H.R. Report 194. Entry 38
29th Cong., 1st sess., Sen. Doc. 1. Entry 343
29th Cong., 1st sess., Sen. Doc. 43. Entry 565
29th Cong., 1st sess., Sen. Doc. 438. Entry 1
29th Cong., 1st sess., Sen. Report 115. Entry 39
29th Cong., 1st sess., H.R. Doc. 2. Entry 343
29th Cong., 1st sess., H.R. Report 298. Entry 503
29th Cong., 2nd sess., Sen. Doc. 75. Entry 549
30th Cong., 1st sess., Sen. Exec. Doc. 1. Entry 207
30th Cong., 1st sess., Sen. Exec. Doc. 7. Entry 188
30th Cong., 1st sess., Sen. Exec. Doc. 23. Entry 2
30th Cong., 1st sess., Sen. Misc. Doc. 11. Entry 287
30th Cong., 1st sess., Sen. Misc. Doc. 22. Entry 657
30th Cong., 1st sess., Sen. Misc. Doc. 26. Entry 656
30th Cong., 1st sess., Sen. Misc. Doc. 148. Entry 227
30th Cong., 1st sess., Sen. Report 11. Entry 549
30th Cong., 1st sess., Sen. Report 226. Entry 230
30th Cong., 1st sess., H.R. Exec. Doc. 8. Entry 207
30th Cong., 1st sess., H.R. Exec. Doc. 41. Entry 188
30th Cong., 1st sess., H.R. Report 37. Entry 39
30th Cong., 1st sess., H.R. Report 299. Entry 549
30th Cong., 1st sess., H.R. Report 421. Entry 241
30th Cong., 1st sess., H.R. Report 458. Entry 287
30th Cong., 2nd sess., H.R. Misc. Doc. 5. Entry 227
31st Cong., 1st sess., Sen. Exec. Doc. 26. Entry 89
31st Cong., 1st sess., Sen. Misc. Doc. 70. Entry 318
31st Cong., 1st sess., H.R. Exec. Doc. 17. Entry 558
31st Cong., 1st sess., H.R. Misc. Doc. 33. Entry 611
31st Cong., 1st sess., H.R. Report 280. Entry 260
31st Cong., 2nd sess., Sen. Exec. Doc. 11. Entry 614
31st Cong., 2nd sess., Sen. Report 275. Entry 639
32nd Cong., 1st sess., Sen. Exec. Doc. 1. Entry 88

32nd Cong., 1st sess., Sen. Report 304. Entry 498
33rd Cong., 1st sess., Sen. Misc. Doc. 67. Entry 226
33rd Cong., 1st sess., H.R. Report 59. Entry 498
33rd Cong., 1st sess., H.R. Misc. Doc. 47. Entry 218
33rd Cong., 1st sess., H.R. Misc. Doc. 53. Entry 393
33rd Cong., 1st sess., H.R. Report 223. Entry 219
33rd Cong., 2nd sess., H.R. Misc. Doc. 8. Entry 226
33rd Cong., 2nd sess., H.R. Report 110. Entry 119
33rd Cong., 3rd sess., H.R. Exec. Doc. 91. Entry 442
34th Cong., 1st sess., Sen. Report 252. Entry 279
34th Cong., 1st sess., H.R. Report 226. Entry 490
34th Cong., 1st sess., H.R. Report 284. Entry 613
34th Cong., 1st sess., H.R. Report 299. Entry 279
34th Cong., 3rd sess., H.R. Report 172. Entry 487
34th Cong., 3rd sess., H.R. Report 244. Entry 195
35th Cong., 1st sess., Sen. Exec. Doc. 35. Entry 321
35th Cong., 1st sess., Sen. Report 305. Entry 119
35th Cong., 1st sess., Sen. Misc. Doc. 218. Entry 119
35th Cong., 1st sess., H.R. Exec. Doc. 103. Entry 330
35th Cong., 1st sess., H.R. Report 293. Entry 401
35th Cong., 1st sess., H.R. Report 372. Entry 488
35th Cong., 1st sess., H.R. Court of Claims Report 161. Entry 119
35th Cong., 2nd sess., H.R. Report 56. Entry 613
35th Cong., 2nd sess., H.R. Report 60. Entry 490
35th Cong., 2nd sess., H.R. Report 151. Entry 37
35th Cong., 2nd sess., H.R. Report 154. Entry 223
36th Cong., 1st sess., H.R. Report 344. Entry 280
36th Cong., 1st sess., H.R. Report 496. Entry 490
36th Cong., 1st sess., H.R. Report 509. Entry 488
38th Cong., 2nd sess., Sen. Exec. Doc. 31. Entry 612
39th Cong., 1st sess., H.R. Exec. Doc. 1. Entry 387
39th Cong., 2nd sess., Sen. Report 156. Entry 317
43rd Cong., 1st sess., Sen. Report 173. Entry 479
45th Cong., 2nd sess., H.R. Report 189. Entry 365
45th Cong., 2nd sess., H.R. Report 425. Entry 119
46th Cong., 2nd sess., H.R. Report 200. Entry 119
46th Cong., 3rd sess., Sen. Report 877. Entry 119
51st Cong., 1st sess., H.R. Exec. Doc. 6, pt. 2. Entry 413
63rd Cong., 2nd sess., Sen. Exec. Doc. 608. Entry 311

INDEX

Figures in parentheses refer to page numbers; all other figures refer to entry numbers, not to pages. Titles of works are indexed in italic. Main author headings of entries, which are arranged alphabetically throughout the bibliography, are not indexed.

420, 432, 438, 461, 637, 674-76, 678
Riley county, Kans., 631
Rio de las Animas Perdidas en Purgatorio, 555
Road to Santa Fe, The, 257
Roads, 487, 488
Robidoux, Antoine, 358, 490, 491, 618
Robidoux, Joseph, 358, 372, 429
Rocky Mountain Adventures, 92
Roenigk, Adolph, 460
Root, George E., 90
Round Grove, (15)
Round Mound, (16)
Routes of Explorations and Surveys, 442
Roy, Jean Baptiste, 495
Royall, W. B., 244
Ruddock, Samuel A., 495
Rugeley, Helen J. H., 249
Russell, Don, 248
Russell, Mrs. Hal, 497
Russell, John, (22)
Russell, Marion, (29), 572
Russell, William H., 91, 125, 394, 498, 514, 515, 616
Russell & Jones, freighters, 498
Russell, Majors & Waddell, (4, 25), 368, 394, 513-15, 616, 665
Ruxton, George F., 259, 298, 358, 485
Ruxton of the Rockies, 499

Sabin, Edwin L., 105, 193
Sage, Rufus B., (20), 112, 266, 358
St. Louis, Mo., 76, 112, 186, 190, 255, 351 358, 420, 438, 462, 463, 616
St. Vrain, Ceran, (17), 38, 39, 112, 172, 177, 236, 258, 266, 275, 358, 438, 503, 504, 551, 603, 625, 679
St. Vrain & McCarty, mail contractors, 89
Saline county, Mo., 708
Saline river region, 407
Salisbury, William W., 367
Salpointe, Archbishop John B., 680
San Antonio, Tex., (6)
Sand creek, 255, 316, 317, 358, 420, 438, 605
Sanderson, J. L., 506. See also Barlow & Sanderson
Sandoval, Felipe, (5), 66, 372
Sanford, Mrs. Byron N., 507
Sanguinet, Charles, (8), 435
San Jose, N.M., 498

San Miguel del Vado, N.M., (16), 91, 177, 255, 347, 358, 420, 438
Santa Fe, N.M., (23), 21, 51, 91, 111, 177, 206, 255, 372, 420, 589, 591, 616, 624, 625, 641
Santa Fe: The Railroad that Built an Empire, 403
Santa Fe and the Far West, 508
Santa Fe Pioneers, (19). See also Texan-Santa Fe Expedition
Santa Fe Republican, 240
Santa Fe Trace Battalion, 122, 124
Santa Fe Trade, The, 252
Santa Fe Trail, The: by W. E. Brown, 91; by R. Duffus, 177; by H. L. James, 328; by Margaret Long, 369; by editors of Look, 371
Santa Fe Trail: an Essay, The, 191
Santa Fe Trail: First Reports, 540
Santa Fe Trail: The Trip Over It in 1863, The, 524
Santa Fe Trail to California, The, 471
Santa Fe Trail Highway Association, 509
Santa Fe Wagon Boss, 203
Sapp, Representative, 195
Sappington, John, 283
Sargent, Kans., 202
Satanta, chief, 263, 358, 438, 500
Satren, Pierre, (5), 70, 71, 372
Scenes and Adventures in the Army, 129, 132, 675
Scenes in the Rocky Mountains, 502
Sears, Ethel M., 652
Second Colorado Cavalry, 4, 91
Second Dragoons, 132, 173, 438
Second Kansas Cavalry, 688
Second William Penn, The, 500
Sedalia, Mo., 286
Sedgwick, John, 438, 457, 493
Segale. See Blandina, Sister
Seligman, Sigmund, 445
Sentinel to the Cimarron, 541
Separate Battalion of Mo. Volunteers, 341, 342
Seth Hays & Co., 413
Settle, Raymond W. and Mary L., 224
Seventy Years on the Frontier, 394
Seven Years' Travel, 231
S. H. Long's Expedition, 327
Shawneetown, Kans., 123
Shepard, Elihu H., 712
Sheridan, Kans., 389